KU-166-425

TREASON

Famous English Treason Trials

The execution of the rebel Jacobite lords on Tower Hill, 18 August 1746 (Museum of London/Bridgeman Art Library, London)

TREASON

Famous English Treason Trials

A L A N   W H A R A M

ALAN SUTTON PUBLISHING LIMITED

First published in the United Kingdom in 1995
Alan Sutton Publishing Limited
Phoenix Mill · Far Thrupp · Stroud · Gloucestershire

Copyright © Alan Wharam, 1995

All rights reserved. No part of this publication may be reproduced, stored in a
retrieval system, or transmitted in any form, or by any means, electronic, mechanical,
photocopying, recording or otherwise, without the prior permission of the publisher
and copyright holder.

British Library Cataloguing in Publication Data

A catalogue record for this book is available from the British Library.

ISBN 0-7509-0991-9

Typeset in 10/12 Plantin.
Typesetting and origination by
Alan Sutton Publishing Limited.
Printed in Great Britain by
Butler & Tanner, Frome, Somerset.

Contents

List of Illustrations

Preface

In *The Treason Trials, 1794* I gave an account of some important trials which occupied the courts for several weeks during the last decade of the eighteenth century; in this book, I have collected a series of treason trials – some famous, some infamous, and some forgotten.

Anyone who has had business in the criminal courts will know that the majority of people who appear there are the weak, the inadequate, the sordid, the greedy, and occasionally the plain evil, but in cases of treason it is quite different. Many of the men – and the one woman – who appear in this book, and in my earlier book, were inspired by honourable motives (although it was often alleged in the indictments that they were instigated by the Devil), and they included some of the most illustrious men of their times. In addition, the conduct of the profession ranged across the whole spectrum, from Sir Edward Coke and Sir John Popham striving to secure the political murder of Sir Walter Raleigh to John Adolphus and Frederick Pollock defending men, whose opinions they abhorred, with the highest degree of professional skill and integrity.

I have, so far as possible, refrained from dealing with matters of law (although this was unavoidable in the two twentieth-century cases which both turned on legal issues). I have, however, retained the conventional abbreviations for the judges and law officers of the crown; these come after the name of the individual, e.g. Smith A.-G. These abbreviations are:

A.-G. and S.-G. – Attorney-General and Solicitor-General
B. and CB – Baron and Chief Baron
J. and CJ – Justice and Chief Justice
LC – Lord Chancellor

Throughout the period covered by this book the English judiciary consisted of the Court of Chancery, in which the Lord Chancellor sat alone, and the three courts of common law: the Court of King's (or Queen's) Bench and the Court of Common Pleas (each consisting of a Chief Justice and three Justices), and the Court of Exchequer consisting of a Chief Baron and three Barons (although, in spite of their name, they had the same qualifications and status as the other judges); these courts were amalgamated into the High Court of Justice in 1875.

Members of the peerage were tried by their peers in the House of Lords; otherwise, serious criminal offences were usually tried at assizes, the Old Bailey being the Assize Court for the County of Middlesex. However, there were two alternative methods for the trial of exceptionally serious crimes: either by referring the case to the Court of King's (or Queen's) Bench, and later the King's (or Queen's) Bench Division of the High Court, or by the appointment of a Special Commission consisting of senior judges appointed for the purpose.

Acknowlegements

I would like to take this opportunity to thank the Cambridge University Library for providing me with photocopies of the reports in the *State Trials*, the Library of the Leeds Metropolitan University, the Library of the Law Faculty of Leeds University, the Leeds Central Reference Library, and especially that remarkable institution, the Leeds Private Library (founded 1768) and its librarian, Geoffrey Forster, and his staff. I also wish to thank Jonathan Falconer and Joanna Pyke of Alan Sutton Publishing for their help, and all those who have provided illustrations for this book. In particular, I wish to thank my agent, John Welch, whom I remember so well half a century ago when he was the senior NCO in the Denstone College Training Corps and was trying, probably without a great deal of success, to instil some military discipline into me, and without whose help this book would never have been published.

Every effort has been made to trace the copyright holder of the autographs of the Cato Street conspirators. I would be grateful for any information that would enable me to do so.

The Treason Acts

High Treason has always been regarded as the most serious of all criminal offences. Even today it still carries the death penalty, which was carried out in a most barbarous manner throughout most of our history, as will be illustrated in some of the cases described in this book (although by the eighteenth century it was becoming customary to commute the sentence to death by hanging). In addition to the physical penalties, all the property of a person convicted of treason was, until the eighteenth century, forfeited to the Crown.

High Treason involves a breach of the allegiance which a subject owes to his or her sovereign; it follows, therefore, that no one under our law can be convicted of treason unless he or she owes allegiance to the Crown. Persons owing allegiance include all natural-born British subjects wherever they may be, and aliens, such as de la Motte, while resident in the United Kingdom and enjoying the protection of the Crown; in the case of William Joyce it was held that a person holding a British passport also owes allegiance. A person can be absolved from his or her allegiance to the Crown; thus the American colonists who had rebelled against the Crown were formally absolved from their allegiance by the Treaty of Paris in 1783. (Although some colonial courts suggested that the colonists had been absolved earlier; and in the USA the date of the Declaration of Independence, 4 July 1776, is usually taken as the day on which allegiance to the Crown was ended, on the ground that the Crown was in breach of its fundamental duties towards its American subjects.)[1]

Prior to 1351 treason under the common law of England was an uncertain and ill-defined offence. Blackstone, in his *Commentaries*, vol. IV, ch. 6, explained that the judges had raised, by 'forced and arbitrary constructions', offences into treason which should not have been regarded as such. Thus, 'accroaching' or attempting to exercise royal power, a very uncertain charge, had been held to be treason, and so had the killing of the king's father or brother, or even his messenger. In order to bring this situation to an end, parliament passed the Treason Act of 1351. Sir Edward Coke explained what happened in his *Institutes*:

> And although nothing can concern the King, his Crown and Dignity more than *Crimen lesae Majestatis*, High Treason; yet at the request of his Lords and Commons, the blessed king by authority of Parliament made the declaration as is aforesaid; and therefore, and for other excellent laws made at this Parliament, this was called *Benedictum Parliamentum*, as it well deserved. For except it be Magna Carta, no other Act of Parliament hath had more honor given unto it by the King, Lords Spiritual and Temporal and the Commons of the Realm for the time being in full Parliament, than this Act concerning Treason hath had.

The standard English text[2] of the Act reads as follows:

> 1. Item, whereas divers opinions have been before this time in what case treason shall be said, and in what not: the king, at the request of the lords and of the commons, hath made a declaration in the manner as hereafter followeth, that is to say:
>   (i) when a man doth compass or imagine the death of our lord the king, of our lady his queen, or of their eldest son and heir;
>   (ii) or if a man do violate the king's companion, or the king's eldest daughter unmarried, or the wife of the king's eldest son and heir;

(iii) or if a man do levy war against our lord the king in his realm;

(iv) or be adherent to the king's enemies in his realm, giving to them aid and comfort in the realm or elsewhere, and thereof be probably attainted of open deed by the people of their condition;

(v) or if a man counterfeit the king's great or privy seal;

(vi) or if a man counterfeit the king's money; and if a man bring false money into the realm counterfeit to the money of England, knowing the money to be false, to merchandize and make payment withal;

(vii) or if a man slay the chancellor, treasurer, or the king's justices of the one bench or the other, justices in eyre, or justices of assize, and all other justices assigned to hear and determine, being in their places doing their offices;

and it is to be understood, that in the cases above rehearsed, that ought to be judged treason which extends to our lord the king, and his royal majesty. And of such treason the forfeiture of the escheats pertaineth to our sovereign lord, as well of the lands and tenements holden of other, as of himself.

2. And because that many other like cases of treason may happen in time to come, which a man cannot think nor declare at this present time: it is accorded, that if any other case, supposed treason, which is not above specified, doth happen before any justices, the justices shall tarry without any going to judgement of the treason, till the cause be shewed and declared before the king and his Parliament, whether it ought to be judged treason or other felony.[3]

The words appended to s. 1(iv) – 'and thereof be probably attainted of open deed' – have in practice been applied to the other heads of treason, notably s. 1(i) on the ground that these offences exist only in the mind and cannot be proved unless evidenced by some open deed or (as it is usually called) 'overt act'. In the case of 'compassing the king's death' the overt act must be one which demonstrates an intention that the king should die; thus in the case of the Pop Gun Conspiracy, *R. v. Crossfield*, the overt acts alleged were the attempts to procure the manufacture of a tube for the discharge of a dart at the king, for this was clearly, if proved, a plan to assassinate him. In some cases, however, the connection was not so clear or so close. Thus a conspiracy to imprison the king came to be regarded as an overt act on the ground that the imprisonment of the king was likely to lead to his death – 'it being an old observation, that there is generally but a short interval between the prisons and the graves of princes'.

In the course of time a body of case-law grew up as to what could, or could not, be treated as an overt act; 'levying war' was treason in itself under s. 1(iii), whereas a conspiracy to levy war was insufficient under s. 1(iii), but could be alleged as an overt act under s. 1(i). According to some writers, a time came when the overt act became the treason in itself, without reference to the intention of the accused, on the ground that if the overt act was proved, that was conclusive evidence of the accused's intention that the king should die – a theory known as 'constructive treason'. However, this theory is quite contrary to the express terms of the Act, and as far as I am aware has no judicial support except in the directions given to the juries in the cases of Thomas Hardy and John Horne Tooke, both of whom were acquitted.[4]

In proceedings for any serious criminal offence, the charge is formulated in a document known as the 'indictment'. In modern times, an indictment must be clearly worded and, where relevant, must specify exactly the Act of Parliament and the section under which the charge is brought; where two or more offences are alleged in the same indictment, they must be specified in two or more separate 'counts'. In earlier times, however, indictments were often long and verbose, the Acts were not specified, and it is often very difficult to determine under which head of treason a person was charged. Thus in the Essex Rebellion, where fighting broke out in the streets of London during the course of an attempt to attack the Tower and seize the queen, the indictment alleged 'compassing the Queen's death' and 'raising an insurrection', but it is impossible to know whether these were intended as two separate charges or whether one was laid as an overt act of the other. A further complication is that, over the years, additional treason acts were passed to extend the law in times of crisis, and one cannot always be sure whether a person was charged under the Act of 1351 or some other Act. This may also have given rise to the belief that 'constructive treasons' were being invented.

Under s. 1(iii), 'levying war in the realm', a person could be charged with levying war directly against the king, as in the case of the Jacobites. After the rebellion of 1745 had been crushed, many prisoners were taken and the gaols of the north of England were full; the authorities were reluctant to inflict a massive revenge – memories were still alive of the gallows and the rotting corpses all over the West Country after the Monmouth rebellion of 1685. So in 1746 nearly 400 prisoners were taken to Carlisle and brought into court in batches of twenty, and told that if they agreed to plead Guilty, then lots would be drawn and one man would be executed and the remainder transported; most of them agreed to this scheme, although some insisted on their right to be tried, and a few of these were acquitted. Altogether, about thirty men were executed at Carlisle, and another twenty at York.

The leaders of the rebellion were, however, taken to London and put on trial there; three lords, Cromarty, Kilmarnock and Balmerino, were arraigned before the House of Lords; Cromarty and Kilmarnock pleaded Guilty; Balmerino, probably because he did not understand the procedure, pleaded Not Guilty but was convicted; Cromarty was pardoned, but Kilmarnock and Balmerino were executed on 18 August 1746 on a scaffold which had been erected on Tower Hill (see cover illustration and frontispiece).

A person could also be charged under this section if he participated in a riot on such a scale that it amounted to levying war, as in the cases of Lord George Gordon and the Chartist rebels. This was known as 'constructive levying of war', but is no evidence for the existence of any other form of constructive treason.

'Adhering to the enemy' under s. 1(iv) is usually straightforward; an 'enemy' is a subject of a foreign power with whom the Crown is at open war – presumably including persons who are engaged in warfare with the Crown even if war has not been declared. There are, however, problems where the overt acts occurred out of the realm, as in the case of Roger Casement; although the ambiguity of this subsection has been known for a long time, parliament has never seen fit to amend it.

In the two centuries after 1351, several new treasons were created by statute. Some of these are enumerated by Blackstone: clipping money, burning houses to extort money, stealing cattle by Welchmen, wilful poisoning, execrations against the king or calling the king opprobrious names by public writing, marrying or deflowering any of the king's children, sisters, aunts, nephews or nieces without the royal licence, derogating from the king's royal style or title, etc. All these treasons were repealed in 1547 and again for good measure in 1553.

Subsequently, the process began again. Similar legislation was passed during the Elizabethan period against the Roman Catholics, and later against the Jacobites and their supporters, and at the time of the wars of the French Revolution, trading with the enemy was made treasonable.

It appears that anyone who is an accessory to treason, as Lady Alice Lisle, may be convicted of the full offence.

According to Sir Walter Raleigh, a person accused of treason could not, at common law, be convicted on the evidence of one witness alone. An Act of 1547 laid down that two lawful witnesses were required to convict a prisoner of treason, unless he willingly and without violence confessed the same, and this was repeated in an Act of 1695. These provisions were repealed by the Treason Act 1945.

Legislation was also passed from time to time to ensure that a person accused of treason had advanced notice of the indictment, of the names of the witnesses who were to be called by the Crown, and of the jurors who would be empanelled to try him, and to enable him to have the same power to subpoena witnesses to give evidence for him as was available to the Crown to compel their appearance against him.

It will be observed that the Act of 1351 is worded in such as way as to exclude all cases except those specifically referred to – a person shall not be convicted of treason unless he falls into one of the categories enumerated. In practice, it has been found difficult – except in wartime cases – to secure convictions. Cases of treachery and espionage in peacetime are not covered by the Act, and are usually dealt with under the Official Secrets Acts; persons involved in riots, even if technically amounting to the levying of war, are usually prosecuted for riot or other offences under legislation relating to public order.

Various offences akin to treason are contained in the legislation relating to the Armed Forces of the Crown. In 1940 parliament passed the Treachery Act, which set out various offences similar to treason, and in particular enabled the prosecution of offenders for adhering to the enemy abroad.

By the autumn of 1795 six years had passed since the French Revolution, and more than two years since France became a republic. In England, enthusiasm for the Revolution had largely evaporated, especially after the execution of the king in January 1793, and England had been at war with France for nearly three years. Nevertheless, there was still some support for revolutionary ideas, and on 27 October 1795 a mass meeting in Copenhagen Fields, attended it has been said by 150,000 people, had passed some subversive resolutions, and there were rumours going around that plans were being made for the assassination of the king. And then, on 29 October, the king's coach was assaulted as he was entering Old Palace Yard for the opening of parliament (see page 105).

Immediately after the assault, the House of Lords held an inquiry into what had occurred, and the evidence was recorded in the Parliamentary Journals. Five witnesses were called. Two, John Walford, a haberdasher of Pall Mall, and John Stockdale, a bookseller of Piccadilly, were special constables who had been escorting the coach on foot, on the right-hand side. While the coach was proceeding along Parliament Street they heard a man shouting 'No war; down with George,' and as the coach entered Palace Yard something struck the window with great velocity; Walford thought it must be a ball or a marble, Stockdale that it was halfpenny. James Parker, one of His Majesty's footmen, was also walking beside the coach when a ball or a marble 'whisked by my face'. He thought that it could not have been thrown by hand and must have come from a gun, or a 'wind gun' for it made no report; he thought it had been fired from a window on the first floor of a house next to the passage leading into the Palace Yard, adjacent to the cathedral. Two Bow Street officers, John Sayer and Christopher Kennedy, saw that the glass of the coach window had been broken –

a small hole with a cracked star round it. They said that there were about thirty or forty people on each side of the road, who hooted and hissed and threw more stones at the coach when the king came out after opening parliament.

It was because of this outrage that parliament now passed the Treason Act 1795, which received the Royal Assent on 18 December. The Act recited that 'Duly considering the daring outrages offered to your Majesty's most sacred person in your passage to and from your Parliament at the opening of this present session, and also the continued attempts of wicked and evil-disposed persons to disturb the tranquillity' of the kingdom, etc., it was therefore enacted that certain new treasons be created. Similar enactments had been passed in other times of crisis, and in essence the new treasons were simply well-established 'overt acts' which now became treasons in their own right.

The enacting section was long and verbose, but the gist of it was that the following were to become treasonable:

(i) Plotting any harm to the King, his heirs and successors;
(ii) Plotting to deprive him of the style and title of the Crown;
(iii) Levying war to induce him to change his policies, or to intimidate Parliament;
(iv) Moving any foreigner to invade the realm.

The Act was passed on a temporary basis – until the end of the existing reign – but was subsequently made permanent. It was repealed in 1848.

CHAPTER ONE

The Essex Rebellion (1601)

The so-called Essex Rebellion was a wild scheme that had been engineered principally by Robert Devereux, the second Earl of Essex, along with William Shakespeare's friend, Henry Wriothesley (the Earl of Southampton), and several commoners: Sir Christopher Blount, Sir Charles Davers, Sir John Davis, Sir Gilly Merrick and Mr Henry Cuffe.

The second Earl of Essex was born in 1566; following the death of his father, his mother, Lettice, married the Earl of Leicester. The second Earl of Essex became one of the queen's favourites at an early age: 'Doth not my lord of Essex now enjoy his Earldom of Essex by the gift of Henry 8th to his father?' said the Attorney-General, Sir Edward Coke, when opening the case for the Crown against the Earls; 'Was not he made Master of her majesty's Horse at 22 years of age? one of her majesty's Council? to be earl marshal of England? general of her majesty's forces in Ireland? and lastly, hath he not received divers gifts and sums of money, to his own use, of her majesty's gracious and princely bounty, to the value of £30,000?'

The queen had been having trouble with the Earl of Essex, but in 1599 she sent him off to command her army in Ireland. He took the Earl of Southampton with him, in spite of the queen's orders to the contrary, and also his stepfather, Sir Christopher Blount, who had recently married Lettice following the death of her second husband. He had 16,000 footmen and 1,300 horse under his command, 'such an army, as he himself said, [as] should make the earth tremble where he went', the Attorney-General was later to say. The scheme of operations was that he was to proceed into the north against the rebel Irish under 'the Arch Traitor Tyrone', but instead he entered into negotiations with Tyrone. Sir Christopher Blount had been wounded and was lying at the 'Castle of Tho. Lee, called Reban', when the earl visited him and told him that: 'He intended to transport a choice part of the army of Ireland into England, and land them in Wales, at Milford, or thereabouts; and so securing his descent thereby, would gather such other forces, as might enable him to march on London.'

This plan evidently came to nothing, and the earl was recalled. Then, in the winter of 1600/1, he and his friends embarked upon another scheme.

They met at Drury House where it was resolved first to take the Tower: Sir Christopher Blount was to hold the gate, Sir Gilly Merrick the hall, Sir John Davis the great chamber, and Sir Charles Davers the privy chamber. The earl was to enter the great chamber and stand between the halberds, that is to say in the corner of the room where the guards usually set up their halberds against the wall, and take possession of them. (When evidence on this point was given, the Lord Admiral interrupted to point out that the guards should not 'use that fashion of setting up their halberds in that manner'.) It was hoped that some of the lords would then come into the great chamber and welcome him, and they would then make their way into the privy chamber. Anyone who resisted would be seized, and they would then send into the City and call a parliament.

This plan seems to have come to the notice of the queen on Saturday 7 February 1601, and she summoned the Earl of Essex to come to the court, but he refused to go. On the following morning she sent a deputation to Essex House.[1]

The deputation consisted of Thomas Egerton, the Lord Keeper of the Seal, Sir John Popham, Chief Justice of the Court of Queen's Bench, the Earl of Worcester and Sir Thomas Knollys, the Comptroller of Her Majesty's Household. They went to the earl's house where a crowd of his supporters was assembled – the Earls of Southampton and Rutland, Sir Christopher Blount, Sir Charles Davers and many other knights and gentlemen. They found the gate shut against them, but after a while they were let in at the wicket. As soon as they were inside, the wicket was shut behind them and their servants were kept outside while the crowd was flocking around them. The Lord Keeper told the Earl of Essex to disband his assembly and lay down his arms, but he refused to obey, so the Lord Keeper told him that if he had any grievance it should be heard. The earl replied that his life was sought and that he would be murdered in his bed.

The crowd then started shouting: 'Away my lord, they abuse you, they betray you, they undo you, you lose time.' So the Lord Keeper put on his hat and invited the earl to speak with him privately, and he commanded them all upon their allegiance to lay down their arms. The Earl of Essex and the deputation went inside the house, and as they were going the crowd shouted out, 'Kill them, kill them!; cast the great seal out of the window; kill them; let us shop them up.'[2] Then the earl took the deputation into a back room, ordered the door to be closed and told them to be patient while he went into London, leaving them under the guard of Sir John Davis and Owen Salisbury who were armed with muskets. They asked to be released, but they were told that they were to be kept there until the earl returned. At about 4 o'clock in the afternoon, Sir Ferdinando Gorges came and rescued them.

While the queen's deputation was imprisoned in Essex House, the earl, accompanied by the Earl of Southampton, Sir Christopher Blount and some others, went into the City. There is little evidence of this escapade in the report of the trial, but according to the history books they went along the Strand, on to St Paul's and then into Gracechurch Street. Here they turned back, but found that Ludgate was barricaded against them, and in a scuffle which then ensued a man was killed. The earl went down to the river and returned home by boat. He began to make his house ready for a siege, but the Lord Admiral arrived and prepared to attack it. The earl surrendered on terms which were: that he might have an honourable trial, that he might deliver his griefs in person to the queen, that he might go in safety, that he might have his minister with him, and that the queen would redeem those who had been with him in the house and who were innocent. The earl was then arrested and taken to the Tower.

The two earls were tried by their peers, the House of Lords, and the commoners subsequently by a Special Commission. The editor of the *State Trials* gives no indication as to the origin of the report of the trial of the earls, but it reads like a detailed record. There are two reports of the trial of the commoners: the longer and more detailed is from 'A MS purchased at the sale of MSS of Peter le Neve, esq. Norroy King of Arms.' It reads as if it was a full report – there are one or two occasions when there is a blank in the text as if the scribe had failed to catch a word or phrase.

On 19 February 1601 the House of Lords assembled in Westminster Hall for the trial of the earls. The Lord Treasurer Buckhurst presided under a canopy of state as High Steward of England, and at a table beside him sat Sir John Popham, Chief Justice of the Court of King's Bench, Sir Edmund Anderson, Chief Justice of the

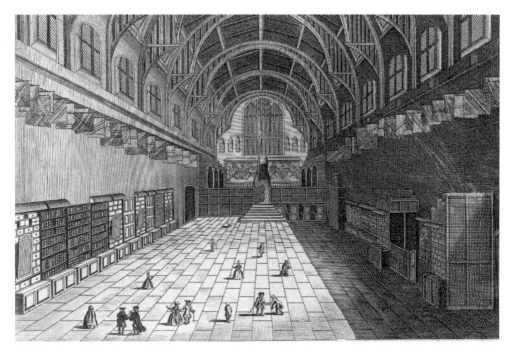

The interior of Westminster Hall; the courts sat in the partitioned areas at the end and sides of the building
(British Museum)

Court of Common Pleas, and Sir William Periam, Chief Baron of the Court of Exchequer, together with Gawdie, Fenner, Walmesley, Warburton and Kingsmill JJ, and Clarke B. Seven serjeants-at-arms came in with maces and laid them down before the High Steward. Beside the High Steward stood the King-of-Arms, and one of her majesty's gentlemen ushers with his white rod in his hand; the Clerk of the Crown and his assistant sat in front of him. Sir Walter Raleigh, the Captain of the Guard, and forty of the queen's guard were in attendance. The High Steward commanded silence and the clerk read the commission. The serjeant-at-arms then read a proclamation that the Lieutenant of the Tower should bring forth the prisoners, the Earls of Essex and Southampton.

The trial commenced when the Lord High Constable of the Tower, the Lieutenant of the Tower and the gentleman porter, the latter carrying the axe, came into the court, followed by the two earls. The gentleman porter stood between the earls, with the edge of the axe away from them, and the two prisoners kissed each other's hands and embraced each other. Then a proclamation was read, which summoned the peers of the realm to appear and answer to their names, 'upon pain and peril that will fall thereon'. Nine earls and sixteen other peers answered to their names.

The Earl of Essex then asked whether he was entitled to challenge any of the peers, and Popham CJ said, 'No'. Coke A.-G. referred to the case of Lord Darcy in the reign of Henry VIII, so the earl let them go on.

The conduct of criminal proceedings at that time bears only a faint resemblance to modern procedure. Most of the evidence consisted of written statements, depositions from witnesses or confessions from other prisoners, rarely supported by oral evidence on oath. These statements appear to have been read by the prosecuting counsel, and cross-examination, if any, was directed to them. The prisoners themselves frequently interrupted the proceedings to make their own statements or to converse with the judges or other men on the bench.

The indictment was read. This document is not printed in the report, but it may be assumed that it was similar to that subsequently preferred against the commoners: 'That on the 8th day of Feb. last, at Essex-house, they conspired the death and disinherison of the queen's majesty, and on that day caused an insurrection of the subjects, and made war in London against the queen, and intended altering the government, state, and religion now established, and to surprize the court at Whitehall.' It then went on to set out the facts relied upon by the prosecution. The two earls pleaded Not Guilty.

Serjeant Yelverton, as Queen's Serjeant and head of the profession, described what had happened, and likened the plot to the sedition of Catiline in Rome:

> for as Catiline entertained the most seditious persons about all Rome to join with him in his conspiracy, so the Earl of Essex had none but Papists, Recusants, and Atheists for his adjutors and abettors in their Capital rebellion against the whole estate of England. My lord, I much wonder that his heart could forget all the princely advancements given him by her majesty, and be so utterly beflinted, as to turn them all to rebellious ends; but it seems this overweighing a man's own conceit, and an aspiring mind to wished honour, is like the crocodile, which is ever growing as long as it liveth.

Their lordships knew, he went on, how the earls had gone into the City with arms and weapons, which made him wonder why they stood upon their trials without confession: 'But my hope is, that God of his mercy, that hath revealed their treasons, will not suffer the rest of his or any others to the hurt of the state, or prejudice to her majesty's most royal person, whom I pray God long to preserve from the hands of her enemies.'

'Amen,' cried the two earls, 'and God confound their souls that ever wished otherwise to her sacred person.'

Sir Edward Coke, the Attorney-General, now followed Serjeant Yelverton. Sir Edward had been born in 1552 and was called to the Bar in 1578. He had been MP for Aldborough, and had held the offices of Recorder of London, Speaker of the House of Commons, Solicitor-General and, since 1593, Attorney-General. He explained the law: 'the thought of Treason to the Prince, by the law is death; and he that is guilty of rebellion is guilty of an intent (by the laws of the land) to seek the destruction of the prince, and so adjudged Treason'. He reiterated what the serjeant had already said, and went on to describe what had happened at Drury House.

At the end of the Attorney-General's speech, the Earl of Essex asked: 'Will your lordships give us our turns to speak, for he playeth the Orator, and abuseth your lordships ears and us with slanders; but they are but fashions of orators in corrupt states.' He went on to say that he and the Earl of Southampton could well answer the charges. However, he was told that he could not speak until after Henry Witherington's examination had been read. This was a statement which confirmed what the Law Officers had said, upon which the Earl of Essex declared:

> I protest before God upon my salvation that I never heard such words as 'Kill him, kill him:' . . . And as for locking up the council, I protest to God it was done in charity, and without disloyalty, but intending only to save them, lest they should take hurt; considering the people abroad in the streets, with a great and sudden outcry, said 'We shall be slain.' At which time we thought our enemies had been come to beset the house, for my intent was no otherwise than loyal to her majesty and them.

The Lord Keeper, the Earl of Worcester and Popham CJ then gave evidence upon their honour that they had heard the words 'Kill them, kill them', although they could not say that they were spoken with the knowledge of the Earl of Essex or at his command. The combined statement of these three men was read; this contained a detailed account of the day of the rebellion and was attested viva voce by Popham CJ.

The Attorney-General turned to the Earl of Essex and asked him: 'Yea, my lord, you had 300 men in arms in your house; why did you not dissolve them, being commanded upon your allegiance from the queen to do it?' The earl replied that they had heard rumours of 'men about my house against them' and it was not in his power suddenly to dissolve them. The Earl of Southampton added: 'Mr Attorney, you speak all this as if it were true as the Gospel.' The Earl of Essex explained that he was defending his house against his enemies, but the Attorney-General replied that this was no excuse, for they had refused to dissolve their company when charged upon their allegiance to do so. After some discussion of other topics, the earl said, 'Well, Mr Attorney, I thank God you are not my judge this day, you are so uncharitable.' 'Well, my lord,' said the Attorney-General, 'we shall prove you anon what you are, which your pride of heart, and aspiring mind, hath brought you unto.'

It appears to have been permissible for anyone present to participate whenever they wished, and at this point Sir Walter Raleigh intervened, to say that 'my lord of Essex had put himself into a strong guard at Essex house, and this is like to be the bloodiest day's work that ever was'.

The Attorney-General intervened again: 'Well, my lord, what can you devise to say for Sir John Davis, another of your adherents, a Papist? for he hath confessed that he is a Papist and a Catholic, and drawn in by Sir Christ. Blount, one of your chiefest counsel, and that he called for a Seminary priest upon his convertment to absolve him.' There followed a discussion as to whether Sir Christopher Blount was a papist.

Then Serjeant Yelverton interrupted: 'Why, my lord, if you deny the raising the power, why should so many men come to your house that day?' The Earl of Southampton protested that he had not more than ten or twelve men with him, which was his usual company – so he was far from purposing to raise a tumult.

The Attorney-General now returned to the evidence and asked for the confession of Sir Ferdinando Gorges to be read. The confession, which Sir Ferdinando Gorges confirmed in person, described the meeting at Drury House and the earl's expedition into London, and also how he had then returned to Essex House with instructions to release Popham CJ.

The examinations of Sir Charles Davers and Sir John Davis confirmed the plan to take the court. The latter said that it was the earl who had written the details down with his own hand; he also stated that he had asked the Earl of Essex how he would deal with offenders, and the earl had replied that he would admit them all to an honourable trial.

Sir Christopher Blount had been examined and had confessed that he had been reconciled to the Pope, and that the purpose of the Earl of Essex was to alter the state of government. The Earl of Rutland said that he had been with the Earl of Essex in the streets of London and had heard him cry out that 'England is bought and sold to the Spaniards.' Lord Cromwel said that he too had gone with the earl into London and heard him say 'Where is the sheriff? Let him bring muskets and pistols; for I am credibly informed out of Ireland, that the kingdom of England is sold to the Spaniard.' And Lord Sandes had also been with the earl and went with him to

Norden's map of London, 1593; by the time of the Essex Rebellion, Leycester House (on the left) had become the home of the Earl of Essex; the Tower of London may be seen on the right (Museum of London)

Ludgate where they were repulsed, and he had heard him cry 'Charge, charge!' and call for his horses.

There the Attorney-General closed his case, and added: 'And do but note, they have all agreed and jumped together, notwithstanding they were all severally examined; but I must needs think it the just judgment of God, in his mercy towards our sovereign, to have the truth so marvellously revealed; coming from them of their own accords, without rack or torture to any of them.'

The Earl of Essex pointed out that all the witnesses had been in fear of their lives, and that his real intention had been to prostrate himself before the queen and put himself at her mercy, and desire her 'that she would . . . have been pleased to have severed some from her majesty, who, by reason of their potency with her, abused her majesty's ears with false informations; and they were Cobham, Cecil and Raleigh'.

The trial again developed into a general conversation. The Lord Admiral wanted to know whether the Earl of Essex had delivered articles in writing for the seizure of the court and the Tower. The Earl of Southampton said it was a foolish action, going through the town – but the plan to have men planted at the court was to protect them from their private enemies. Cobham asked the Earl of Essex why he had laid such imputations against him, and the earl said he had forgiven him. Then Francis Bacon intervened; he was one of Her Majesty's Counsel, but it is not clear in what capacity he was acting: 'It is evident that you, my lord of Essex, had planted a pretence against the government: and now, under colour of excuse, you must lay the cause upon particular enemies.' He told the tale of Pisistratus, who, with the purpose of subverting the kingdom, entered the city and 'cut his body over-thwart' so that the citizens might think he had been in danger:

> and so by this means held the same conceit as you and your complices did; entering the city of London, persuading yourselves, if they had undertaken your cause, all would have gone well on your side. And now, my lord, all you have said, or can say, in answer to these matters, are but shadows; and therefore, methinks, it were your best course to confess, and not to justify.

The earl now turned to Mr Secretary Cecil and said that he had heard him tell one of his fellow-counsellors, 'That none in the world but the Infanta of Spain had right to the crown of England.' So Sir Robert Cecil joined in: 'The difference between you and me is great; for I speak in the person of an honest man, and you, my lord, in the person of a Traitor.' He demanded to know the name of the counsellor: 'name him, name him, name him if you dare, if you dare, I defy you; name him if you dare'. Then the Earl of Southampton said it was Mr Comptroller, so Sir Robert requested the Lord High Steward to send a messenger to the queen to request the attendance of Mr Comptroller Knollys.

There seems to have been a short adjournment until Mr Comptroller arrived, and the Lord High Steward asked him if he had heard Sir Robert Cecil say that no one but the infanta had right to the crown of England. He replied: 'I remember that once in Mr Secretary's company, there was a book read, that treated of such matters; but I never did hear Mr Secretary use any such words, or to that effect.' Whereupon Sir Robert 'thanked God that though the Earl stood there as a traitor, yet he was found an honest man; . . . I beseech God to forgive you for this open wrong done unto me, as I do openly pronounce I forgive you from the bottom of my heart'. 'And I, Mr Secretary,' said the earl, 'do clearly and freely forgive you with all my soul; because I mean to die in charity.'

The Earl of Southampton then made a long speech in which he pleaded that he had acted innocently and in ignorance of the law, and he submitted himself to the mercy of the queen. The Earl of Essex endeavoured to explain why he and his friends had gone to London: he had sent for the sheriff and Mr Alderman Watts to come to see if they were demeaning themselves loyally and to put themselves in their hands, upon which the Attorney-General interrupted to ask him why he was crying out that England belonged to the Spaniards. The Earl of Southampton protested that he had never heard the Earl of Essex say anything of the sort, and that he had never intended treason and had acted only to assist the Earl of Essex in his private quarrel. The Earl of Essex then made another long speech in which he referred to a quarrel between the Earl of Southampton and Lord Grey, but he protested he had no malice – not even to his private enemies – and had intended no harm to the queen and had never sought the crown of England.

Bacon then delivered what was in effect the closing speech for the prosecution: 'Well, my lord, may it please your grace, you see how weakly he hath shadowed his purpose, and how slenderly he hath answered the objections against him.' He now drew another historical parallel, this time from the rebellion of the Duke of Guise, who had come upon the Barricadoes at Paris in his doublet and hose, attended by eight men; when the king took up arms against him, he was glad to yield himself, and said that the occasion was a private quarrel.

Robert Devereux, second Earl of Essex
(1566–1601) (National Portrait
Gallery)

The Lieutenant of the Tower was then instructed to withdraw his prisoners from the bar, and the peers retired to a private place behind the canopy and the chair of state. They sent for the two Chief Justices and the Chief Baron to advise them on the law, which they did on two points:

> That in case where a subject attempteth to put himself into such strength, as the king shall not be able to resist him, and to force and compel the king to govern otherwise than according to his own authority and direction, it is manifest rebellion;
>
> That in every Rebellion the law intendeth as a consequent the compassing the death and deprivation of the king, as foreseeing that the rebel will never suffer the king to live or reign, who might punish or take revenge of his treason and rebellion.

After half an hour the peers returned, and the Lord High Steward asked each in turn whether Robert, Earl of Essex was guilty of treason or not. Each in turn, bending his body and laying his left hand upon his right side, said: 'Guilty, my lord, of High Treason.' The same procedure was followed in the case of the Earl of Southampton. The prisoners were then brought back to the bar, and the Clerk of the Crown asked them what they could say as to why they should not have judgment of death.

The Earl of Essex said that, having been brought within the compass of the law, he was willing to die. He declared that he was 'free of Popery and Atheism', and he would die in the faith he had professed. The Earl of Southampton again pleaded that he had acted in ignorance of the law, he had spent the best part of his patrimony in her majesty's service, and he submitted himself to her mercy.

The Lord High Steward suggested to the Earl of Essex that he too should seek the mercy of the queen, to which he replied in yet another speech in which, at first, he appeared to be turning down the suggestion, but in conclusion he said: 'Mistake me not, nor think me so proud, that I will not crave her majesty's mercy, for I protest . . . I do crave her majesty's mercy with all humility; yet I had rather die than live in misery.'

The Lord High Steward then exhorted them to prepare themselves for God, and told them that he must now proceed to judgment, to which the Earl of Essex replied cheerfully: 'Yea, my lord, with a very good will I pray you go on.' So the Lord High Steward proceeded: 'You must go to the place from whence you came, and there remain during her majesty's pleasure; from thence to be drawn on a hurdle through London streets, and so to the place of execution, where you shall be hanged, bowelled, and quartered; your head and quarters to be disposed of at her majesty's pleasure, and so God have mercy on your souls.'

The Earl of Essex now embarked on yet another speech, beginning: 'My lord, I am not a whit dismayed to receive this sentence, for I protest death is as welcome to me as life. . . . And I think it fit my poor quarters that have done her majesty true service in divers parts of the world, should be sacrificed and disposed of at her majesty's pleasure. . . .' Then he requested that the queen would grant him permission to have the same preacher to comfort him that he had had since his troubles began, and that the Constable of the Tower and Lord Howard would take the sacrament with him. Their lordships promised that this request would be passed on to the queen, to which he replied: 'I humbly thank your lordships.' Then the serjeant-at-arms proclaimed that the peers might take their ease and depart, and that the Commission was dissolved.

The Earl of Southampton was reprieved; the queen was at one time minded to reprieve the Earl of Essex also, but changed her mind. While he was awaiting death, he made his last written confession in which he said that he had indeed intended to seize the court and the Tower, and to have called a parliament. He called himself a burden to the commonwealth to be spewed out; he desired his life to be shortened for he knew that the queen could not be safe as long as he was alive. Finally, he desired a private death, to avoid the acclamations of the people.

This last request was granted. A scaffold was erected in the courtyard of the Tower, and early in the morning of 25 February 1601 two doctors of divinity and the minister of the church in the Tower went to his room, and he gave thanks that his dangerous designs had failed. He thanked the queen for granting that he should not be executed in public lest 'his mind might be disturbed by the acclamations of the public, protesting that he had now learned how vain a thing the blast of popular favour and applause was', and he repeated that he deserved to be spewed out. He was brought to the scaffold. Several peers and aldermen of London were there, and Sir Walter Raleigh 'who if we may believe himself, came with an intent to make answer if anything should be objected against him by the earl at his death; but others thought he came to feed his eyes with a sight of the earl's sufferings, and to satiate his hatred with his blood', but he was warned to keep away, and retired to watch the execution from the Armoury. The earl acknowledged his sins and besought the queen and her ministers to forgive him, and gave thanks that he had never been a Papist or an Atheist. The executioner asked his forgiveness and he forgave him. The earl laid his head on the block, and repeated the opening lines of Psalm 51, and said: 'In humility and obedience I prostrate myself to my deserved punishment: Thou, O God! have mercy on thy prostrate servant: Into thy hands, O Lord! I commend my spirit.' His head was taken off with the third stroke, but the first took away all sense and motion.

On 5 March the other conspirators – Sir Christopher Blount, Sir Charles Davers, Sir John Davis, Sir Gilly Merrick and Henry Cuffe – appeared before a Special Commission at Westminster Hall. The commission consisted of the Earl of Nottingham (Lord High Admiral), Lord Hunsdon (Lord Chamberlain), Mr Secretary Cecil, Sir John Popham CJ, Sir John Fortescue (Chancellor of the Exchequer), Mr Secretary Herbert, and 'divers of the judges'. Popham CJ acted as *de facto* president of the court as well as chief witness for the prosecution.

Serjeant Yelverton opened the case for the Crown, and was followed by Coke A.-G., who asked for Merrick and Cuffe to be removed for a time for pestering the bar. Coke A.-G. dealt first with Blount, who interrupted to say that, as a result of wounds which he had received, he was scarce *compos mentis*. However, Coke A.-G. pressed on and described various treasonable conspiracies in the past: an insurrection by the labourers of Kent against the Statute of Labourers, a rising by the prentices of London against the Lord Mayor for allowing other prentices to be whipped for making a rout in Southwark, and a rising in Oxfordshire to overthrow closes and restore tillage. All these had been held to be treason, so how much more so was a conspiracy to take the Tower and the City, and possess the court and call a parliament. This was a case like the story of Richard II and Henry IV Part I: 'This treason's bird hath been long a-hatching, like unto an elephant's whelp, long a-breeding, but bred in a hollow tree, and discovered before it was fledged.' And they had invented a buzz that the Earl of Essex was to be murdered by Sir Walter Raleigh, when really they planned to murder him.

It was while the Attorney-General was addressing the Court that Mr Secretary Cecil asked for a ruling whether in a case 'When men were actors and abettors in such a matter, whether the law charged them not in this point with direct Treason against the Person of the prince?' and the judges affirmed that this was so.

Evidence relating to the arrival and imprisonment of the counsellors on the Sunday morning was repeated, and it was at this point in the trial that Popham CJ cross-examined Sir Christopher Blount from the bench: 'Why they stood at the great chamber door with muskets charged and matches in their hands; which, through the key-hole, the L.C.J. said, he discerned?' Sir John Davis answered on behalf of Sir Christopher Blount: he said that he had wished to go to London with the others, but the Earl of Essex had charged him with the custody of the counsellors, and he had had to pacify the captain of the guard, Owen Salisbury, who was very violent and 'so disordered he doubted what he would attempt'. Popham CJ said that they had not been afraid – 'if they did take their lives, it was but the cutting off of a few years' – and when he had been invited to leave, he had replied 'as they came together, so they would go together, or die together'. Sir John Davis further explained that, to assure their lordships that no harm was intended, he had gone upstairs and persuaded the Countess of Essex to come and join them, and he had prepared a dinner for them from such provisions as were available in the house, but, said Popham CJ, 'My lord keeper and he told Davis, they would eat none of my lord's meat.'

While the Attorney-General was describing the escapade into London, Sir Christopher Blount confessed that he had gone with the Earl of Essex and had charged the forces at Ludgate, but 'denied the killing of . . . [the scribe had probably failed to hear the man's name and there is a gap in the MS].'

Coke A.-G. then embarked on a long account of the events that had taken place in Ireland. This account is far from clear, although whether this was because he had failed to brief himself properly or because the scribe was having difficulty in following what he was saying, I cannot tell. He also explained why this evidence had not been placed before the court at the trial of the Earl of Essex: 'but the cause was, one, the shortness of time; another, because all the lords were satisfied, and said there was Treason full enough proved against him, and it satisfied to condemn him'. There was also some discussion as to how much Sir Christopher Blount, who had been seriously injured and was lying ill at the time, had known of the Irish conspiracy. Finally, the Attorney-General closed his case against Sir Christopher by saying: 'the action of breaking out into that it did, it was a great mercy of the queen's that in *flagrante crimine* he was not, according to the martial law, presently put to the sword', although it is not clear whether he was referring to the Earl of Essex or Blount.

Flemming S.-G. then opened the case against Sir Charles Davers, but Sir Charles intervened to say that he perceived that his act had extended to treason, although he intended no harm to the queen's person, and said he was sorry he had so far forgotten himself to plead Not Guilty. Sir Ferdinando Gorges' confession was then read, and Mr Secretary Cecil explained that the reason why he too had not been prosecuted was because he had been responsible for rescuing the counsellors from Essex House.

Sir Christopher Blount said that he had known nothing of the plot until the earl had sent for him, and he was more to be commiserated as he had married the earl's mother:

> I must needs confess that heretofore, I having done much to her majesty's service, adventured my life many times, as the marks of this my wretched carcase will shew; hazarded my fortune when it was at the best, and all for the honour of her majesty, and in her service, and yet she never vouchsafed notice of me or my service;

but he now confessed himself Guilty and cast himself on Her Majesty's mercy.

It was now the turn of Francis Bacon, who opened the case against Sir John Davis in the form of a diatribe, in which he referred to the protestations of innocence which had been made:

> And this stile of protestation that no harm was intended to the sovereign, was common in traitors. Manlius, the lieutenant of Catiline, had that very protestation; but the proceeding in such in this, as no long discoursing needs to prove it Treason, the act itself was Treason.

He declared that Sir John had been a plotter from the start:

> The second plot was in taking of the court, and in this consultation he was *penna Philoso-phi-scribentis*; you were clerk of that Council-Table, and wrote all: and in the detaining of the privy-counsellors, you were the man only trusted. And . . . you held it a stratagem of war to detain pledges, and was meant to have carried the lord-keeper with the Great Seal into London; and to have had with you the lord-chief-justice, a man for his integrity, honoured and well-beloved of the citizens; and this Achitophel plot you thought to have followed.

Sir John could no longer suffer in silence, and told Mr Bacon that, if with good manners he might, he would long since have interrupted and saved a great part of his labour, for he intended to plead Guilty. 'But in that you call me Clerk of that Council, let me tell you, sir Charles Davers was writing, but his hand being bad, I was desired to take pen and write.'

The Lord Admiral then reminded the court that Sir John had been responsible for detaining the lords in Essex House:

> The case was hard with these worthy counsellors: for by God he swore, though these counsellors had been in the house, yet being as he was, general of the forces, and sent to force the house, he [the Lord Admiral] must and would have battered and blown it up,

though it had been the death of them as well as the rest; and had all his own sons been there, he would have done it.

Then the Attorney-General 'took in hand' the evidence against Mr Cuffe, who appears to have been employed by the Earl of Essex as a secretary or librarian, and Sir Gilly Merrick. To Cuffe he said that

> he was the arrantest Traitor that ever came to that bar; he was Poly . . . . the very seducer of the earl. . . . For the *polypragma*, this fellow, the cunning coiner of all plots, how to intrap a worthy gentleman.[3]

Mr Secretary Cecil said that the Earl of Essex himself had confessed that Cuffe was a principal instigator, and added that:

> he must needs speak of a difference he found between noble and generous-minded men and others baser born: from the earls and other gentlemen of birth and good house, all their confessions came freely and liberally from them without concealment or covering any thing with untruths. By Cuffe, and some others of baser sort, nothing would be confessed, but what they were convicted of, and shadowed with untruths so far as their wits could do it.

Cuffe defended himself vigorously:

> If a man may be excused of Treason by committing nothing, I am clear. Yet the number of matters heaped upon me, and the inferences and inforcements of the same, used against me to make me odious, make me seem also a monster of many heads in this business; but since by the law all accusations are to be believed, and facts weighed, as by evidence they are proved; and things best proved by being singled; I beseech Mr Attorney that we may insist upon some point certain, and not as in a stream have all things at once brought upon me with violence.

He said that he had spent all the day of the rebellion locked up in his chamber among his books, and never appeared until all was surrendered to the Lord Admiral. 'To conclude me to be a Traitor, because I was in a house where treason was committed; by the same reason if a lion had been there locked in a grate, he had been in case of treason.' It was true, that as a servant who longed for the honour of his master, he had often wished to see him recalled to the court and restored to her majesty's former favour, but he had never aspired to anything other than to see him restored to the position in which he had been before.

Then the Attorney-General told Cuffe that he would give him a cuff that should set him down, and called for the earl's confession to be read. This was plainly against Cuffe, and Cecil asked what he meant by having a parliament, to which Cuffe replied that 'it was conceived these things would work great alteration; and for settling of all things, they thought, that shortly would follow a Parliament'. The Attorney-General closed his case by saying that 'it was meant that Cuffe should have been the Speaker of that Parliament'.

As for Sir Gilly, Coke A.-G. urged first:

> that he was the man who fortified Essex house against the queen's forces; and if God had not otherwise guided it, that day he had been the death of a noble person, the lord Burleigh, for he set one with a musket-shot to shoot at him, but missing the lord Burleigh, captain Lovel's horse was killed under him at Essex-gate with that shot. . . . And the story of Henry 4th, being set forth in a play, and in that play there being set forth the killing of a king upon a stage: the Friday before, sir Gilly and some others of the earl's train having an humour to see a play, they must needs have the play of Henry 4th. The players told them that was stale, they should get nothing of playing of that, but no play else would serve; and sir Gilly gives 40 shillings to Philips the player to play this, besides whatsoever he could get.

The confession of a man called Thomas Johnson was then read. He said that he had seen Sir Gilly all that day, walking in his doublet and hose up and down the house, with muskets following him, and that he had gone down to the banqueting hall with his hat full of shot. To this Sir Gilly responded that he was trying to save the counsellors from the fury of Owen Salisbury, who had sworn that if the house was forced he would send them all to the Devil. This was followed by the confession of one Watts, who said that:

> there was a watch in the house all Saturday night, and none of the company went to bed, but for a while's rest threw themselves upon their beds in their cloaths; and that sir Gilly Merrick caused certain hogsheads to be broken up, to fortify against the tennis-court. That the earl had 100 muskets in the house, but wanted flaskets and such other furniture for them.

This was virtually the end of the case, but the Attorney-General, determined to have the last word with the jury, read out part of the confession of the Earl of Essex, in which he had acknowledged that he was worthily spewed out.

The jury was out for half an hour, and found all five prisoners Guilty; and Popham CJ asked them if they had anything to say why judgment should not be given against them.

Sir Christopher Blount made a long speech. He said that he had nothing to say to excuse himself, or to extenuate his fault, except that he had acted out of his over-love for that unhappy earl, the Earl of Essex: 'I left all to adventure with the earl in service for her majesty into Portugal, at Cales, the Islands, and in Ireland.' Finally, he requested a private audience with the Lord Admiral; this was granted, and the two men met in the Court of Wards after the court rose.

Sir Charles Davers said that he now confessed himself Guilty, and asked the favour of the queen 'that I may be beheaded', and Sir Christopher Blount intervened again to make the same request.

Sir John Davis appealed for mercy and expressed the hope that his wife would not be afflicted for his offence, and Sir Gilly Merrick prayed that his wife and children should be pitied.

Cuffe complained that he had had £350 seized upon in his chamber – he did not say what had happened to it. He also requested that the law would be satisfied with his life without torturing or quartering of his flesh.

Popham CJ, not satisfied with having presided over the trial and given evidence against the accused and having cross-examined them from the bench, now addressed his victims. He was sorry, he said, to see that anyone was so ill affected to the state as to plot against it. Should it be said in the world that Englishmen, after forty-three years of peace under a queen who was admired by all the world, should become weary of her government? He was sorry to think that Englishmen should excuse themselves by ignorance of the law, which all subjects were bound to know. And some of them were Christians: 'Where, I pray, did you ever read or hear that it was lawful for the subject to command or restrain his sovereign? It is a thing against the law of God, and all nations.' And then, after advising them to take care of their souls, he pronounced the formal judgment.

On 13 March Cuffe and Merrick were drawn to Tyburn. Cuffe delivered a long speech in which he declared that he had had nothing to do with the commotion, but 'was shut up the whole day within the house, where I spent the time in very melancholy reflections'. Here he was interrupted by Merrick and advised not to

Sir John Popham (*c.* 1531–1607). In his youth he was a highwayman, but he was called to the Bar and became Chief Justice of the Court of King's Bench in 1592; in this capacity he was the presiding judge at the trials of the Earl of Essex, Sir Walter Raleigh and the Gunpowder Plot conspirators (National Portrait Gallery)

'palliate his crime by specious pretences', but he went on again until he was interrupted a second time, and 'so began to apply himself to his devotions, which he managed with a great deal of fervour'. He was then despatched by the executioner. Merrick briefly entreated those noblemen who stood nearby to intercede with the queen to stay further proceedings against those who had unwarily espoused the unhappy cause before he too was despatched.

On 18 March Sir Christopher Blount, Sir Charles Davers and Sir John Davis were executed on Tower Hill. Sir Charles made a short speech in which he craved the pardon of God, the queen, and Lord Grey. Sir Christopher Blount, on the other hand, in spite of his 'imperfection of speech, and God knows, a weak memory, by reason of my late wound', delivered a long address in which he said that he had first become aware of the discontentment of the Earl of Essex three years previously, but had never discussed it again until the earl came to visit him at Reban. Here the sheriff interrupted him and told him that his hour had come, but Lord Grey and Sir Walter Raleigh told the sheriff to allow him to continue. When Sir Christopher heard Sir Walter's voice he thanked God that he was there and begged for his forgiveness, to which Sir Walter replied that he willingly forgave him, but then reminded him that he had been regarded as a principal provoker of the Earl of Essex and had advised him to transport his army from Ireland into England: 'You shall do well to tell the truth, and to satisfy the world.'

Sir Christopher then addressed Lord Grey and the others on horseback round the scaffold and admitted that he knew of the plan to make a descent upon England and to march upon London, but he knew it was dangerous and would cost much blood:

And although it be true, that (as we all protested in our Examinations and Arraignments) we never resolved of doing hurt to her majesty's Person; . . . yet, I know, and must confess, that if we failed in our ends, we should (rather than have been disappointed) even have drawn blood from herself.

Then he beseeched God to preserve the queen, and asked for forgiveness. He turned away from the rail to the executioner, 'prepared himself to the block, and so died very manfully and resolutely'.

CHAPTER TWO

The Trial of Sir Walter Raleigh (1603)

The editor of the *State Trials* has reprinted a note to Wilson's *Life of James I*[1] which reads as follows:

> This conspiracy of Sir Walter Raleigh's is variously represented by the Historians and Writers of that time, but acknowledged by all of them to have been a Riddle of State.

This is a fair summary of all that is known of this affair. The 'evidence' that emerged at the trial of Sir Walter – not a shred of which would have been admissible under the modern rules of evidence – was self-contradictory, and much of the case for the Crown consisted simply of insults delivered by the Attorney-General. In so far as one can piece the story together, it appears that there was a plan, initiated by two Roman Catholic priests, William Watson and William Clarke, to seize the king and the Tower, depose the privy counsellors, and declare liberty of religion. Also, several other men, notably Lord Grey, George Brooke, Sir Griffin Markham, Bartholomew Brookesby and Anthony Copley, were parties to this plan. There was another plan, involving Lord Cobham (Brooke's brother), to depose the king and to replace him by his cousin, Arabella Stuart.[2] A third plan, also involving Lord Cobham, was to raise money for a rebellion and to call in the Spaniards for their assistance. Whether these plans, if they existed at all, were linked together, and whether any or all of them were instigated by Sir Walter Raleigh, or whether he was a party to them, one cannot say.

The two priests, together with Brooke, Markham, Brookesby and Copley, were arraigned at Winchester on 15 November 1603. They were all convicted, according to Sir Dudley Carleton in a letter which he wrote to Mr John Chamberlain on 27 November, 'upon their own confessions, which were set down under their own hands, as Declarations; and compiled with such labour and care, to make the matter they undertook seem very feasible, as if they had feared they should not say enough to hang themselves'.

Sir Walter was tried at Winchester on 17 November 1603. The commissioners who were appointed to hear the case were Henry Howard (Earl of Suffolk and Lord Chamberlain), Charles Blunt (Earl of Devonshire), Lord Henry Howard, Robert Cecil (Earl of Salisbury), Edward Lord Wotton of Morley, Sir John Stanhope (Vice-Chamberlain), Sir John Popham (Chief Justice of the Court of King's Bench), Sir Edmund Anderson (Chief Justice of the Court of Common Pleas), Gawdie and Warburton JJ, and Sir W. Wade. It will be noted that, although in those days the judges were in the personal appointment of the monarch, James I had retained the services of Popham and Anderson CJJ, and Sir Edward Coke was still Attorney-General.

The editor of the *State Trials* gives no indication as to the origin of the report, but it gives the appearance of a transcript of a shorthand note.

The indictment set out:

> That he [Raleigh] did conspire, and go about to deprive the King of his government; to raise up sedition within the realm; to alter religion, to bring in the Roman Superstition and to procure foreign enemies to invade the kingdom.

It is doubtful whether these charges would have fallen within the provisions of the Treason Act 1351, but they might been covered under Acts passed in 1571 and 1584.

The indictment then went on to allege that, on 9 June, Lord Cobham and Sir Walter Raleigh had conferred at Durham house on 'how to advance Arabella Stuart (who was a cousin of the King) to the crown'. It alleged that they had agreed with Count Aremberg (the Austrian ambassador) to obtain 600,000 crowns for the purpose, and that Lord Cobham should go to Albert, Archduke of Austria, to obtain money from him, and thence to Spain to obtain further assistance. Also that they had agreed that Arabella should be induced to write letters to the archduke, the King of Spain, and the Duke of Savoy, promising to establish a firm peace between England and Spain, to tolerate the Popish religion, and to be 'ruled by them in contracting her marriage'. Finally, that Lord Cobham should return via Jersey (where Sir Walter was Captain of the Isle) and arrange the distribution of the money.

The indictment also claimed that Lord Cobham and his brother, Brooke, had given their assent to these measures, and that they had said 'That there would never be a good world in England, till the king (meaning our sovereign lord) and his cubs (meaning his royal issue) were taken away.' Furthermore, that Sir Walter had falsely written a book against the title of the king, and had instigated Brooke to incite Arabella to write the letters referred to, and had instigated Lord Cobham to write letters to Aremberg and deliver the letters to Matthew de Laurency for obtaining the 600,000 crowns. Lastly, that Lord Cobham was going to give 8,000 crowns to Sir Walter, and 10,000 to Brooke.

The trial commenced in an orderly manner. Sir Walter pleaded Not Guilty; a jury was empanelled and he was invited to challenge any of them, but he declined. He asked if he might be allowed to deal with each point as it arose, but Popham CJ told him that he could say what he wished after 'the king's learned council [*sic*] have delivered all the evidence'.

Serjeant Heale, the king's serjeant, then opened the case for the Crown, and set the tone for what was to follow:

> You have heard of Raleigh's bloody attempts to kill the king and his royal progeny, and in place thereof to advance Arabella Stuart. The particulars of the indictment are these: First, that Raleigh met with Cobham the 9th of June, and had conference of an invasion, of a Rebellion, and an Insurrection, to be made by the king's subjects, to depose the king, and to kill his children, poor babes that never gave offence. . . . Since the Conquest, there was never the like Treason. But out of whose head came it? Out of Raleigh's, who must also advise Cobham to use his brother Brooke to incite the lady Arabella to write three several Letters, as aforesaid in the Indictment. . . . As for the lady Arabella, she, upon my conscience, hath no more Title to the crown than I have, which before God I utterly renounce. . . . Now, whether these things were bred in a hollow tree, I leave to them to speak of, who can speak far better than myself.

He sat down, and the Attorney-General then embarked upon a tirade of abuse, spattered with malice, unsupported either by the facts set out in the indictment or by the evidence which was to follow:

> We carry a just mind, to condemn no man, but upon plain evidence. Here is Mischief, Mischief *in summo gradu*, exorbitant Mischief. . . . Mischief is ever underpropped by falsehood or foul practices: and because all these things did concur in this Treason, you shall understand the main, as before you did the bye.[3] The Treason of the bye consisteth in these Points: first, that the lord Grey, Brook, Markham, and the rest, intended by force to surprize the king's court; which was a Rebellion in the heart of the Realm, yea, in the heart of the

heart, in the Court. They intended to take him that is a sovereign, to make him subject to their power, purposing to open the doors with musquets and cavaliers, and to take also the Prince and Council: then under the king's authority to carry the king to the Tower; and to make a stale[4] of the Admiral.

Watson, the priest, was to be made Lord Chancellor, Brooke Lord Treasurer, and 'a hole must be found in my Lord Chief Justice's coat', Grey must be Earl Marshal and Master of the Horse: 'So you see, these Treasons were like Sampson's foxes,[5] which were joined in their tails, though their heads were severed.'

Here Sir Walter Raleigh intervened to say that he was not charged with the bye, which was the treason of the priest. 'You are not,' retorted the Attorney-General, and went on:

> My lords, you shall observe three things in the Treasons: 1. They had a watch-word (the king's safety); their pretence was *Bonum in se*; their intent was *malum in se*; 2. They avouched Scripture; both the priests had *scriptum est*; perverting and ignorantly mistaking the Scriptures; 3. They avouched the common law, to prove that he was no king until he was crowned.

Then he came to the 'evidence', the most forcible being that 'when a man, by his accusation of another, shall, by the same accusation, also condemn himself, and make himself liable to the same fault and punishment: this is more forcible than many witnesses'.

From then on, any semblance of regularity in the proceedings broke down. At one point the Attorney-General appears to have been accusing Sir Walter of planning to murder the king's children, to which Sir Walter replied: 'To whom speak you this? You tell me news I never heard of.'

Sir Edward Coke (1552–1634). As Attorney-General, from 1594 to 1606, he prosecuted the Earl of Essex, Sir Walter Raleigh and the Gunpowder Plot conspirators. He was Chief Justice of the Court of King's Bench, from 1613 to 1617; following his resignation (or dismissal) he returned to Parliament, and wrote his *Institutes* (By courtesy of the Inner Temple; photo: Courtauld Institute of Art)

'Oh sir, do I?' said the Attorney-General. 'I will prove you the notoriest traitor that ever came to the bar. After you have taken away the king, you would alter religion . . .'

'Your words cannot condemn me; my innocency is my defence. Prove one of these things wherewith you have charged me, and I will confess the whole indictment. . . .'

'Nay, I will prove all: thou art a monster; thou hast an English face, but a Spanish heart. Now you must have Money. . . .'

'Let me answer for myself.'

'Thou shalt not.'

'It concerneth my life.'

Popham CJ now intervened: 'Sir Walter Raleigh, Mr Attorney is but yet in the general: but when the king's counsel have given the Evidence wholly you shall answer every particular.'

'Oh! do I touch you?' asked the Attorney-General.

Now Lord Cecil, a friend of the accused, asked: 'Mr Attorney, when you have done with this General Charge, do you not mean to let him answer every particular?'

'Yes,' said the Attorney-General, 'when we deliver the Proofs to be read.' Then, after a lurid account of the evidence, he said: 'I think you meant to make Arabella a Titular Queen, of whose Title I will speak nothing; but sure you meant to make her a stale. Ah! good lady, you could mean her no good.'

'You tell me news, Mr Attorney,' said Sir Walter.

'Oh sir! I am the more large, because I know with whom I deal: for we have to deal today with a man of wit.' Then he went on to refer to Raleigh's 'Machiavellian and devilish policy': 'Now then see the most horrible practices that ever came out of the bottomless pit of the lowest hell. . . . You are the absolutest traitor that ever was.'

'Your phrases will not prove it. . . . I do not hear yet, that you have spoken one word against me; here is no Treason of mine done: if my Lord Cobham be a traitor, what is that to me?'

'All that he did was by thy instigation, thou Viper; for I *thou* thee, thou traitor.'

'It becometh not a man of quality and virtue, to call me so: But I take comfort in it, it is all you can do.'

'Have I angered you?'

'I am in no case to be angry.'

'Sir Walter Raleigh,' said Popham CJ, 'Mr Attorney speaketh out of the zeal of his duty, for the service of the king, and you for your life; be valiant on both sides.'

The Clerk of the Crown Office now read out Lord Cobham's examination, which he had given, it is thought, under interrogation before the Privy Council. He confessed that he had a passport to go to Spain to deal with the king for 600,000 crowns, and said that nothing would be done until he had spoken to Sir Walter Raleigh. He 'breathed out oaths and exclamations against Raleigh, calling him Villain and Traitor; saying that he had never entered into these courses, but by his instigation, and that he would never let him alone. Besides, he spoke of Plots and Invasions; of the particulars whereof he could give no account, though Raleigh and he had conferred of them.'

Sir Walter dealt with all this in no uncertain terms:

Let me see the Accusation: This is absolutely all the evidence can be brought against me; poor shifts! You gentlemen of the jury, pray understand this. This is that which must either condemn, or give me life; which must free me, or send my wife and children to beg their bread about the streets: this is that must prove me a notorious Traitor, or a true subject to the king. Let me see my Accusation, that I may make my Answer.

The clerk said that he had already read the whole of the examination, so Sir Walter embarked upon his defence. He had never heard of Arabella Stuart, he said, and Lord Cobham was no babe to be guided by others. As for Spain, he knew that the king was penniless – the Jesuits, 'who were wont to have such large allowance, were fain to beg at the church door'. And his only discussion with Lord Cobham was about 'matters of profit; as the ordering of his house, paying of his servants board-wages, &c.'

So the prosecution had another of Lord Cobham's examinations read out, in which, after Cobham had read a note in Sir Walter's writing, he had exclaimed: 'Oh Villain! Oh Traitor! I will now tell you all the truth.' The examination continued: 'His [Cobham's] purpose was to go into Flanders, and into Spain, for the obtaining the aforesaid Money; and that Raleigh had appointed him to meet in Jersey as he returned home, to be advised of him about the distribution of the Money.'

Popham CJ now joined in. He had been staying at Richmond, he said, on account of the plague, but he was sent for because Lord Cobham was refusing to sign his declaration. Popham CJ told him that it would be a 'contempt of high nature' if he refused to sign, so he had signed it. Lord Cecil intervened again: he had been at Windsor when news of a plan to seize the king had been disclosed, but he doubted whether Sir Walter was involved. Then the Attorney-General repeated what Lord Cobham had told his brother, Brooke: 'You are fools, you are on the bye, Raleigh and I are on the main; we mean to take away the king and his cubs.'

This drew from Sir Walter the question: 'Hath Cobham confessed that?'

'This is spoken by Mr Attorney,' said Popham CJ, 'to prove that Cobham's speech came not out of passion.'

'Let it be proved that Cobham said so,' said Sir Walter.

The Attorney-General now made another long speech, in which he said:

> It had been better for you to have kept in Guiana, than to have been so well acquainted with the state of Spain. Besides, if you could have brought Spain and Scotland to have joined, you might have hoped to prevail a great deal the better. . . . Then you say, you never talked with Cobham but about leases and letting lands, and ordering his house; I never knew you Clerk of the Kitchen, &c. If you had fallen on your knees at first, and confessed the Treason, it had been better for you.

There followed some discussion on the law, in which Sir Walter argued that the witness must confront the accused face to face, and that two witnesses were required to secure a conviction on a charge of treason: 'You try me by the Spanish Inquisition, if you proceed only by the Circumstances, without two Witnesses.'

'This is a treasonable speech,' said the Attorney-General.

'. . . Good my lords, let it be proved, either by the laws of the land, or the laws of God, that there ought not to be two witnesses appointed.'

Popham CJ, after referring to some statutes which he said had been repealed, said: 'It sufficeth now if there be Proofs made either under hand, or by oaths. . . .'

'It may be an error in me,' said Sir Walter, 'and if those laws be repealed, yet I hope the equity of them remains still; but if you affirm it, it must be a law to posterity. The proof of the Common Law is by witness and jury: let Cobham be here, let him speak it. Call my accuser before my face, and I have done.'

'You have read the letter of the law, but understand it not,' said the Attorney-General, and then went on: 'Now I come to prove the Circumstances of the Accusation to be true. Cobham confessed he had a passport to travel. . . . You say he promised to come home by Jersey, to make merry with you and your wife.'

'I said in his return from France, not Spain,' said Sir Walter. 'All this is but one accusation of Cobham's, I hear no other thing; to which accusation he never subscribed nor avouched it. I beseech you, my lords, let Cobham be sent for, charge him on his soul, on his allegiance to the king; if he affirm it, I am guilty.'

Lord Cecil asked if the accusation was evidence without Cobham's subscription: 'I desire to be resolved by the Judges, whether by the law it is not a forcible argument of evidence,' and the judges replied that it was.

'By the rigour and cruelty of the law it may be forcible evidence,' said Sir Walter.

'That is not the rigour of the law, but the justice of the law,' said Popham CJ.

'Oh my lord, you may use equity.'

'That is from the king; you are to have justice from us.'

Anderson CJ added: 'The law is, if the matter be proved to the jury, they must find you guilty; for Cobham's accusation is not only against you, there are other things sufficient.'

Then more evidence was read. Copley confessed he had been offered 1,000 crowns to be in this action, and Brooke said that there had been letters between Cobham and Aremberg for a sum of money to surprise the king. Yet another confession from Lord Cobham, dated 18 July, said: 'If the money might be procured, then a man may give pensions.' And one from Laurency: 'Within five days after Aremberg arrived, Cobham resorted to him. That night that Cobham went to Aremberg with Laurency, Raleigh supped with him.'

Upon this the Attorney-General commented: 'Raleigh must have part of the Money, therefore now he is a traitor. The crown shall never stand one year on the head of the king (my master) if a Traitor may not be condemned by Circumstances: for if A. tells B. and B. tells C. and C. D. &c. you shall never prove Treason by two witnesses.'

It now transpired that Sir Walter himself had been examined and his declaration was read, in which he said that Cobham had offered him 8,000 crowns for the furtherance of peace between England and Spain: 'I had thought it had been one of his ordinary conceits, and therefore made no Account thereof.' He now repeated this before the court, adding: 'Let me be pinched to death with hot irons, if ever I knew there was any intention to bestow the money on discontented persons.'

Lord Cecil now returned to the question of Lord Cobham's evidence, and a further argument on the law ensued. 'Sir Walter Raleigh presseth, that my Lord Cobham should be brought face to face,' he said, '. . . If we sit here as commissioners, how shall we be satisfied whether he ought to be brought, unless we hear the judges speak?'

'This thing cannot be granted,' said Popham CJ, and Gawdie J. added: 'The Statute you speak of concerning two witnesses in case of Treason, is found to be inconvenient, therefore by another law it was taken away.'

'The common trial of England is by Jury and Witnesses,' said Sir Walter.

'No, by examination,' said Popham CJ, 'if three conspire a Treason, and they all confess it; here is never a witness, yet they are condemned.'

Warburton J. now joined in the discussion: 'I marvel, Sir Walter, that you being of such experience and wit, should stand on this point; for so many horse-stealers may escape, if they may not be condemned without witnesses. If one should rush into the king's Privy-Chamber, whilst he is alone, and kill the king (which God forbid) and this man be met coming out with his sword drawn all bloody; shall he not be condemned to death?'

'I know not how you conceive the law,' said Sir Walter.

'We do not conceive the law,' said Popham CJ, 'but we know the law. . . . There must not such a gap be opened for the destruction of the king, as would be if we should grant this. You plead hard for yourself, but the law pleads as hard for the king. . . .'

'The king desires nothing but the knowledge of the truth,' said Sir Walter, 'and would have no advantage taken by severity of the law. If ever we had a gracious king, we have now. . . . Good my lords, let my Accuser come face to face and be deposed.'

Popham CJ brought the discussion to a close: 'You have no law for it; God forbid any man should accuse himself upon his oath!'

The Attorney-General added for good measure: 'The law presumes, a man will not accuse himself to another. You are an odious man. . . . Now you shall hear of some stirs to be raised in Scotland.' So another part of Copley's examination was read, in which he said 'the stirs in Scotland came out of Raleigh's head', and also part of Sir Walter's own examination: 'The way to invade England, were to begin with Stirs in Scotland.' Sir Walter added, 'I think so still: I have spoken it to divers of the Lords of the Council, by way of discourse and opinion.'

'Now let us come to those words "of destroying the king and his cubs,"' said the Attorney-General.

'O barbarous! If they, like unnatural villains, should use those words, shall I be charged with them? . . . Do you bring the words of these hellish spiders, Clarke, Watson, and others, against me?'

'Thou hast a Spanish heart,' retorted the Attorney-General, 'and thyself art a spider of hell; for thou confessest the king to be a most sweet and gracious king, and yet hast conspired against him.'

Sir Walter Raleigh (1552–1618) and his son
(National Portrait Gallery)

More examinations were read. Brooke had asked Cobham what was meant by 'this Jargon, the Bye and the Main?' and said that Cobham had told him that Cobham and Raleigh were on the main: 'by the Main was meant the taking away of the king and his issue', and Brooke thought 'on his conscience it was infused into his brother's head by Raleigh'. When Cobham had been asked if he had ever said that 'It will never be well in England, till the king and his cubs were taken away,' he had said that he would say no more on that score. Sir Walter then exclaimed, 'I am not named in all this: there is a law of two sorts of Accusers; one of his own knowledge, another by hearsay.'

There followed more discussion on the law, until they started talking about the book which, Cobham had said, he had had from Raleigh and passed on to Brooke. Sir Walter explained that he had found this book in the old Lord Treasurer's study after his death, and Lord Cecil, his son, took up the story from there. Sir Walter had requested Lord Cecil's permission to search his father's papers for some cosmographical studies of the Indies. Lord Cecil had allowed him to do so, and said:

> whosoever should then search his study may in all likelihood find all the notorious Libels that were writ against the late queen; and whosoever should rummage my study, or at least my Cabinet, may find several against the king, our Sovereign Lord, since his accession to the throne.

To which Sir Walter added: 'And I do own, as my Lord Cecil has said, that I believe they may also find in my house almost all the Libels that have been writ against the late queen.'

'You were no Privy Counsellor,' said the Attorney-General, 'and I hope never shall be.'

'He was not a sworn counsellor of state,' said Lord Cecil, 'but he has been called to consultations.'

'I think it a very severe interpretation of the law,' said Sir Walter, 'to bring me within compass of Treason for this Book, writ so long ago, of which nobody had read any more than the Heads of Chapters, and which was burnt by G. Brook without my privity.'

There was some discussion about the contents of this book, and it was alleged that Sir Walter had burnt it, but he said, 'I burned it not. . . . Here is a book, supposed to be treasonable; I never read it, commended it, or delivered it, nor urged it.'

'Why, this is cunning,' said the Attorney-General.

'Every thing that doth make for me is cunning, and every thing that maketh against me is probable.'

Next they turned to discuss a man called Kemish, who was said to have brought a letter from Sir Walter to Lord Cobham, and was thought to have been threatened with the rack: 'was not the keeper of the rack sent for, and he threatened with it?' asked Sir Walter. To which Sir W. Wade, one of the commissioners, replied: 'When Mr Solicitor and myself examined Kemish, we told him he deserved the Rack, but did not threaten him with it.' In one of his examinations, Lord Cobham had said that Kemish had brought a message to him from Sir Walter, 'that he should be of good comfort, for one witness could not condemn a man for treason'.

'Kemish added more,' said Sir Walter. 'I never bade him speak those words.'

The Attorney-General tried to interrupt, but Lord Cecil said: 'It is his last Discourse; give him leave, Mr Attorney.' Sir Walter continued:

> I am accused concerning Arabella, concerning Money out of Spain. My L.C. Justice saith, a man may be condemned with one Witness, yea, without any Witness. Cobham is guilty of

many things, *conscientia mille testes*; he hath accused himself, what can he hope for but mercy? My lords, vouchsafe me this grace; let him be brought, being alive, and in the house; let him avouch any of these things, and I will confess the whole Indictment, and renounce the king's mercy.

'Let us not scandal the innocent,' said Lord Cecil, referring to Arabella Stuart, 'she is as innocent of all these things as I, or any man here.'

It now transpired that Arabella was present in court, standing beside the Lord Admiral, who declared: 'The lady doth here protest upon her salvation, that she never dealt in any of these things; and so she willed me to tell the court.'

Sir Walter pointed out that this whole business had originated with Lord Cobham: 'Were it not for his accusation, all this were nothing,' and again he demanded that Lord Cobham should be brought to face him: 'If you grant me not this favour, I am strangely used; Campion was not denied to have his accusers face to face.'[6]

'Since he must needs have justice,' said Popham CJ, 'the acquitting of his old friend may move him to speak otherwise than the truth.'

'He is a party, and may not come,' said the Attorney-General, 'the law is against it.'

Lord Cecil intervened again: 'I am afraid my often speaking (who am inferior to my lords here present) will make the world think I delight to hear myself talk,' but now began to distance himself from his friend: 'You know the law of the realm (to which your mind does not contest), that my Lord Cobham cannot be brought. . . . Then, Sir Walter, call upon God, and prepare yourself. . . . Excepting your faults (I call them no worse), by God, I am your friend. The heat and passion in you, and the Attorney's zeal in the King's service, makes me speak this.'

The Attorney-General concluded the matter by saying: 'For the lady Arabella, I say she was never acquainted with the matter. Now that Raleigh had conference in all these Treasons, it is manifest. The Jury hath heard the matter.'

Now at last he called a witness, the only person to give evidence in the presence of the court. This was a man called Dyer, a pilot, who had met a Portuguese gentleman in Lisbon, and upon him 'enquiring what countryman I was, I said, an Englishman. Whereupon he asked me, if the king was crowned? And I answered, No, but that I hoped he should be shortly. Nay, saith he, he shall never be crowned; for Don Raleigh and Don Cobham will cut his throat ere that day come.'

'What infer you from this?' asked Sir Walter.

'That your Treason has wings,' said the Attorney-General.

In the face of assertions such as this, how could Sir Walter defend himself?

He did his best. He pointed out to the jury that there was no cause so doubtful that the king's counsel could not make it good against the law, they had produced nothing but Cobham's accusation, and it was on the strength of this that they would have men delivered up to be slaughtered, and their wives and children turned out into the streets to beg.

The Crown seem to have regarded this as a sort of closing speech for the defence, and Serjeant Philips replied on behalf of the prosecution. However, all he said was to repeat the terms of the indictment, adding that there was nothing against Cobham's accusation except the bare denial of the defendant – and the bare denial of a defendant was no evidence to the court to clear him.

Sir Walter replied: 'If truth be constant, and constancy be in truth, why hath he forsworn that that he hath said? You have not proved any one thing against me by direct Proofs, but all by circumstances.'

'Have you done?' asked the Attorney-General. 'The king must have the last word.'

'Nay, Mr Attorney, he which speaketh for his life, must speak last. . . . I appeal to God and the king in this point, whether Cobham's Accusation be sufficient to condemn me.'

'The king's safety and your clearing cannot agree. I protest before God, I never knew a clearer Treason.'

'I never had intelligence with Cobham since I came to the Tower.'

'Go to, I will lay thee upon thy back, for the confidentest Traitor that ever came at a bar. Why should you take 8,000 crowns for a peace?'

Once again, Lord Cecil intervened: 'Be not so impatient, good Mr Attorney; give him leave to speak.'

'If I may not be patiently heard, you will encourage Traitors, and discourage us. I am the king's sworn servant, and must speak; if he be guilty, he is a Traitor; if not, deliver him.' Thereupon the Attorney-General 'sat down in a chase' and refused to say anything else, but the commissioners intreated him, so he made another long speech and repeated all the 'evidence'. When Sir Walter interrupted him, and said he did him wrong, the Attorney-General declared: 'Thou art the most vile and execrable Traitor that ever lived.'

'You speak indiscreetly, barbarously and uncivilly.'

'I want words sufficient to express thy viperous Treasons.'

'I think you want words indeed, for you have spoken one thing half a dozen times.'

'Thou art an odious fellow, thy name is hateful to all the realm of England for thy pride.'

'It will go near to prove a measuring between you and me, Mr Attorney.'

'Well, I will now make it appear to the world, that there never lived a viler viper upon the face of the earth than thou.'

At this, the Attorney-General pulled a letter out of his pocket. He said that Raleigh had taken an apple and pinned a letter to it and thrown it into Cobham's window. In the letter he had written that it was doubtful whether they would be proceeded against, and had added: 'Do not do as my lord of Essex did; take heed of a preacher; for by his persuasion he confessed, and made himself guilty.' 'If this be not enough to prove him a traitor,' the Attorney-General commented, 'the king my master shall not live three years to an end.'

Here the Attorney-General produced a letter which Lord Cobham had written, and he read it out, adding some interjections of his own:

> I have thought fit to set this down to my lords, wherein I protest on my soul to write nothing but the truth. I am now come near the period of my time, therefore I confess the whole truth before God and his angels. Raleigh, four days before I came from the Tower, caused an apple [Attorney-General: 'Eve's apple'] to be thrown in at my chamber window; the effect of it was, to intreat me to right the wrong that I had done him, in saying, 'that I should have come home by Jersey;' which under my hand to him I have retracted. His first Letter I answered not, which was thrown in the same manner; wherein he prayed me to write him a Letter, which I did. He sent me word that the Judges met at Mr Attorney's house, and that there was some good hope the proceedings against us should be stayed: he sent me another time a little tobacco. . . . He told me, the States had audience with the king [Attorney-General: 'Ah! is not this a Spanish heart in an English body?']. He hath been the original cause of my ruin. . . . He advised me not to be overtaken with preachers, as Essex was; and that the king would better allow of a constant denial, than to accuse any.

'Oh, damnable atheist,' commented the Attorney-General after reading this out.

'I bid a poor fellow throw in the Letter at his window,' explained Sir Walter, 'written to this purpose; "You know you have undone me, now write three lines to justify me."'

Popham CJ asked him what he had to say of the letter, and he replied that Cobham was a base, dishonourable, poor soul. To which the Attorney-General retorted, 'Is he base? I return it into thy throat on his behalf: But for thee, he would have been a good subject.'

'I see you are not so clear a man as you have protested all this while,' said Popham CJ. 'For you should have discovered these matters to the king.'

Now it was Sir Walter's turn to play his best card. He in his turn pulled a letter out of his pocket, which Lord Cobham had written to him, and he asked Lord Cecil to read it as he knew the writing;

> Seeing myself so near my end, for the discharge of my own conscience, and freeing myself from your blood, which else will cry vengeance against me; I protest upon my salvation I never practised with Spain by your procurement. . . . So God have mercy upon my soul, as I know no Treason by you.

'Now I wonder how many souls this man hath!' said Sir Walter. 'He damns one in this Letter, and another in that.'

'Here was much ado,' records the report. The Attorney-General alleged that the letter had been 'politicly and cunningly urged from Lord Cobham', and Popham CJ willed that the jury might now be satisfied.

This was the end of the evidence, but Sir Walter now argued that, even if everything alleged against him was true, it still could not amount to treason against King James since it had all occurred during the reign of Queen Elizabeth.[7] Indeed, although the indictment alleged that all these events had taken place in the summer of 1603, no precise dates had been mentioned in any of the so-called evidence that had been placed before the court.

The jury withdrew and returned in less than a quarter of an hour with a verdict of Guilty. Serjeant Heale demanded judgment against the prisoner, and the Clerk of the Crown asked him if he had anything to say why judgment should not be passed upon him.

> My lords, the jury have found me guilty: they must do as they are directed. I can say nothing why judgment should not proceed. You see whereof Cobham hath accused me: you remember his Protestations, that I was never guilty. I desire the king should know of the wrongs done unto me since I came hither.

'You have had no wrong, Sir Walter,' said Popham CJ.

> Yes, of Mr Attorney. I desire my lords to remember three things to the king. 1. I was accused to be a practiser with Spain: I never knew that my Lord Cobham meant to go thither; I will ask no mercy at the king's hands, if he will affirm it. 2. I never knew of the practice with Arabella. 3. I never knew of my Lord Cobham's practice with Aremburg, nor of the surprizing Treason.

Popham CJ said that he was satisfied that Lord Cobham had accused him truly, and Sir Walter submitted himself to the king's mercy. The Lord Chief Justice now delivered a long homily to the prisoner:

> It is best for man not to seek to climb too high, lest he fall; nor yet to creep too low, lest he be trodden on. . . . You have been taken for a wise man, and so have shewed wit enough this day. . . . Two vices have lodged chiefly in you; one is an eager ambition, the other corrupt covetousness. Ambition, in desiring to be advanced to equal grace and favour, as you have

been before time. . . . For your covetousness, I am sorry to hear that a gentleman of your wealth should become a base spy for the enemy, which is the vilest of all other. . . . Let not any devil persuade you to think there is no eternity in Heaven: for if you think thus, you shall find eternity in Hell-fire. . . . I never saw the like Trial, and hope I shall never see the like again.

He then pronounced the death sentence in the usual form:

You shall be had from hence to the place whence you came . . . and from thence you shall be drawn upon a hurdle through the open streets to the place of execution, there to be hanged and cut down alive, and your body shall be opened, your heart and bowels plucked out, and your privy members cut off, and thrown into the fire before your eyes; then your head to be stricken off from your body, and your body shall be divided into four quarters, to be disposed of at the king's pleasure: And God have mercy upon your soul.

Sir Walter now asked the Earl of Devonshire and the other lords, that they would request that his death should be honourable and not ignominious; they promised to use their utmost endeavours. The court then rose, and Sir Walter was taken to the castle.

Sir Dudley Carleton was present throughout these proceedings, and in his letter to John Chamberlain on 27 November he wrote that Sir Walter had conducted his case 'with that temper, wit, learning, courage and judgment, that save that it went with the hazard of his life, it was the happiest day he ever spent. And so well he shifted all advantages that were taken against him, that were not *fama malum gravius quam res*, and an ill name half hanged, in the opinion of all men, he had been acquitted.' Sir Dudley went on to describe how the news was brought to the king:

The two first . . . were Roger Ashton and a Scotchman; whereof one affirmed, That never any man spoke so well in times past, nor would do so in the world to come; and the other said, That whereas when he saw him first, he was so led with the common hatred, that he would have gone a hundred miles to see him hanged, he would, ere he parted, have gone a thousand to have saved his life. In one word, never was man so hated, and so popular, in so short a time.

The two peers, Lord Cobham and Lord Grey, were tried separately towards the end of the month. A meeting of the House of Lords, consisting of eleven earls and nineteen barons, was convened at Winchester for the purpose; Lord Ellesmere LC presided as Lord Steward. Lord Cobham confessed some of the charges and denied others. He denied having anything to do with Arabella, and he claimed that Raleigh had stirred him up to discontent and had propounded a scheme for the Spaniards to invade and to land at Milford Haven. When his brother's accusation was read against him, he said his brother was 'an incompetent accuser, baptizing him with the name of a viper; and laid to his charge (though far from the purpose) the getting of his wife's sister with child'. When asked about the two letters, 'the one excusing, the other condemning, Raleigh', he said that: 'the last was true, but the other was drawn from him by device in the Tower, by young Harvey the lieutenant's son, whom Raleigh had corrupted, and carried intelligence between them'. 'Having thus,' Sir Dudley continued, 'accused all his friends, and so little excused himself, the peers were not long in deliberation what to judge; and after sentence of condemnation given, he begged a great while for life and favour, alleging his confession as a meritorious act.'

Lord Grey's conduct was very different. He spoke with great assurance, and made a long and eloquent speech, holding the House all day, from eight in the morning till eight at night. However, the evidence, in the confessions of Brooke and Markham, showed that he was acquainted with the plan to seize the court. He was found Guilty, and when asked if he had anything to say, replied: 'The house of the Wiltons had spent many lives in their prince's service, and Grey cannot beg his. God send the king a long and prosperous reign, and to your lordships all honour.'

In his letter, Sir Dudley Carleton then went on to discuss what was likely to happen to the convicted prisoners: 'They say the priests shall lead the dance tomorrow; and Brooke next after: for he proves to be the knot that tied together the three conspiracies; the rest hang indifferent betwixt mercy and justice, wherein the king hath now subject to practise himself.' He added that the lady of Pembroke was doing her best to procure Raleigh's pardon.

On 11 December Sir Dudley wrote another letter to Mr Chamberlain, this time from Salisbury: 'I may as well leap in where I left . . . and proceed in an order of narration; since this was a part of the same play, and that other acts came betwixt, to make up a tragical comedy.' He then described the execution of Watson, Clarke and Brooke.

As for the others, there was, according to Sir Dudley, much discussion at court as to what should be done. The Lords of the Council advised the king to show mercy, but one clergyman, Patrick Galloway, preached as hotly against the moderation of justice as if it had been one of the seven deadly sins. The king himself made it clear that he would make his own decision and, late on Wednesday night, warrants were signed and sent to Sir Benjamin Tichborne for the execution of Markham, Lord Grey and Lord Cobham, in that order, at 10 o'clock on Friday.

'A fouler day could hardly have been picked out, or fitter for such a tragedy,' wrote Sir Dudley. Markham was brought out first, and he prepared himself for the block. It was at this moment that the sheriff was accosted by John Gib, a Scottish groom of the bedchamber, and on his return to the scaffold he told Markham that his execution would be postponed for two hours. So the sheriff took him away and locked him up in the great hall 'to walk with Prince Arthur'.[8]

Lord Grey was now led to the scaffold, escorted by a troop of young courtiers and looking so cheerful that 'he seemed a dapper bridegroom'. He fell on his knees and made a long confession and prayer, 'which held us in the rain for more than half an hour', until he was told by the sheriff that he had received word from the king to change the order of execution and that Lord Cobham was to go first. So he too was led to Prince Arthur's hall.

Now it was Lord Cobham's turn. He came to the scaffold with good assurance and contempt of death. He said prayers and was about to take his farewell when the sheriff stopped him. Lord Grey and Markham were now brought back, and as they knew no more than the onlookers what was about to happen, they 'looked strange one upon the other like men beheaded, and met again in the other world'.

Sir Dudley then continued:

> Now all the actors being together on the stage (as use is at the end of a play,) the sheriff made a short speech unto them, by way of the interrogatory of the heinousness of their offences, the justness of their trials, their lawful condemnation, and due execution there to be performed; to all which they assented; then, saith the sheriff, see the mercy of your prince, who, of himself, hath sent hither to countermand, and given you your lives. There was then no need to beg a *plaudite* of the audience, for it was given with such hues and cries, that it went from the castle into the town, and there began afresh. . . . Raleigh, you must think (who had a window open that way), had hammers working in his head, to beat out the meaning of this stratagem.

Raleigh was to have been executed on the following Monday, but he too was reprieved. He, Lord Cobham and Lord Grey were all confined in the Tower; Markham, Brookesby and Copley were all banished.

The whole scheme nearly miscarried, as Sir Dudley explained in the final paragraph of his letter:

> I send you a copy of the king's letter, which was privately written the Wednesday night, and the messenger despatched the Thursday about noon. But one thing had like to have marred the play; for the letter was closed, and delivered him unsigned; which the king remembered himself, and called for him back again. And at Winchester, there was another cross adventure; for John Gib could not get so near the scaffold, that he could speak to the sheriff, but was thrust out amongst the boys, and was fain to call out to Sir James Hayes, or else Markham might have lost his neck. . . . From Salisbury this 11th of Dec. 1603. Your's, &c. Dudley Carleton

Fourteen years Sir Walter Raleigh spent in the Tower, occupying himself with writing. Then a proposition was put to the king by Sir Ralph Winwood, the Secretary of State, that Sir Walter should go to Guiana where he had reported that there was a rich mine of gold. The king gave his support to the scheme, and commissioned Sir Walter as the admiral of a fleet to undertake the expedition, but when Count Gondamar, the Spanish ambassador, heard about it, he protested on the ground that it was hostile to his country, and it was agreed that no outrages should be committed against any of Spain's subjects. Sir Walter and the king agreed that the plans should be kept secret, but written details were in the hands of Count Gondamar before the expedition sailed.

Sometime in the summer of 1617 Sir Walter sailed in the *Destiny* with about a dozen other ships. Some of his men died of a fever, and the expedition was delayed by contrary winds. When they reached Guiana in November, the mine turned out to be a chimera. They attacked and plundered Santo Thoma, a Spanish colony, in breach of the terms of the commission, and it was here that one of Sir Walter's sons was killed. In the governor's closet they found a copy of the secret paper relating to the adventure which Count Gondamar had obtained, and soon afterwards, one of Sir Walter's men, Captain Remish (or Kemish), who had reported the existence of the mine in the first place and had encouraged the adventure, committed suicide in the cabin of the *Convertine*.

On his return to Plymouth, Sir Walter was arrested by Sir Lewis Steukley, Vice-Admiral of the County of Devon. Count Gondamar told the king that Sir Walter was a pirate, and demanded that he be put to death. It was decided to 'proceed against him under his old condemnation, for having had experience upon a former Trial, they cared not to run the hazard of a second.'

And so, on 28 October 1618, Sir Walter was brought to the bar of the Court of King's Bench at Westminster. Sir Edward Coke, who had prosecuted him in 1603, was now Chief Justice of that court, and Serjeant Yelverton was now Attorney-General. The latter asked for judgment to be enforced, and the Clerk of the Crown read out the record of the conviction and judgment, and asked Sir Walter if he had anything to say. He replied that his voice was weak by reason of the ague, but Coke CJ said that it was audible enough. So Sir Walter argued that the King's Commission to proceed in a voyage beyond the seas, as an admiral with powers of martial law over his officers and men, constituted a pardon – as, indeed, he had been advised by Francis Bacon, Lord Verulam LC: 'One would think that by this royal patent, which gave him power of life and death over the king's liege people, Sir Walter Raleigh should become *rectus in curia*, and free from all old convictions.' But Coke CJ interrupted him and told him that his commission could not help him; nothing but an express pardon would suffice. So Sir Walter simply put himself at the mercy of the king, and Coke CJ then gave his judgment. He told Sir Walter that he had had an honourable trial and had been justly convicted, that the king had spared him but that he had stirred up new offences, and concluded with his prayers that God would have mercy on his soul.

That night Sir Walter wrote two long letters: one to the king, one to his wife.

He told the king that he submitted himself to the will of God, and would suffer whatever should please His Majesty to inflict upon him.

The letter to Lady Raleigh begins:

> You shall now receive, my dear wife, my last words in these my last lines. My love I send you, that you may keep it when I am dead; and my counsel, that you may remember it when I am no more. . . . First, I send you all the thanks which my heart can conceive, or my words can rehearse, for your many travails, and care taken for me. . . . Secondly, I beseech you, for the love you bare me living, do not hide yourself many days, but by your travels seek to help your miserable fortunes, and the right of your poor child. Thy mourning cannot avail me, I am but dust . . .

He went on to deal with his property, and then continued:

> I cannot write much, God he knows how hardly I steal this time while others sleep, and it is also time that I should separate my thoughts from the world. Beg my dead body, which was living denied thee; and either lay it at Sherburne (and if the land continue) or in Exeter church by my father and mother. . . . My dear wife, farewell. Bless my poor boy. Pray for me, and let my good God hold you both in his arms. Written with the dying hand of sometime thy husband, but now alas overthrown. Walter Raleigh.

At 9 o'clock on the following morning, he was taken to a scaffold in Old Palace Yard, Westminster. He said he was ill: 'If I shall shew any weakness, I beseech you to attribute it to my malady,' and asked for the Lords Arundel, Northampton and Doncaster, who came down to the scaffold. Then he made a long speech, mostly about the expedition to Guiana and his arrest at Plymouth, and why he had not fled to France when he had the opportunity. He gave an account of how some of his men had mutinied and threatened to cast him into the sea or lock him up in his cabin, and how there had been rumour that he had never intended to go to Guiana at all, or never intended to return. Addressing the Earl of Arundel, he said: 'My lord, being in the gallery of my ship, at my departure, I remember your honour took me by the hand and said, You would request one thing of me, which was, That whether I made a good voyage or a bad, I should not fail, but to return again into England; which I then promised you, and gave you my faith I would; and so I have.' The earl replied that that was true.

Sir Walter referred to other 'false slanders' – that he had taken much money on his voyage, and that he had persecuted the Earl of Essex at his execution. He concluded: 'And I protest, as I shall appear before [God], this that I have spoken is true, and I hope I shall be believed.'

Then a proclamation was made that all men should depart from the scaffold. Sir Walter gave his hat and cap and some money to some of his friends, and thanked the Earl of Arundel for his support. He put off his doublet and gown, and asked the headsman to show him the axe: 'I prithee let me see it, dost thou think I am afraid of it?' He felt along the edge and said to the sheriff: 'This is a sharp medicine, but it is a physician that will cure all diseases.' The executioner knelt down and asked for his forgiveness, which he gave. He lay on the block and the headsman threw down his own cloak so as not to spoil the prisoner's gown, and then struck off his head with two blows. His head was displayed on each side of the scaffold and then put into a red leather bag, his velvet gown thrown over it, and it was carried away in a mourning coach of Lady Raleigh's.

He was 66 years old.

CHAPTER THREE

The Gunpowder Plot Trial (1606)

The principal source of information relating to the Gunpowder Plot is the speech delivered by James I to parliament on 9 November 1605, and subsequently printed for circulation at home and for despatch to English ambassadors abroad. This document, known as the King's Book,[1] recounts how the plot was discovered through the services of Lord Monteagle (who may have been a government spy), and contains a description of the plot itself based chiefly on the confession of Guy Fawkes (which was probably extracted under torture) and of Thomas Winter (which may have been a forgery).

The plot has been the subject of many books, articles, theses and letters. Nevertheless, the details of the plot itself seem to have been accepted in general, in spite of the dubious nature of the sources. There has, however, been much controversy as to the extent of the government's knowledge of what was going on. Some historians accept the orthodox story, including the part played by Lord Monteagle, at its face value, but there is a strong school of thought that believes that the government, and Robert Cecil (Earl of Salisbury and Secretary of State) in particular, knew about the plot before it was officially 'discovered' and allowed it to mature until its disclosure would cause the maximum damage to the Roman Catholics. An extreme version of this theory is that the plot was actually instigated by Cecil himself to discedit the Catholics. If the government did know about the plot in advance, then it must almost necessarily follow that the story of its 'discovery' by Lord Monteagle was fabricated and that Monteagle himself was in the employment of the government.

In this account I have not become involved in these controversies, but have simply recounted the orthodox version for the benefit of those readers whose knowledge of the plot is simply that Guy Fawkes was found guarding a store of gunpowder in a vault under the House of Lords.

Many men were involved in the plot, and a brief outline of the dramatis personae may be of assistance to readers. Dates of birth are given where known:

Bates, Thomas. A servant of Catesby. Executed 30 January 1606.

Catesby, Sir Robert (b. 1573). A member of a distinguished Catholic family with estates in Warwickshire and Northamptonshire. A charismatic character – six feet tall, handsome and elegant, with the courage of a lion (the family crest) and a brilliant swordsman. The leader and organizer of the plot. Killed at Holbeach, 8 November 1605.

Digby, Sir Everard (b. 1578). A friend of Gerard. Joined the plot in October 1605. Executed 30 January 1606.

Fawkes, Guy (b. 1570). From a Yorkshire family. At school at York with the Wright brothers. A professional soldier. Executed 31 January 1606.

Garnet, Henry (he also went under various aliases) (b. 1555). The Superior of the Jesuits in England. Executed 3 May 1606.

Gerard, John (b. 1564). A Jesuit. Implicated in the plot, but he escaped.

Grant, John. Husband of Dorothy Winter (the sister of the Winter brothers). Executed 30 January 1606.

Keys, Robert. Executed 31 January 1606.

Percy, Thomas (b. 1560). A great-grandson of the 4th Earl of Northumberland. Killed at Holbeach, 8 November 1605.

Rookwood, Ambrose (b. ?1578). Executed 31 January 1606.

Tesimond, Oswald (b. 1563). A Jesuit. Implicated in the plot, but he escaped.

Tresham, Francis (b. ?1567). Died in custody before trial.

Winter, Robert. Wounded and captured at Holbeach. Executed 30 January 1606.

Winter, Thomas (b. 1572). Executed 31 January 1606.

Wright, Christopher (b. ?1570). Killed at Holbeach, 8 November 1605.

Wright, John (b. ?1568). Killed at Holbeach, 8 November 1605.

At about 7 o'clock one Saturday evening in October 1605, Lord Monteagle was sitting in his room in London waiting to go to his supper. He had sent a footman on an errand across the road, and a tall stranger met him and handed him a letter, telling him to deliver it to his master. Lord Monteagle opened the letter. He was perplexed by its contents, and thought it might be some foolish 'pasquil' to scare him from attending parliament, but he thought it best not to conceal the letter, so he took it to the King's Palace at Whitehall, and handed it to the Earl of Salisbury, the king's principal secretary. The earl commended him, and said that this was a matter to be taken seriously. So the earl in turn reported the matter to the Lord Chamberlain, who was responsible for overseeing all places of assembly, as well as the king's private houses. They in turn consulted the Lord Admiral and the Earls of Worcester and Northampton, and they all decided to place the matter before the king.

The king had been hunting at Royston, and he returned to London on the following Thursday. The next day the Earl of Salisbury approached him in his gallery and showed him the letter, which read as follows:

> My Lord; Out of the love I bear to some of your friends, I have a care of your preservation;
> therefore I would advise you, as you tender your life, to devise some excuse, to shift off your

The leading members of the Gunpowder Plot (National Portrait Gallery)

attendance at this parliament. For God and man have concurred to punish the wickedness of this time. And think not slightly of this advertisement, but retire yourself into your country, where you may expect the event in safety. For, though there be no appearance of any stir, yet I say, they shall receive a terrible blow this parliament, and yet shall not see who hurts them. This counsel is not to be condemned, because it may do you good, and can do you no harm, for the danger is past as soon as you have burnt the Letter; and I hope God will give you grace to make good use of it; to whose holy protection I commend you.

The king read the letter twice and said that he thought it was to be treated seriously, for the style seemed more quick and witty than was to be expected in a pasquil or libel. This surprised the earl who said he thought that it was more likely the work of some fool or madman, and pointed out the sentence 'for the danger is past, as soon as you have burnt the Letter'. This, he said, was likely to be the saying of a fool – for if the danger was past as soon as the letter was burnt, then the warning was of little value. But no, said the king. Taking the sentence with the earlier one: 'they shall receive a terrible blow this parliament', he conjectured that the danger was of some sudden explosion of gunpowder. 'For no other insurrection, rebellion, or whatsoever other private and desperate attempt could be committed, or attempted, in time of parliament, and the authors thereof unseen, except only if it were by a blowing up of gunpowder, which might be performed by one base knave in a dark corner.' Making the phrase 'as soon as' mean 'as quickly as' the warning referred to the suddenness and quickness of the danger 'which should be as quickly performed and at an end, as that paper should be a blazing up in the fire'.

So the king expressed the wish that the under-rooms of the parliament house should be thoroughly searched before the opening of parliament. The earl was surprised: the king was usually reckless rather than cautious, and as a result had exposed himself to many dangers, but he made some merry jest, as was his custom, and left the king. The following day, he returned, accompanied by the Lord Chamberlain, and it was agreed that a search should be carried out on the afternoon before the meeting of parliament.

So that afternoon the Lord Chamberlain and Lord Monteagle searched the lower rooms, and found a great store of billets and faggots and coal in a vault under the upper house. They asked Whyneard, the keeper of the wardrobe, what it was, and he told them that Thomas Percy had hired the house and the vault underneath it to store his wood and coal there. At the same time the Lord Chamberlain noticed a man standing in the corner, who said he was Percy's man and was looking after his house for him.

The Lord Chamberlain returned to the king and spoke to him in his private gallery. There were several privy counsellors there too: the Lord Treasurer, the Lord Admiral, and the Earls of Salisbury, Worcester and Northampton. He reported what he had seen, and that Lord Monteagle had told him that, as soon as he heard that Thomas Percy was in possession of the house, he became suspicious on account of Percy's 'backwardness in religion', but at the same time, because of his long friendship towards him, he thought that the letter might have come from him. The Lord Chamberlain added that he was surprised at the amount of wood and coal in the house, when Thomas Percy rarely resided there, and he also thought that Percy's man 'looked like a very tall and desperate fellow'.

The king's fears were now increased, and he insisted that the house should be thoroughly searched and that the billets and coal should be searched to the bottom in case they were covering powder. The counsellors agreed, but on the other hand they were worried that if a search was carried out and nothing was revealed – if 'this letter should prove to be nothing but the evaporation of an idle brain' – this would result in a 'general scandal of the king and the state, as being so suspicious of every light and frivolous toy'; more particularly as Thomas Percy was a close relative of the Earl of Northumberland, who was one of the king's greatest subjects and counsellors. There was further discussion and eventually it was decided to carry out a search, making the excuse that Whyneard had missed some of the king's hangings, and that the rooms should be 'narrowly ripped for them'.

Sir Thomas Knevet was employed to carry out the search. He was a gentleman of the king's privy chamber, a justice of the peace for Westminster, and a man of unswerving fidelity to the old queen and to the new king. He went to parliament house about midnight with a small band of men, and finding 'Thomas Percy's alledged man standing without the doors, his clothes and boots on, at so dead a time of night, he resolved to apprehend him'. He then searched the house and found a small barrel of gunpowder under the billets and coal, and then the others, thirty-six barrels in all, great and small. When he searched the man, he found on him three matches and all the other instruments required for blowing up the powder. This man then immediately confessed his guilt, adding 'That, if he had happened to be within the house, when he took him, . . . he would not have failed to have blown him up, house and all.'

Sir Thomas Knevet returned to the palace and reported the findings to the Lord Chamberlain and the Earl of Salisbury, who immediately warned the rest of the council and, although it was now 4 o'clock in the morning, they all went to the king's bedchamber, where the Lord Chamberlain 'being not any longer able to conceal his joy for the preventing of so great a danger, told the king, in a confused haste, that all was found and discovered, and the traitor in hands and fast bound'. The prisoner himself was brought before the council and examined, but he, putting on a 'Roman resolution', refused to disclose anything of significance. He refused to name his accomplices or to answer any question which might reveal the plot, and took the whole blame upon himself. He said he 'was moved, only for religion and conscience sake, denying the king to be his lawful sovereign, or the Anointed of God, in respect he was a heretick', and he said he was John Johnson, a servant of Thomas Percy. The following day, however, he was taken to the Tower, where he remained for two or three days. He was then re-examined and the rack was shown to him: his mask of Roman fortitude dropped. He said that his real name was Guy Fawkes, and he made a full deposition.

He described how some eighteen months previously he had been in the Low Countries when he was approached by Thomas Winter and invited to join a Catholic plot against the king. They in turn brought in Robert Catesby, Thomas Percy and John Wright, who all took a vow of secrecy. Catesby suggested that the plot should be achieved with gunpowder, by making a mine underneath the upper house of parliament. So Thomas Percy hired a house nearby, and from there, early in December 1604, they started digging. By Christmas they had reached the wall, which they found was three yards thick, and by February they were only halfway through. They were now joined by two other men, Christopher Wright and Robert Winter, and they all stayed in the house, with powder and shot, resolved to die there rather than yield or be taken. While they were mining through the wall, they heard a rushing noise in a cellar, as of coal being moved, and when Fawkes went to investigate he found that the cellar was to let, so Thomas Percy hired it. They had already brought twenty barrels of powder[2] into the house, so these were moved into the cellar and covered with faggots and coal. It was Easter now, and parliament was prorogued until the autumn, so they dispersed, while Percy, who had the key to the cellar, laid in more powder and wood. Fawkes himself returned in September, and he too added to the store. They also resolved, when 'this act should have been performed', that some of their confederates should surprise the Lady Elizabeth, the king's daughter, who was living at Lord Harrington's house in Warwickshire, and proclaim her queen.

As soon as it became known that the plot was discovered, on Tuesday 5 November, Catesby and Percy set off for Warwickshire and were followed by Thomas Winter and the two Wright brothers. John Grant, another papist, went to the stables of a man called Benocke, 'a rider of great horses', carried off seven or eight of his horses, and met the other conspirators at Sir Everard Digby's house in Dunchurch. Sir Everard had organized a hunt that day, although 'his mind was, Nimrod-like, upon a far other manner of hunting, more bent upon the blood of reasonable men than brute beasts'. They now tried to organize an open rebellion. They collected such armour, horses and powder as they could, and thought to augment their number 'by running up and down the country . . . (dreaming to themselves, that they had the virtue of the snow-ball, which, being little at the first, and tumbling down from a great hill, groweth to a great quantity, by increasing itself with the snow that it meeteth by the way)'. But they could not assemble more than eighty men, and their own servants kept stealing from them and deserting.

The common people, mystified by Grant's removal of the horses from Benocke's stables, and seeing what they could only regard as some 'publick misbehaviours', refused to give them any support or even a cup of drink. Sir Robert Verney, the sheriff of Warwickshire, chased them out of his county into Worcestershire, where Sir Robert Walsh continued the pursuit on his own initiative, for the royal proclamation, declaring them traitors, had not yet reached him.

They fled to Holbeach in Staffordshire, where the sheriff invited them to surrender, but they replied 'That he had need of better assistance, than of those few numbers that were with him before he could be able to command or controul them.' However, while the sheriff and his men were preparing to assault the house, and while the rebels were preparing to defend it, an explosion occurred inside it. Several of the rebels were seriously injured, so they opened the gates and let the sheriff's men rush in. Catesby and Percy were killed, both by the same shot, and Winter was taken, injured but alive. Others were killed, or stripped of their clothes and left to die of the cold, or taken to the local jail, where they were kept until they were sent to London where a huge crowd collected to see them as 'the rarest sort of monsters'.

Following his arrest, Thomas Winter made a confession in the presence of the Privy Council. He described how, early in 1603, very soon after the king's accession, he received a summons from Robert Catesby, so he went to see him in Lambeth. Catesby said that it was necessary that they should not forsake their country, but should deliver her from her servitude and replant the Catholic religion without any foreign help. And he had thought of a way of doing so, 'in a word, it was to blow up the Parliament house with gunpowder'. Winter pointed out the difficulties, the want of a house and of someone to dig the mine, and the noise they would make in the digging, and so on, but Catesby said simply: 'Let us give an attempt.' He asked Winter to go to Henry Garnet, the Constable of the State of the Catholics in England, who was in exile at the time, to inform him of the plan, and to bring back someone who was best fitted to carry out the work; he suggested Guy Fawkes.

So Winter went to Flanders and met Guy Fawkes. They sailed back to England together and landed at Greenwich, where they took a pair of oars and rowed to Catesby's lodgings in London.

Sometime later in the summer there was a meeting in a house near St Clement's: Winter, Catesby and Fawkes were there, and also John Wright and Thomas Percy. They took an oath of secrecy, and heard mass and received the sacrament. Catesby had heard that Mr Whyneard had a house to rent just by the parliament house, so Percy was sent to take it. Fawkes, calling himself Percy's servant under the name of John Johnson, received the keys of the house. About this time they heard that parliament was to be prorogued until the following February, so they separated and arranged to meet again in the autumn. In the meantime they rented a house in Lambeth where they could store their gunpowder and wood so that it could be conveyed by boat to Percy's house, and Robert Keys was employed to look after it.

They planned to start digging the mine in the autumn, but some Scottish peers were holding a conference in Percy's house so work was postponed until December. Percy and Wright joined them and they equipped themselves with tools and baked meats, so as to avoid sending out for provisions. They entered the house late at night, and saw no one until Christmas Eve. By then they had dug as far as the wall of parliament house, propping up the mine with timber as they went.

While the work was in progress, they were discussing what they would do after the explosion. They expected that both the king and the prince his heir would be in parliament and would be killed. The next in line of succession was the king's second son, and Percy said that he would be able to enter his room without suspicion, and undertook to carry him away. It would be easy to surprise the Lady Elizabeth, and take her to Catesby's house near Ashby. They would save as many peers as they could who were Catholics, but they would not inform any foreign princes in advance, for they did not know if they would approve of their scheme, and they could not bind them to secrecy.

They now heard that parliament had again been prorogued until the autumn. They brought over all the powder from Lambeth to Percy's house, and they carried on digging for a time, until they found the opportunity to hire the cellar. Until now, Catesby had borne the cost of the whole operation – maintaining the conspirators, the expenses of the houses which had been hired, and providing the gunpowder. They now enlisted the help of Sir Everard Digby, who promised £1,500, and Francis Tresham, who promised £2,000. Percy said that he could raise £4,000 from the Northumberland estates, and provide ten 'gallopping horses'. Winter and Fawkes themselves bought some new powder as they thought that the first was dank. At about this time, they learnt that parliament was to meet on 5 November, so towards the end of October they all met at a house called White-Webbes in Enfield Chase to make their final arrangements.

Two days later Winter received information that Lord Monteagle had been warned of the plot and had passed on the letter to the Earl of Salisbury. Winter returned to White-Webbes to tell Catesby what had happened and advised him to leave the country, but Catesby said he was 'resolved to send Mr Fawkes to try the uttermost, protesting, if the part belonged to himself, he would try the same adventure'.

On Friday 1 November Winter, Catesby and Tresham met at Barnet, and discussed who had sent the letter to Lord Monteagle, but they could not imagine who had done so. On the following evening Winter met Tresham at Lincoln's Inn Fields, and

Tresham reported that the Earl of Salisbury had passed the letter on to the king. So Winter gave up the plan for lost, and said so to Catesby who now decided to fly, but to wait for Percy to agree. However, when they saw Percy on the Sunday, he said that he 'would needs abide the uttermost trial'.

They were all in confusion now: Catesby resolved to go into the country, and Percy was intending to follow. At 5 o'clock on the Tuesday morning John Wright (or his brother Christopher) came to Winter to tell him that all was discovered, so Winter told him to go to Percy and bid him be gone. Winter himself went down to parliament house, found the guard standing there who would not let him pass, and heard one of them say, 'There is a treason discovered, in which the king and the lords should have been blown up.' Realising now that all was known, he went to his stable, took his gelding, and rode to Dunchurch to meet Catesby. However, he never caught up with him, and on Friday he received news that Catesby, Ambrose Rookwood and John Grant had all been burnt with powder. He was advised to flee, but said first that he would see the body of his friend, and bury him.

When he reached Holbeach, however, he found Catesby reasonably well, and with him were Percy, the Wright brothers, Rookwood and Grant. They said that they meant to die there and Winter said that he would stay with them. At about 11 o'clock the sheriff's men came to besiege the house. Winter walked into the courtyard and was shot in the shoulder and lost the use of one arm. Both the Wright brothers were killed and Rookwood was injured.

> Then said Catesby to me (standing before the door they were to enter) Stand by me, Tom, and we will die together. Sir, quoth I, I have lost the use of my right arm, and I fear that will cause me to be taken. So, as we stood close together, Mr Catesby, Mr Percy, and myself, they two were shot, as far as I could guess, with one bullet, and then the company entered upon me, hurt me in the belly with a pike, and gave me other wounds, until one came behind, and caught hold of both my arms. And so I remain, Yours, &c.

And thus Winter concluded his confession.

On 27 January 1606 Robert and Thomas Winter, Guy Fawkes, John Grant, Ambrose Rookwood, Robert Keys and Thomas Bates appeared for trial before a Special Commission at Westminster; Sir Everard Digby was tried separately later on the same day.

The commissioners were the Earls of Nottingham, Suffolk, Worcestershire, Devonshire, Northampton, and Salisbury. Once again, Popham CJ was the senior judge, assisted by Thomas Fleming CB and Warburton J. The indictment alleged that Henry Garnet, the Superior of the Jesuits within the realm of England, and Oswald Tesimond, a Jesuit, together with the defendants and Robert Catesby, Thomas Percy, John and Christopher Wright, 'lately slain', and Francis Tresham, 'lately dead', had all conspired to restore the Roman Catholic religion and:

> did conclude and agree, with Gunpowder, as it were with one blast, suddenly, traitorously and barbarously to blow up and tear in pieces our said sovereign lord the king, the excellent, virtuous, and gracious queen Anne, his dearest wife, the most noble prince Henry, their eldest son, and future hope and joy of England; and the lords spiritual and temporal, the reverend judges of the realm, the knights, citizens and burgesses of parliament, and divers other faithful subjects of the king in the said parliament; [and] should surprize the persons of the noble ladies Elizabeth and Mary, daughters of our said sovereign lord the king, and falsely and traitorously should proclaim the said lady Elizabeth to be queen of the realm.

The indictment then went on to set out the details of the scheme to dig a mine under parliament house and fill the cellar with gunpowder, and, in addition, 'divers great iron bars and stones', no doubt with the intention of making the explosion more effective. Also to procure horses and armour, and to encourage an open rebellion against the king. No statute was mentioned, but a plot to kill the king was clearly 'compassing the death of the King' within the provisions of the Act of 1351.

Sir Edward Philips, the King's Serjeant, opened the case for the Crown. He said that the defendants were all Jesuits: 'all grounded Romanists and corrupted scholars, of so irreligious and traitorous a school'. Sir Edward Coke A.-G. described the case as

> the greatest treasons that were ever plotted in England, and concern the greatest king that ever was of England. . . . I desire that I may with your patience be somewhat more copious, and not so succinct, as my usual manner hath been; and yet I will be no longer than the very matter itself shall necessarily require.

He explained why there had been 'no speedier expedition' in bringing the case to trial; it was right that 'things of great weight and magnitude slowly proceed'. Some of the offenders had only recently been arrested, and 'heretical, treasonable and damnable books' only recently discovered. Twenty-three days had been spent in examinations: Guy Fawkes might have been hanged under the name of 'John Johnson' before his true identity had been disclosed.

This offence, the Attorney-General continued, was *primae impressionis* and therefore *sine nomine*, without any adequate name to describe it, for it would have involved the death not only of the king, but of the whole kingdom. It was unprecedented and without all measure of iniquity, and 'to their treasons were added open rebellion, burglary, robbery, horse-stealing, &c. . . . For it had three roots, all planted and watered by Jesuits, and English Romish Catholicks; the first root in England, in December and March; the second in Flanders, in June; the third in Spain, in July'. For Thomas Winter and Oswald Tesimond had gone to Spain to invite the Spaniards to invade, and to discuss whether they should land a large army in Essex or Kent ('where note, by the way, who was then lord Warden of the Cinque Ports'[3]), or a small one at Milford Haven. And 'because that in all attempts upon England, the greatest difficulty was ever found to be the transportation of horses;[4] the Catholicks in England would assure the king of Spain to have always in readiness for his use and service, 1,500 or 2,000 horses, against any occasion or enterprize.'

All this had happened, he said, while the old queen was still alive, but after her death Christopher Wright went to Spain and found Guy Fawkes there also encouraging the King of Spain to invade England. He thought that Catesby and Tresham had been involved, too, in the treason of the Earl of Essex and of Watson and Clarke, but when these plans failed, 'they fell to the powder-plot'.

The Attorney-General went on, quoting lengthy passages from Latin and the Bible, to enumerate all those who were involved in the plot. He pointed out that when Catesby's servant, Thomas Bates, had been inveigled into the plot, he was made to swear an oath of secrecy, and when he confessed to Tesimond the priest, the latter resolved and encouraged him in the action and gave him absolution. Next, he enumerated the intended victims: the king, their liege lord, the queen, 'a most gracious and graceful lady, a most virtuous, fruitful, and blessed vine, who hath happily brought forth such olive-branches, as that . . . her memory shall be blessed of all our posterity', the royal issue male, 'the future hope, comfort, joy, and life of our state. And as for preserving of the good lady Elizabeth the king's daughter, it should

only have been for a time to have served for their purposes . . . and then God knoweth
what would have become of her.' And to conclude:

> all the most honourable and prudent counsellors, and all the true-hearted and worthy
> nobles, all the grave judges and sages of the law, all the principal knights, gentry, citizens
> and burgesses of parliament, the flower of the whole realm. *Horret animus*, I tremble even to
> think of it: Miserable desolation! no king, no queen, no prince, no male issue, no
> counsellors of state; no nobility, no bishops, no judges! . . . Miserable, but yet sudden had
> their ends been, who should have died in that fiery tempest, and storm of gunpowder.

The conspirators, said the Attorney-General, had chosen parliament as the scene of
their crime because they believed it was there that unjust laws had been passed. That
therefore was the fittest place to do justice, and it was 'justice Fawkes, a man like
enough to do according to his name. If by what law they meant to proceed; it was
gunpowder law, fit for justices of hell.' So he asked what laws they were complaining
about. For the first ten years of the old queen's reign Catholics came to the English
churches and services without scruple, but when a bull was issued, in which the
queen was accursed and deposed, and her subjects discharged from their allegiance, a
law was passed against bringing in the bull. Then Campion, the Jesuit, came to
England to put the bull into effect and to circulate treasonable books, so another law
was passed against recusants and seditious books, subject to a fine. Yet the Jesuits still
came and the queen was excommunicated, so that eventually, in the twenty-seventh
year of her reign, it was made treasonable for any Catholic priest to come into
England. And he pointed out that in the five years of Queen Mary some 300 persons
were put to death for their religion, but in the forty-four years of Elizabeth only thirty
priests and five of their supporters were executed.

Finally, the Attorney-General gave his own version of the collapse of the plan:

> Observe a miraculous accident which befel in Stephen Littleton's house, called Holbach in
> Staffordshire, after they had been two days in open rebellion, immediately before the
> apprehension of these traitors: for some of them standing by the fireside, and having set two
> pound and a half of powder to dry in a platter before the fire, and underset the said platter
> with a great linen bag full of other powder, containing some fifteen or sixteen pounds; it so
> fell out, that one coming to put more wood on the fire, and casting it on, there flew a coal
> into the platter, by reason whereof the powder taking fire and blowing up, scorched those
> who were nearest, as Catesby, Grant, and Rookwood, blew up the roof of the house: and the
> linen bag which was set under the platter being therewith suddenly carried out through the
> breach, fell down in the court-yard whole and unfired; which if it had took fire, would have
> slain them all there, so that they never should have come to this trial . . .

He concluded by attempting to link the gunpowder plot with Sir Walter Raleigh:

> Before Raleigh's treason was discovered, it was reported in Spain that Don Raleigh and Don
> Cobham should cut the king of England's throat. I say not that we have any proofs, that
> those of the Powder-Plot were acquainted with Raleigh, or Raleigh with them: but as before
> was spoken of the Jesuits and priests, so they all were joined in the end, like Sampson's
> Foxes in the tails, howsoever severed in their heads.

The confessions of all the prisoners were then read and acknowledged by them in
open court, together with some of the declarations of their dead comrades. They were
all found Guilty by the jury. On being asked why judgment should not be pronounced
upon them, Thomas Winter asked that he and his brother should be hanged,
although Robert Winter himself asked for mercy. Fawkes said that he was unaware of

some of the conferences which had been mentioned in the indictment. Keys said that his estate and fortunes were desperate, Bates craved mercy, and Grant stood mute for a while, but then said that he was guilty of conspiracy intended but not effected. Ambrose Rookwood alone spoke at any length, saying that he had been drawn into the plot by his friend Catesby, and that it was his first offence, and he submitted himself to the king's mercy.

It was evening when Sir Everard Digby was arraigned, the indictment being almost identical to that under which the other conspirators had been charged. Sir Everard confessed to treason, and made a short speech in which he said that he had been drawn into the plot from his friendship with Catesby, and his other two motives were the cause of religion and that he feared that harsher laws would be passed against the Catholics. He begged that his wife, sisters and creditors should not be penalized, he prayed the pardon of the king, and entreated that he should be beheaded.

Coke A.-G. replied briefly ('for it grew now dark'), and dealt with the points which he had raised:

> O how he doth now put on the bowels of nature and compassion, in the peril of his private and domestical estate! But before, when the publick state of his country, when the king, the queen, the tender princes, the nobles, the whole kingdom were designed to a perpetual destruction; where was then this piety, this religious affection, this care?

Sir Everard interrupted to say that he deserved death and was only begging for mercy, and Coke A.-G. replied by quoting from a Psalm: 'Let his wife be a widow, and his children vagabonds, let his posterity be destroyed, and in the next generation let his name be quite put out.'

The Earl of Northampton then delivered a long homily in which he commented that the new Trojan horse 'might be brought within the walls of the parliament, with a belly stuffed, not as in old time with armed Greeks, but with hellish gunpowder', and enlarged upon the disloyalty of the Catholics.

Popham CJ, now speaking for the first time, pronounced judgment, and when the court rose Sir Everard said, 'if I may but hear any of your lordships say, you forgive me, I shall go more chearfully to the gallows', and they replied, 'God forgive you, and we do.'

On the following Thursday Sir Everard Digby, Robert Winter, Grant and Bates were drawn on a hurdle to a scaffold by St Paul's churchyard, where they were executed.

Next day, Thomas Winter, Rookwood, Keys and Fawkes, now known as 'the devil of the vault', were drawn to the Old Palace in Westminster. Winter said little, except to protest that he died a Catholic, and so 'with a very pale and dead colour, went up the ladder, and, after a swing or two with a halter, to the quartering block was drawn, and there quickly despatched'. Rookwood confessed his offence and asked God to bless the king and the royal family, but suddenly, at the last moment, 'to mar all the pottage with one filthy weed . . . he prayed God to make the king a catholick, otherwise a papist', and he too died affirming that he was a Catholic. Keys said nothing, but 'went stoutly up the ladder; where, not staying the hangman's turn, he turned himself off with such a leap, that with the swing he brake the halter, but, after his fall, was quickly drawn to the block, and there was quickly divided into four parts'.

Finally came Fawkes. He made a short speech and seemed to be sorry for what he had done and asked forgiveness:

Old Palace Yard, Westminster. Guy Fawkes, Thomas Winter, Robert Keys and Ambrose Rookwood were executed here; so too was Sir Walter Raleigh (Museum of London)

His body being weak with torture and sickness, he was scarce able to go up the ladder, but yet with much ado, by the help of the hangman, went high enough to break his neck with the fall . . . to the great joy of the beholders, that the land was ended of so wicked a villainy.

Henry Garnet was arraigned on 28 March 1606, in the Guildhall, where a sort of pulpit had been erected to serve as a dock.

In his opening speech for the prosecution, Coke A.-G. described Henry Garnet in the following terms:

He is . . . a man of many names, Garnet, Wally, Darcy, Roberts, Farmer, Philips: and surely I have not commonly known and observed a true man, that hath had so many false appellations: he is by country an Englishman, by birth a gentleman, by education a scholar, afterwards a corrector of the common law print, with Mr Tottle as printer; and now he is to be corrected by the law. He hath many gifts and endowments of nature, by art learned, a good linguist, and by profession a Jesuit, and a superior, as indeed he is superior to all his predecessors in devilish Treason; a doctor of Jesuits, that is, a doctor of five DDs, as dissimulation, deposing of princes, disposing of kingdoms, daunting and deterring of subjects, and destruction.

At the outset of his speech, the Attorney-General said that he would only touch little upon the evidence, but it turned out to be one of the longest so far recorded in the reports. It was largely an attack upon the Jesuits, who were spreading a tale 'that king-killing and queen-killing was not indeed a doctrine of theirs, but only a fiction and policy of our state, thereby to make the popish religion to be despised and in disgrace'. Garnet, who had been examined twenty times, the last occasion being only two days before the trial, had come into England in July 1586, after it had been made treasonable by statute for any Romish priest to enter the country, just at the time when the Spanish Armada was being prepared. After that hostile invasion in 1588, the Jesuits 'fell again to secret and treasonable practices', and in 1592 they planned to kill the queen because the state of England was such that 'unless mistress Elizabeth be suddenly taken away, all the devils in Hell will not be able to prevail against it, or shake it'. There were other plots in 1594 and 1597, and the Pope had issued two bulls and sent them to Garnet to promote the Catholic religion after the queen's death.

When James I had come to the throne he had granted a general pardon, which Garnet had taken out under his own name, Henry Garnet of London, but not under any of his aliases. No sooner had he done so than Catesby approached him to ask whether it was justifiable, for the good of the Catholic cause against heretics, 'amongst many nocents to destroy and take away some innocents also', to which he had replied:

> that if the advantage were greater to the Catholic part, by taking away some innocents together with many nocents, then doubtless it should be lawful to kill and destroy them all. And to this purpose he alleged a comparison of a town or city which was possessed by an enemy, if at the time of taking thereof there happen to be some friends within the place, they must undergo the fortune of the wars in the general and common destruction of the enemy.

Following this advice, Catesby had embarked on the Gunpowder Plot, and they all confessed and received absolution from Garnet. In October 1605 Garnet met the conspirators at Coughton in Warwickshire and openly prayed for the success of the plot.

Sometime after, when Garnet had been arrested and was in the Tower, he had written a letter to his friend Rookwood who was also under arrest in the Gatehouse – an innocuous letter,

> but in the margin, which he had made very great and spacious, where there remained clean paper, he wrote cunningly with the juice of an orange, or of a lemon, to publish his innocency, and concerning his usage; and there denieth those things which before he had freely and voluntarily confessed; and said, that for the Spanish Treason, he was freed by his majesty's pardon; and as for the Powder Treason, he hoped for want of proof against him, to avoid that well enough.

Garnet's 'express and voluntary confessions' were then read, together with those of his accomplices. The 'trial' then developed into a theological debate, with Garnet defending himself against the charge of equivocation. As for the alleged power of the Pope to depose princes, that 'was by all other Catholic princes tolerated without grievance'. As to what he had been told, he 'might not disclose [the Powder Treason] to any, because it was a matter of secret confession, and would endanger the life of divers men'.

The Attorney-General made another speech, and the Earl of Northampton also spoke at great length. He referred to the bulls:

> The two Bulls that in the late queen's time entered the land (with a purpose by their loud lowing to call all their calves together, for the making of a strong party, at the shutting up of the evening, against your dread sovereign), were grazed in your pastures, Mr Garnet; or to speak more properly (because they durst not endure the light, nor admit the air) they were stall-fed at your crib, as yourself confess. . . . You say the Bulls were after sacrificed in the fire by yourself: But not before the king's good angel had cut their throats.

Garnet said that he was bound by the secrets of the confession, so the Earl of Nottingham asked him 'if one confessed this day to him, that to-morrow morning he meant to kill the king with a dagger, he must conceal it?' and he replied that he must conceal it.

So far, Popham CJ had kept quiet, but now he joined in and asked him if he had not instigated the whole business. Garnet replied, 'No, my lord, I did not.'

Garnet now desired the jury not to credit any of those things of which there was no direct proof, and the Earl of Salisbury asked 'Mr Garnet, is this all you have to say? if it be not, take your time, no man shall interrupt you.' Garnet answered 'Yea, my lord,' and then the Attorney-General humbly desired the commissioners that, if he had forgotten anything, their lordships would be pleased to remind him of it, and he was assured by the Earl of Salisbury that he had done very well, painfully and learnedly. So the jury retired, and returned within a quarter of an hour with a verdict of Guilty. Mr Waterhouse, the Clerk of the Crown, asked Garnet why judgment should not be pronounced, and he replied 'that he could say nothing, but referred himself to the mercy of the king and God Almighty'. Popham CJ made 'a pithy preamble of all the apparent Proofs and Presumptions of his guiltiness, and gave Judgment, that he should be hanged, drawn and quartered'. The Earl of Salisbury asked if he had anything else to say, and Garnet answered: 'No, my lord; but I humbly desire your lordships all to commend my life to the king's majesty; saying, That at his pleasure he was ready either to die or live, and do him service.'

And so the Court rose.

More than a month later, on 3 May, Garnet was taken to a scaffold set up at the west end of St Paul's Church. The Recorder of London was present, at the king's request, and he asked Garnet to confess his treason before the crowd, but he replied that his voice was so low, and his strength gone, that the people would not hear him. However, he spoke to those who were with him on the scaffold and said that he had had only 'a general knowledge' of the plot from Mr Catesby, and that he could not disclose anything which had been said to him in confession.

The recorder then led Garnet to the scaffold to make a public confession, which he did:

> I confess I have offended the king, and am sorry for it, so far as I was guilty, which was in concealing it; and for that I ask pardon of his majesty. The Treason intended against king and state was bloody, myself should have detested it, had it taken effect. And I am heartily sorry that any Catholicks ever had so cruel a design.

He knelt at the foot of the ladder and asked if he might have time to pray and was told 'he should limit himself, none should interrupt him', but he kept looking round as if he might be reprieved at the last moment, until the recorder told him 'not to deceive himself; he was come to die, and must die'. So he climbed the ladder and prayed for the royal family and for the Catholics, and crossed himself saying, 'Let me always remember the cross.' He was turned off and hung until he was dead.

CHAPTER FOUR

The Trial of Alice Lisle (1685)

Alice Lisle was the daughter of Sir White Beconshaw, descended of an ancient and honourable family, and the wife of John Lisle who had been a member of the Long Parliament, and had sat as a judge in the tribunal that had convicted Charles I. During the Commonwealth he was appointed Lord President of the High Court of Justice, but after the Restoration he and his wife went to live in Lausanne where he regularly attended the church near the town gate. It was known that his life was in danger, and he was warned not to go to this church as it would be easy for an assassin to make his escape through the gate, but he ignored the warning. During August 1664 two suspicious characters came to lodge at Vevey, and then for a week in Lausanne. Mr Lisle heard about them and sent his landlord to find out who they were, but they gave a good account of themselves, and no reason could be found for having them removed.

On Thursday 11 August one of these men went to a barber's shop, pretending that he wanted something for his teeth. When he saw Mr Lisle go past, he left the shop and followed him to the churchyard, where he 'drew a carabine from under his cloak' and shot Mr Lisle in the back. The recoil of the carabine blew off the murderer's hat and he dropped the weapon, but he ran to the gate where his companion was waiting for him, mounted, and leading a second horse. The pair galloped away and were never heard of again. Mr Lisle was killed.

After the murder, Alice returned to Hampshire and lived at Moyle's Court, her husband's home, near Ringwood. Charles II was succeeded by James II, and in the summer of 1685 the Duke of Monmouth, claiming to be the legitimate heir to the throne, landed at Lyme and began to assemble an army. About a month later, on Monday 6 July, he met the king's army at Sedgemoor. He was defeated and taken prisoner, taken to London, and, on 15 July, was executed on Tower Hill. The rebels appear to have had close associations with Nonconformist dissenters, who at that time were subject to legal disabilities and criminal penalties. The rebel army dispersed, and sought refuge where they could. At the end of July, two rebels, John Hicks (who was a dissenting minister) and Richard Nelthorp, were found hiding in Moyle's Court. Ironically, the father of Colonel Penruddock, the officer who carried out the search, had been sentenced to death by John Lisle during the Commonwealth.

Early in August the king appointed Sir George Jefferies, Chief Justice of the Court of King's Bench, to preside over a commission on the Western Circuit. The gaols were full of prisoners who had been caught but had not been summarily executed by Colonel Percy Kirke, now the commanding officer of the region. Kirke was recalled, and Sir George Jefferies was appointed Commander in Chief of the West with the rank of Lieutenant-General.[1] So far as I know, such a combined appointment was unique in English legal and military history.

George Jefferies was born in 1748. He became a member of Inner Temple at the age of fifteen and was called to the Bar in 1768. He immediately demonstrated a prodigious professional talent, and an equally prodigious talent for copious drinking with attorneys, the aristocracy, and the king. He soon became a leading member of

Sir George Jeffreys (or Jefferies) (1645–89). As Chief Justice of the Court of King's Bench in 1683 he presided over the 'Bloody Assize'. He was appointed Lord Chancellor in 1685, and at the time of the Revolution of 1688 he tried to flee the country but was found and taken to the Tower. He died there soon afterwards (The National Trust; photo: Courtauld Institute of Art)

the Old Bailey and the commercial bar, and was appointed Common Serjeant of the City of London at the age of twenty-three, Recorder seven years later, and soon afterwards Chief Justice of Chester. In 1683, still only thirty-five, he became Chief Justice of the Court of King's Bench. At this time he was a most popular judge – on his return from the Western Circuit in 1684, 500 horsemen, it is said, went out to meet him. His tour of the Northern Circuit that same summer resembled a royal progress – he was wined and dined in all the county towns, at Hull the bells were rung to greet him, and Carlisle welcomed him with a 15-gun salute. On the bench he was acquiring a reputation for interrupting witnesses and taking a firm line with convicted prisoners; he described a Lancashire magistrate as 'a snivelling canting fanatical rascal'; and by this time he was suffering from the stone, and was no doubt in constant discomfort if not acute pain.

The Lord Chief Justice seems to have treated the conviction of Alice Lisle as a foregone conclusion, and it is said that he obtained a promise from the king that she would not be pardoned. He opened his Assize at Winchester on 27 August, and Alice Lisle was immediately put on trial. The indictment was a relatively short document, in which the prisoner was accused of giving aid and comfort to John Hicks, at Ellingham in the County of Hampshire, well knowing that he was a traitor who had been in rebellion against the king.

It appears that there was no published, contemporaneous record of the trial, and only a few brief references in the history books of the period. Then the report materialized, without any provenance, in the 1719 edition of the *State Trials*. From there it was reprinted, again without any provenance, in Howell's edition, and for two centuries it was the principal evidence upon which the disreputation of Jefferies CJ rested. Then, in 1928, J.G. Muddiman published a paper in *Notes and Queries*,[2] in which he contended that the report was a forgery fabricated for the sole purpose of defaming the Lord Chief Justice, and he declined to include an account of the case in his book on the Bloody Assizes which he wrote for the Notable British Trials series.

Having studied the report with great care I am satisfied that it is, basically at least, a true record. If it was a forgery it is certainly a very remarkable piece of fiction! I would, however, be prepared to admit that some of the more outrageous remarks attributed to Jefferies CJ may have been added later. As for the facts of the case it is very difficult to believe that anyone could have had a motive for inventing them.

The trial began in an orderly fashion. The prisoner pleaded Not Guilty, and, as she was infirm ('being thick of hearing'), she asked to be allowed to have some friends to stand beside her and keep her informed of what was happening. Matthew Browne was assigned for this purpose. The jurors were called and the prisoner was invited to challenge any whom she chose, which she did (including one member of the grand jury who had expressed a desire to sit on the petty jury at the trial).

Mr Mundy opened the case and repeated briefly the gist of the indictment. The Solicitor-General, Mr Henry Pollexfen, who was also the Leader of the Circuit, was leading counsel for the Crown, and he set out the facts, as alleged by the prosecution, in rather greater detail. He stated that, after their defeat, the rebels were forced, 'like vagabonds, to skulk up and down', and John Hicks went to Warminster and sent a messenger, one Dunne, to Lady Lisle to ask her if she would receive him. She returned an answer that she would do so, but with a particular direction that they should come late at night. Accordingly Hicks and Dunne went there late in the evening, accompanied by another rebel, one Nelthorp. When they came to the house, they turned their horses loose, and Lady Lisle provided food and drink for Hicks and Nelthorp. The next morning, Colonel Penruddock came to the house, and searched it and found Hicks and Nelthorp hiding there, together with Dunne, the messenger, and he arrested them.

After this, Alice Lisle started to speak: 'My lord, as for what is said concerning the rebellion, I can assure you, I abhorred that rebellion as much as any woman in the world.' She was interrupted by the Lord Chief Justice to tell her that the 'common and usual methods of trial' must be observed. He told her that she would be fully heard when it came to her turn to make her defence – she should first hear what her accusation was, and should ask any questions of the witnesses that she wished, and when their testimony was concluded then

> You shall be heard to make your own defence, and have full scope and liberty to inlarge upon it as long as you can: it is a business that concerns you in point of life and death; all that you have or can value in the world lies at stake, and God forbid that you should be hindered, either in any time or any thing else, whereby you may defend yourself.

He added that the court was obliged to take care that the defendant suffered no detriment or injury, for though they sat there as judges by the authority of the king, they were also accountable to the King of Kings, and they were therefore obliged by their oaths and their consciences to do her justice: 'And by the grace of God we shall do it, you may depend upon it. And as to what you say concerning yourself, I pray God with all my heart you may be innocent.'

Then, turning to the Solicitor-General, he said: 'Pray call your witnesses.'

The Solicitor-General called three witnesses, Messrs Pope, Fitzherbert and Taylor, who were all sworn together. Pope gave evidence first, describing how he had been taken prisoner by the rebels and had been taken to Keinsham where he was put under guard, along with four or five other prisoners, in Sir Thomas Bridges's stables. While they were there, Mr Hicks

> who is now in Salisbury gaol, and there I saw him yesterday; he came and asked for the prisoners. . . . Then he desired to know how we were dealt with, whether we were kindly used or no? I replied, no, for we had but a piece of bread these two days. He made me answer, that he was sorry for that, for it was otherwise intended.

At the end of his story, the Lord Chief Justice (who was already taking the conduct of the case out of the hands of counsel) asked Pope if he was sure that the man he had seen in Salisbury was the same as had spoken to him at Keinsham, and he replied that he was. Fitzherbert and Taylor then confirmed Pope's evidence. The prisoner was asked if she wished to ask any questions, but she replied 'No, my lord.'

Mr James Dunne was then called, and the Solicitor-General prefaced his evidence by pointing out that the dates would be of particular importance. The battle of 'King's-Edgemore' was on 6 July, the Duke of Monmouth and Lord Grey had been taken at Ringwood three or four days later, and on 26 July Dunne was sent with a message to the prisoner. Dunne would tell the court all the circumstances, but 'I must acquaint your lordship, that this fellow, Dunne, is a very unwilling witness; and therefore . . . we do humbly desire your lordship to examine him a little the more strictly.'

So the Lord Chief Justice addressed the witness:

> Hark you, friend. . . . According as the counsel that are here for the king seem to insinuate, you were employed as a messenger between these persons. . . . Now mark what I say to you, friend: I would not by any means in the world endeavour to fright you into any thing, or any ways tempt you to tell an untruth, but provoke you to tell the truth, and nothing but the truth, that is the business we are come about. . . . I charge thee, therefore, as thou wilt answer it to the great God, the judge of all the earth, that you do not dare to waver one tittle from the truth, upon any account or pretence whatever. . . . For that God of Heaven may justly strike thee into eternal flames, and make thee drop into the bottomless lake of fire and brimstone, if thou offer to deviate the least from the truth, and nothing but the truth. . . . Now come and tell us, how you came to be employed upon such a message, what your errand was, and what was the issue and result of it?

Dunne then told his story, in answer to questions put to him by the Lord Chief Justice. The gist of it was that one Friday night, some time after the battle, a 'short black man' came to his house in Warminster and asked him to take a message for a Mr Hicks to 'my Lady Lisle', about 26 miles away, to ask if she would entertain Mr Hicks. So the following day, he set out and went to Lady Lisle's bailiff. 'Ay, who was that bailiff? tell us his name,' said the Lord Chief Justice, 'I love to know men's names.' His name was Carpenter, and he asked him if his lady would entertain Mr Hicks, but he had replied that he would have nothing to do with it and sent him to Lady Lisle. However, she said that they might come to her house on Tuesday, in the evening.

The Lord Chief Justice recapitulated Dunne's evidence. The Solicitor-General and a Mr Coriton, presumably a junior counsel for the Crown, managed to ask a couple of questions – Did Lady Lisle ask any questions? Did she believe that Dunne knew

Mr Hicks? – to which he replied that he could not tell. Then again the Lord Chief Justice took over the interrogation: 'Mr Dunne, Mr Dunne! Have a care, it may be more is known of this matter than you think for. . . . Truth never wants a subterfuge, it always loves to appear naked, it needs no enamel, nor any covering; but lying and snivelling, and canting and Hicksing, always appear in masquerade. Come, go on with your evidence.'

So Dunne proceeded with his account. He had returned home, and the same man came to see him again and he told him to come back on Tuesday. On Tuesday, at 7 o'clock in the morning, three men came to his house: the little black man, a 'full fat black man' and a thin black man. They stayed in Dunne's house until about 11 o'clock and then set off, via Deverel, Chilmark and Sutton, to Salisbury Plain, where 'one Barter met me' to show them the way. The Lord Chief Justice immediately asked how he had found the way the first time, and Dunne now explained that when he had reached the plain on the Saturday, he lost his way and asked some twenty people how to get to Moyle's Court where Lady Lisle was. Eventually he had spoken to John Barter who took him there, and on the way home he had spent the Saturday night at Fovant.

There was then a long discussion as to the route they had taken, via Chalk, Rocksborne and Fordingbridge, and why it was a different route from the one taken by Dunne on the Saturday, and whether he had promised Barter any reward. 'Half-a-crown, my lord, and half-a-crown I gave him,' said Dunne. It now emerged that the 'little black man' had not travelled with them on the Tuesday, but on this occasion the

Moyle's Court became derelict during the nineteenth century, but was fully restored shortly before this photograph was taken in about 1900. The house was probably built by John Lisle during the Commonwealth or by his widow after her return from Switzerland, and stands on the site of an older building (note the Tudor-style chimney incorporated into the side of the house.) The old stable block can be seen to the left of the house (*Country Life* Picture Library)

'black man' gave Barter five shillings. Dunne now named the others as Hicks and Nelthorp, although he swore that he did not know the latter's name until after his arrest. They rode on through the evening, discharging Barter about eight miles from Moyle's Court, and then they lost their way again. So Dunne was sent to Marton to find someone to help them. 'Now I must know that man's name,' said the Lord Chief Justice, 'and look to it, you tell me right, for it may be I know the man already, and can tell at what end of the town the man lives too.' Dunne said that he could not remember, but added, 'My lord, I can go to the house again if I were at liberty.' Eventually he remembered, the name was Fane. 'Thou sayest right,' said the Lord Chief Justice, 'his name was Fane truly, thou seest I know something of the matter.' So Fane showed them the way to Moyle's Court, but left before they arrived. A young girl came to the door and let them in, but it was dark and he saw nothing more. Hicks and Nelthorp were let in, but Dunne was left outside with no 'entertainment' except for a bit of cake and cheese he had brought with him. He did not see Lady Lisle. The Lord Chief Justice asked him 'What hadst thou for all thy pains?'

'Nothing but a month's imprisonment, my lord,' replied Dunne.

The Lord Chief Justice was quick to comment:

> Thou seemest to be a man of a great deal of kindness and good-nature; for, by this story, there was a man thou never sawest before . . . and because he only had a black beard, and came to thy house, that black beard of his should persuade thee to go 26 miles, and give a man half a crown out of thy pocket to shew thee the way, and all to carry a message from a man thou never knowest in thy life, to a woman thou never sawest in thy life neither; that thou shouldst lie out by the way two nights, and upon the Sunday get home, and there meet with this same black bearded little gentleman, and appoint these people to come to thy house upon the Tuesday; and when they came, entertain them three or four hours at thy own house, and go back again so many miles with them, and have no entertainment but a piece of cake and cheese that thou broughtest thyself from home, and have no reward, nor so much as know any of the persons thou didst all this for, is very strange.

Dunne said he thought that the men were in debt, and the Lord Chief Justice asked what his trade was. He said he was a baker. 'I believe thou dost use to bake on Sundays, dost thou not?' asked the Lord Chief Justice.

'No, my lord, I do not.'

'But thou canst travel on Sundays to lead rogues into lurking-holes: It seemeth thou hast a particular kindness for a black beard.'

It now emerged that 'the little black man' had lent Dunne a horse to take the message on the Saturday: 'How came he to trust thee with his horse?'

'The Lord knows, my lord.'

'Thou sayest right,' said the Lord Chief Justice, 'the Lord only knows, for by the little I know of thee, I would not trust thee with two-pence.'

However, on the Tuesday Dunne had ridden his own horse and left it at Lady Lisle's stable, and the other two had let their horses loose at the gate.

The Solicitor-General now intervened to ask Dunne if he was not aware that the country was being searched for the rebels that had fled from the battle, but he said that Hicks had told him that he and the other man were debtors. He said he did not know what had become of the horses, and that he had slept in one of the chambers – a girl had shown him the way. He had seen no one else in the house and he had taken his own horse to the stable, but 'no body helped me to horse-meat'.

'Why,' asked the Lord Chief Justice, 'thy horse did not feed on thy cake and cheese, did he?'

'There was hay in the rack, my lord.' The stable door was not locked, he went on, he had 'plucked up the latch'. Carpenter the bailiff had taken him to the stable and brought hay for his horse. No, he had not drunk anything in the house. He had not seen anyone that night except Carpenter and the girl. Then the Lord Chief Justice addressed him:

> Now prithee tell me truly, where came Carpenter unto you? I must know the truth of that; remember that I gave you fair warning, do not tell me a lie, for I will be sure to treasure up every lie that thou tellest me, and thou may be certain it will not be for thy advantage . . . But assure thyself I never met with a lying, sneaking, canting fellow, but I always treasured up vengeance for him.

So Dunne said that he and the other two had met Carpenter after they had come to the gate, and nobody else was there. Carpenter had opened the stable door for him. To which the Lord Chief Justice replied:

> Why thou vile wretch, didst not thou tell me just now, that thou pluckedst up the latch? Dost thou take the God of heaven not to be a God of truth, and that he is not a witness of all thou sayest? . . . Did not you tell me that you opened the latch yourself, and that you saw nobody else but a girl? How durst you offer such horrid lies in the presence of God and of a court of justice? . . . You see, gentlemen, what a precious fellow this is, a very pretty tool to be employed upon such an errand, a knave that no body would trust for half a crown between man and man, but he is the fitter to be employed about such works; what pains is a man at to get the truth out of these fellows! and it is with a great deal of labour, that we can squeeze one drop out of them!

Again, the Lord Chief Justice demanded to know if he had seen anyone else that night, where he had slept, whether he had been given a drink: 'it is hard that thou hadst not one cup of drink to thy cake and cheese'.

'My lord, I had never a drop.'

'No, nor did nobody ask you to eat or drink?'

'No, my lord.'

'Thou art the best natured fellow that ever I met with, but the worst rewarded.'

There were further questions as to when he had first heard the names of Hicks and Nelthorp, and what had happened to their horses, and then the Solicitor-General said he would 'set him by for the present' and call Barter. The Lord Chief Justice asked the prisoner if she wanted to ask any questions, and she said No. 'Perhaps her questions might endanger the coming out of all the truth,' commented the Lord Chief Justice, 'and it may be she is well enough pleased to have him swear as he does; but it carries a very foul face upon my word.'

Barter was sworn, and the Solicitor-General said he thought he was an honest man and would tell the truth, and the Lord Chief Justice said:

> Friend, you know your soul is at pawn for the truth of what you testify to us; the other fellow thou seest has been prevaricating with us all this while, and swearing off and on, and scarce told one word of truth, I know very well: Now I know as much of thee as I do of him, therefore look to thyself, and let the truth and nothing but the truth come out.

Barter described how Dunne had come to his house on the Saturday and asked the way to Moyle's Court, and having nothing else to do, he rode with him. Dunne had a letter which he produced for Mr Carpenter, but he refused to meddle with it so Dunne had taken it in to Lady Lisle while he waited in the kitchen. Then Lady Lisle came and asked him where he came from, and he said he was a Wiltshire man. She

asked him if he made bricks, and if he could she would give him ten acres of land, but
he said he could not. Then she went back to Dunne and he heard them laughing
together. When they were going away he asked Dunne what they had been laughing at
and Dunne replied, 'my lady asked, whether I knew anything of the concern? And
that he answered her, no; this the fellow told me was what she laughed at.'

After this, Barter continued, he could neither eat nor drink nor sleep for trouble of
mind, so he went to Colonel Penruddock, and told the colonel where he had arranged
to meet Dunne on the Tuesday. Penruddock had said that he would come and arrest
them there, but for some reason he changed his mind, and came to take them in the
house. So Barter had ridden with them ten miles, and then went home. Nelthorp had
given him five shillings and half a crown and two shillings and sixpence – but he did
not know Nelthorp's name until after he had been taken. He also said that Dunne had
told him that the two men had half a thousand pounds a year apiece, and added that
he had a 'very fine booty for his part and should never want money again', which was
when he gave him half a crown.

Dunne was now recalled. He denied that he had shown Carpenter a letter, he
denied saying that they had 'God knows how many thousand pounds a year a-piece',
but he admitted telling Lady Lisle, when she asked whether Barter was acquainted
with the concern, that he knew nothing of the business.

'What business was that?' asked the Lord Chief Justice.

'Does your lordship ask what that business was?'

'Yes, it is a plain question: What was that business that my lady asked thee, whether
the other man knew?' Dunne paused, so the Lord Chief Justice went on: 'Remember
friend, thou art upon thy oath; and remember withall, that it is not thy life, but thy soul
that is now in danger; therefore I require from thee a plain answer to a very plain
question: What was that business my lady enquired after, whether the other fellow knew,
and thou toldest her, he did not.' Again, Dunne said nothing. 'He is studying and
musing how he shall prevaricate; but thou hadst best tell the truth, friend. . . . Look
thee, if thou canst not comprehend what I mean, I will repeat it to thee again. . . . Thou
sayedst thy lady asked thee, whether he knew of the business; and thou toldest her, he
did not. Now let us know what that business was?'

'I cannot mind it, my lord, what it was.'

'. . . What was that business?'

'That business that Barter did not know of?'

The Lord Chief Justice told him that God could not endure a lie, and asked him
yet again: 'What was that business you and my lady spoke of?'

Dunne paused for 'half a quarter of an hour', and then said, 'I cannot give an
account of it, my lord.'

His lordship now tried a different approach.

Oh blessed God! Was there ever such a villain upon the face of the earth. . . . Dost thou
believe that there is a God? . . . Dost thou believe that that God can endure a lie? . . . Dost
thou think that that God of truth may immediately sink thee into hell-fire if thou tellest a lie?
. . . Dost thou believe, that he knows the business that you and my lady the prisoner were
talking of, as well as you do? . . . Dost thou then believe, that any discourse between you,
though never so private, private from the Almighty, All-knowing God?

Dunne assented to all these questions, so once again the Lord Chief Justice said:
'Now tell us what was the business you spoke of.' Again Dunne said nothing, and now
for the first and only time throughout the trial, Montague CB, who was presumably

sitting beside Jefferies CJ on the bench, joined in and repeated the question. By now, no doubt, the witness's mind had gone blank. Again and again the Lord Chief Justice attacked him in the most outrageous terms:

> Gentlemen of the jury, you take notice of the strange and horrible carriage of this fellow. . . . O blessed Jesus! What an age do we live in, and what a generation of vipers do we live among? . . . Thou wretch! all the mountains and hills in the world heaped upon one another, will not cover thee from the vengeance of the great God for this transgression of false witness-bearing.

At one point Dunne said, 'I cannot tell what to say, my lord,' and then, 'My lord, pray ask the question over again once more and I will tell you.'

So the Lord Chief Justice did what he was asked:

> I will so, and I will ask it with all the calmness, and seriousness, and candour, that I can; if I know my own heart, it is not in my nature to desire the hurt of any body, much less to delight in their eternal perdition; no, it is out of tender compassion to you that I use all these words. . . . Therefore I ask you, with a great desire that thou may'st free thyself from so great a load of falsehood and perjury, tell me what the business was you told the prisoner, the other man Barter did not know?

And Dunne, after another evasive answer, said: 'She asked me whether I did not know that Hicks was a nonconformist?' But the Lord Chief Justice said there must be something more to it than that: 'Dost thou think, that after all this pains that I have been at to get an answer to my question, that thou can'st banter me with such sham stuff as this? Hold the candle to his face, that we may see his brazen face.'

The report gives no indication as to when the trial had started, but there is reason to believe that some felons had been tried earlier in the day, so it may now have been late in the evening.

Dunne said that he was telling the truth – that was all.

'That is all nonsense; dost thou imagine that any man hereabouts is so weak as to believe thee.'

'My lord, I am so baulked, I do not know what I say myself; tell me what you would have me say, for I am cluttered out of my senses.'

The Lord Chief Justice replied:

> Why prithee, man, there is nobody baulks thee but thy own self; thou art asked questions that are as plain as any thing in the world can be: it is only thy own depraved naughty heart that baulks both thy honesty and understanding, if thou hast any; it is the studying how to prevaricate, that puzzles and confounds thy intellect: but I see all the pains in the world, and all compassion and charity is lost upon thee, and therefore I will say no more to thee.'

The Solicitor-General then recalled Barter to ask him what Dunne had told him concerning these people, and Barter said that Dunne had told him that he had concealed them in his house ten days before. Dunne immediately denied this, so Barter went on: 'I know not whether you did or no, but you told me so.' Barter said he had wondered how he had been able to keep them there without their being discovered while the search was going on, and Dunne had told him that he kept them in a chamber during the day and they had walked out at night, for the searches were usually carried out at night. He had also told Barter that he would never lack money again as long as he lived. Dunne denied this too, so the Lord Chief Justice told 'you gentlemen of the king's counsel, and others that are concerned, that you take notice and remember what has passed here, and that an information of perjury be preferred against this fellow'.

Alice Lisle, from a fresco by Edward Ward, entitled *Alice Lisle Concealing the Fugitives after the Battle of Sedgemoor* (1857). The original is in the House of Commons. There is no reason to believe that the people represented here are true likenesses of those involved (House of Commons; photo: Royal Commission on the Historical Monuments of England)

Colonel Penruddock now gave evidence. He described how Barter had come to see him on the Monday and he had arranged to meet him and some people between 9 and 11 o'clock on the following day at Salisbury Plain because he thought they were rebels who were going to Mrs Lisle's house. However, they must have gone another way for he missed them on the plain, so early next morning he took some soldiers and they beset Lady Lisle's house. Carpenter had come out and confessed that there were strangers in the house, 'but pray, says he, do not tell my mistress of it'. So they went in and found Hicks and Dunne in the malt-house; the latter was 'covered with some sort of stuff there'. At this point Lady Lisle had appeared on the scene and Colonel Penruddock told her that he was sure she was harbouring rebels, which she denied. So they searched again and found Nelthorp hiding in a hole by the chimney.

The Lord Chief Justice recalled Dunne yet again, and asked him why he had hid in the malt-house, and Dunne replied that he was frightened of the noise so he had left his chamber and gone to hide there.

'Alack-a-day! That is very strange, that thou should'st hide thyself for a little noise, when thou knewest nothing of the business, nor wert acquainted with anything of the matter at all. . . . It seems you told Barter, that you apprehended them to be rebels?'

'I apprehend them for rebels, my lord?'

'No, no, you did not apprehend them for rebels, but you hid them for rebels. But did you say to Barter, that you took them to be rebels?'

'I take them to be rebels!'

'You blockhead, I ask you, did you tell him so?'

'I tell Barter so!'

'Ay, is not that a plain question?'

'I am quite cluttered out of my senses; I do not know what to say.'

A candle was now held nearer to his nose, and the Lord Chief Justice closed the discussion by saying: 'But to tell the truth, would rob thee of none of thy senses, if ever thou hadst any.'

The Solicitor-General then resumed his examination of Colonel Penruddock: 'Pray, Colonel Penruddock, did you tell her you came to search for rebels?' The colonel explained that he and his men had surrounded the house for some time before anyone answered them, until some ladies, he thought they were Lady Lisle's daughters, looked out of the window, and he had told them there were rebels in the house. When he met Lady Lisle, she said that she knew nothing of any strangers being in the house. Lady Lisle herself then spoke: 'My lord, I hope I shall not be condemned without being heard.'

'No, God forbid, Mrs Lisle; that was a sort of practice in your husband's time; you know very well what I mean: But God be thanked, it is not so now; the king's courts of law never condemn without hearing.'

The prosecution then called a Mr Dowding, who confirmed what Colonel Penruddock had said – they had 'beset the house round, some to the back gate, some to the fore gate; we called almost half an hour before we got in'.

While he was giving his evidence, Lady Lisle interrupted: 'My lord, this fellow who now speaks against me, broke open my trunk, and stole away a great part of my best linen; and sure, my lord, those persons that rob me, are not fit to be evidences against me, because it behoves them that I be convicted, to prevent their being indicted for felony.'

But the Lord Chief Justice took no notice, and Dowding went on to say that he had identified Hicks in Salisbury Gaol where he had admitted that he had been at Keinsham in the Duke of Monmouth's army.

Mrs Carpenter, the bailiff's wife, was called, and she described how the men had come at night to Lady Lisle's house and lodged there: 'but I never made the bed,' she said. She had prepared some supper for them at Lady Lisle's orders and taken it up to the chamber where they lay, and her husband had put it on their table in Lady Lisle's presence. Carpenter himself then gave evidence and confirmed what his wife had said. He denied that he had seen a letter, as Barter had alleged, but he agreed that he had taken Dunne to the stable. He had taken up some beer to Hicks and Nelthorp, but had not given any to Dunne.

Then Mr Rumsey, presumably another member of the team of prosecuting counsel, told his Lordship that Dunne was now prepared to tell all, so Dunne gave yet another version of his story. He had never entertained these men in his house, he said, but when he had gone to Moyle's Court on the Saturday, Lady Lisle had asked him whether Hicks had been in the army. 'I told her, I could not tell, I did not know that he was.' She had asked him if there would be anyone else, and he had replied that he believed there was. When they arrived on the Tuesday, someone took the two horses, and after he had set up his own horse, he and Carpenter and Lady Lisle had gone to join Hicks and Nelthorp. Mr Carpenter or a maid had brought in the supper and set it on the table, and though he did eat and drink with them, he could not tell what they were talking about.

'Was there nothing of coming from beyond seas, who came from thence, and how they came?' asked the Lord Chief Justice, 'come, tell us what was the discourse?' Dunne said he did not remember. The Lord Chief Justice changed the subject, and asked whether Nelthorp's name had been mentioned, adding: 'I will assure you, Nelthorp told me all the story before I came out of town.' Dunne now said that Lady Lisle had asked Hicks who the other gentleman was, and he said it was Nelthorp.

The Lord Chief Justice then asked Dunne if there had been any discourse about the battle, and Dunne replied: 'My lord, I will tell you, when I have recollected it, if you will give me time till to-morrow morning.'

'Nay, but we cannot stay so long, our business must be despatched now. . . . What say'st thou? Prithee tell us what the discourse was.'

'My lord, they did talk of fighting, but I cannot exactly tell what the discourse was.'

'And thou saidst thou did eat and drink with them in the same room?'

'I did so my lord, I confess it.'

'And it was not a little girl that lighted thee to bed, or conducted thee in?'

'It was not a little girl.'

'Who was it then?'

'It was Mr Carpenter, my lord.'

'And why didst thou tell so many lyes then? . . . I pity thee with all my soul, and pray for thee, but it cannot but make all mankind to tremble and be filled with horror, that such a wretched creature should live upon the earth: Prithee be free, and tell us what discourse there was.'

'My lord, they did talk of fighting, but I cannot remember what it was.'

This was the end of the case for the Crown. Mr Jennings said: 'My lord, we have done, we have no more witnesses.'

Then the Lord Chief Justice addressed the court:

Then you that are for the prisoner at the bar, now is your time to make your defence; you hear what is charged upon you, and what a kind of shuffling here has been to stifle the truth; and I am sorry to find the occasion to speak it, that under the figure and form of religion, such practices should be carried on. What have you to say for yourself?

Alice Lisle replied:

My lord, that which I have to say to it is this: I knew of nobody's coming to my house but Mr Hicks, and for him I was informed that he did abscond, by reason of warrants out against him for preaching in private meetings, but I never heard that he was in the army, nor that Nelthorp was to come with him; and for that reason it was, that I sent to him to come by night: but for the other man, Nelthorp, I never knew it was Nelthorp, I could die upon it, nor did not know what name he had, till after he came into my house; but as for Mr Hicks, I did not in the least suspect him to have been in the army, being a Presbyterian minister, that used to preach, and not to fight.

Then said the Lord Chief Justice:

But I will tell you, there is not one of those lying, sniveling, canting Presbyterian rascals, but one way or other had a hand in the late horrid conspiracy and rebellion; upon my conscience I believe it, and would have been as deep in the actual rebellion, had it any little success, as that other fellow Hicks; their principles carry them to it; Presbytery has all manner of villainy in it, nothing but Presbytery could lead that fellow Dunne to tell so many lies as he has told here; for shew me a Presbyterian, and I will engage to shew a lying knave.

Alice Lisle responded: 'My lord, I abhorred both the principles and practices of the late rebellion.'

'I am sure you had great reason for it.'

'Besides, my lord, I should have been the most ungrateful person living, should I have been disloyal, or acted any thing against the present king, considering how much I was obliged to him for my estate.'

'Oh then! Ungrateful! Ungrateful adds to the load which was between man and man, and is the basest crime that any one can be guilty of.'

And now for the first time, Lady Lisle raised the vital point of law: '. . . But my lord, I am so told, and so I thought it would have been, that I should not have been tried as a traitor for harbouring him, till he was convict for a traitor.' She repeated that she did not know of Nelthorp's coming, she had never heard his name mentioned and if he had told her 'I had then remembered the proclamation.' As to the assertion that she had denied having Nelthorp in her house: 'I was in great consternation and fear of the soldiers, who were very rude and violent, and could not be restrained by their officers from robbery, and plundering my house.'

She begged his Lordship not to harbour an ill opinion of her because of the rumours which were going about concerning her attitude towards Charles I – she had in no way been consenting to his death. As for Mr Hicks, she knew that he was a Nonconformist minister, and as there were warrants out for the arrest of Nonconformist ministers, she had been willing to give him shelter. She did not know Mr Nelthorp, but she had heard of him in the proclamation and she would never have hazarded her life by sheltering him.

> And for that whiteheaded man that speaks of my denying them, as I said before, he was one of them that rifled and plundered my house, and tore open my trunk; and if I should not be convicted, he and the rest of them may be called to account for what they did, for they ought not to have meddled with my goods. Besides, my lord, I have a witness that can testify what Mr Nelthorp said, when he was examined before——

The Lord Chief Justice interrupted her in mid-sentence and told her that that would signify little: 'But if you have any witnesses, call them.' So she called George Creed, who said that he had heard Nelthorp say that Lady Lisle did not know of his coming, and did not know his name, and that he had never told her his name, until after he was taken by Colonel Penruddock. 'Well, this is nothing,' said the Lord Chief Justice, 'she is not indicted for harbouring Nelthorp, but Hicks. . . . Have you any more to say for yourself?'

'My lord, I came but five days before this into the country——'

'Nay, I cannot tell when you came into the country, nor do I care; it seems you came time enough to harbour rebels.'

Lady Lisle said that she had stayed in London throughout the rebellion, she knew the king was her sovereign and she knew her duty to him. She could not fight for him herself, but 'My son did; he was actually in arms on the king's side in this business; I instructed him always in loyalty, and sent him thither; it was I that bred him up to fight for the king.'

'Well, have you done?'

'Yes my lord.'

'Have you a mind to say anything more?'

'No, my lord.'

Then she remembered something else – another point of law: 'My, lord, I beseech you afford me your patience and advice; Keinsham, where Mr Hicks is said to be in arms, does not lie in this county.'

'That is nothing: but the treason you committed was in this county.'

Once again she repeated that she did not know that Hicks had been in the army, and again the Lord Chief Justice asked her if she had anything more to say. But now she had no more to say, so his lordship addressed the jury.

He said that this was a case of great weight, and they had been detained in an endeavour to find out the truth – the jury was not sitting there on any other errand but to find out the truth according to their oath – 'That you shall well and truly try, and true deliverance make, between our sovereign lord the King and the prisoner at the bar, according to the evidence,' and he asked them to let the court know the truth of the fact by a 'sincere and upright verdict'.

His lordship then said that he was going to repeat the evidence, but instead of doing so he delivered a lengthy sermon on the infinite goodness of God in restoring King Charles II and preserving his successor from rebellion, a rebellion instigated by men who called themselves ministers of religion and 'cry out that they are fighting the Lord's battle, when they are attempting to kill the lord's anointed'. This was what had brought this poor unfortunate woman into this deplorable condition. After more in the same vein, he gave his ruling on the law:

> Gentlemen, I must tell you for law, of which we are the judges, and not you, That if any person be in actual rebellion against the King, and another person (who really and actually was not in rebellion) does receive, harbour, comfort and conceal him that was such, a receiver is as much a traitor, as he who indeed bore arms;

and he added:

> That there are sufficient testimonies to satisfy you that this woman did receive and harbour him, is that which is left to your consideration.

It was only then that he returned to the evidence and reviewed the facts of the case, pointing out that the prisoner 'directed the particular time wherein they should come, and that was at night; and no prudent person would receive strangers in such a season without some extraordinary ground for it. . . . Works of darkness always desire to be in the dark: works of rebellion and such are never done in the light.' Then he mentioned Barter, and said that Lady Lisle had 'promised him so many acres of land in Carolina'. This was a strange observation, for Carolina had not been mentioned, according to the report, when Barter was giving evidence, or at any time during the trial.

Then, turning to the prisoner again, he declared that she pretended to religion and loyalty and had wept at the death of King Charles the Martyr, and had owned great obligations to Charles II, but no sooner was he in the grave than she had entertained rebels against his successor: 'I will not say what hand her husband had in the death of that blessed martyr, she has enough to answer for her own guilt; and I must confess that it ought not one way or other to make any ingredient into this case what she was in former times.' However, it was his duty to remind the jury that when Colonel Penruddock came to search her house, she said that she had no one in it, which was an aggravation of the offence testified by Colonel Penruddock himself, 'whose father was likewise a martyr and died for his fidelity to the crown; and who was the judge of that father, we all know very well'. Finally he charged the jury to do their duty and deliver their verdict according to conscience and truth.

When he had concluded, Lady Lisle said, 'My lord, if your lordship please——'

But the Lord Chief Justice interrupted: 'Mistress, you have had your turn, you cannot now be heard any more after the jury is charged.'

'My lord, I did not know Nelthorp, I declare it, before he was taken.'

'You are not indicted for Nelthorp, but we are not to enter into dialogues now, the jury must consider of it.'

'Pray, my lord,' said a member of the jury, 'some of us desire to know of your lordship, in point of law, whether it be the same thing, and equally treason, in receiving him before he was convicted of treason, as if it had been after.'

'It is all the same, that certainly can be no doubt; for, if in this case Hicks had been wounded in the rebels army, and had come to her house and there been entertained, but had died there of his wounds, and so could never have been convicted, she had nevertheless been a traitor.'

The jury were out for about half an hour, while the Lord Chief Justice expressed his impatience and wondered why, in so plain a case, they needed to retire, and he was going to warn them that if they did not come quickly, he would adjourn and 'let them lie all night'. Then they returned – but not with a verdict. The foreman said that they 'have some doubt upon us, whether there is sufficient proof that she knew Hicks to have been in the army'.

'There is as full proof as proof can be; but you are judges of the proof, for my part I thought there was no difficulty in it.'

'My lord,' said the foreman, 'we are in some doubt of it.'

'I cannot help your doubts: was there not proved a discourse of the battle and of the army at supper-time?'

'But, my lord, we are not satisfied that she had notice that Hicks was in the army.'

'I cannot tell you what would satisfy you: Did she not enquire of Dunne, whether Hicks had been in the army? And when he told her he did not know, she did not say she would refuse him if he had been there, but ordered him to come by night, by which it is evident she suspected it; and when he and Nelthorp came, discoursed with them about the battle and the army. Come, come, gentlemen, it is plain proof.'

'My lord, we do not remember that it was proved that she did ask any such question when they were there.'

'Sure you do not remember any thing that has passed? Did not Dunne tell you there was such discourse, and she was by and Nelthorp's name was named? But if there were no such proof the circumstances and management of the thing is as full a proof as can be; I wonder what it is you doubt of?'

While the jury were out, Lady Lisle, who was over seventy, had dropped off to sleep in the dock, but she was awake now and said: 'My lord, I hope——', but the Lord Chief Justice interrupted her: 'You must not speak now.' So the jury retired a second time and 'laid their heads together for near a quarter of an hour, and at length agreed', and brought in a verdict of Guilty.

According to a different version, added in footnotes to the *State Trials*, the jury found the prisoner Not Guilty three times, until at last, in a great fury and a transport of rage, the Lord Chief Justice threatened them with attaint of treason, and so they finally brought in a verdict of Guilty.

The Clerk of Arraigns then announced: 'See to her, jailor, she is found guilty of high treason; and prepare yourself to die.' And the Lord Chief Justice addressed the jury:

Gentlemen, I did not think I should have had any occasion to speak after your verdict, but finding some hesitancy and doubt among you, I cannot but say, I wonder it should come about; for I think in my conscience, the evidence was as full and plain as could be, and if I had been among you, and she had been my own mother, I should have found her guilty.

On the following day Alice Lisle was brought back to the bar (along with several other prisoners who were also to receive sentence of death). When asked if she had anything to say, she was silent, and the Lord Chief Justice addressed her:

. . . I cannot but lament the deplorable condition of you, Mrs Lisle, a gentlewoman of quality and of fortune, so far stricken in years, therefore ought to have had more discretion: one, who all your life-time have been a great pretender to, and professor of, religion, and of that religion which bears a very good name, the Protestant religion. . . .

There is no religion whatever (except that hypocritical profession of theirs which deserves not the name of religion, I mean the canting, whining, presbyterian, phanatical profession), that gives the least countenance to rebellion or faction; and I cannot but lament to find you involved in that herd.

And I cannot but deplore it withal, as a most sad and dismal thing, that in this little case so many perjuries should be added to the crime of treason, such as for my part I cannot but tremble to remember. . . .

Then he made certain observations which suggested that he knew more than had been given in evidence, implying that a party of Nonconformists had been invited to hear Hicks preach while he was staying at Moyle's Court:

Even since last night, there has been but too much discovered how far you were concerned; no, it is not unknown who were sent for upon the Monday night, in order to have that rebellious, seditious fellow to preach to them, what directions were given to come through the orchard the back and private way, what orders were given for provision, and how the horses were appointed to be disposed.

Finally, after adjuring her to repent and disclose the truth, he passed sentence:

That you, Mrs Lisle, be conveyed from hence to the place from whence you came, and from thence you are to be drawn on a hurdle to the place of Execution, where your body is to be burnt alive till you are dead. And the Lord have mercy upon your Soul.

He passed sentence of death upon the convicted felons, and then turned again to Lady Lisle:

Look you, Mrs Lisle, when I left his majesty, he was pleased to remit the time of all executions to me: that where-ever I found any obstinacy or impenitence, I might order the executions with what speed I should think best: therefore, Mr Sheriff, take notice, that you are to prepare for the execution of this gentlewoman this afternoon. But withal, I give you, the prisoner, this intimation: we that are the judges shall stay in town an hour or two; you shall have pen, ink, and paper, brought to you, and if in the meantime you employ that pen, ink and paper and this hour or two well, (you understand what I mean) it may be you will hear further from us, in a deferring the execution.

At that stage of the proceedings, some of the clergy of Winchester interceded for Lady Lisle, and she was respited for four days, until Wednesday 2 September. On the Sunday a letter was sent by M. St John and E. Abergavenny to the Earl of Clarendon, the Lord Privy Seal, stating that many false reports had been made of Alice Lisle, and

The Great Hall of Winchester Castle was the scene of the trials of Sir Walter Raleigh and Alice Lisle; it remained the Assize Court for Hampshire until 1974, when it was replaced by new purpose-built courts, and is now open to the public. Note the Round Table on the wall, traditionally believed to have been King Arthur's Table, though it was probably made in the late thirteenth century (Hampshire County Council)

asking him to intercede with the king for her reprieve – the earl read the letter to the king. At the same time, a petition from Alice Lisle, dated 31 August, was also presented to the king in which she simply begged his majesty 'that execution may be altered from burning to beheading, and may be respited four days', to which the king responded 'That he would not reprieve her for one day; but for altering the Sentence he would do it, if there were any precedents for it.' Precedents were shown to him, and so a warrant was drawn up to the effect that Alice Lisle's head should be severed from her body, and that her head and body should be delivered to her relatives to be privately and decently interred. The execution was carried out on a scaffold in the market-place at Winchester. Before she died, she handed a letter to the sheriff, addressed Gentlemen, Friends and Neighbours. After saying that she died in the expectation of forgiveness for her sins, she went on:

> My crime was entertaining a nonconformist minister, who is since sworn to have been in the late Duke of Monmouth's army. I am told, if I had not denied them, it would not have affected me. I have no excuse but surprise and fear; which I believe my jury must make use of to excuse their verdict to the world.
>
> I have been told, the court ought to be counsel for the prisoner, instead of which, there was evidence from thence; which, though it were but hearsay, might possibly affect my jury. My defence was such as might be expected from a weak woman: but such as it was, I did not hear it repeated again to the jury. But I forgive all persons that have done me wrong, and I desire that God will do likewise.
>
> I forgive Colonel Penruddock, though he told me, he could have taken those men before they came to my house.
>
> As to what may be objected, that I gave it under my hand that I had discoursed with

Nelthorp, that could be no evidence to the court or jury, it being after my conviction and sentence.

I acknowledge his majesty's favour in altering my sentence: and I pray God to preserve him, that he may long reign in peace, and the true religion flourish under him.

Two things which I have omitted to say, which is, that I forgive him that desired to be taken from the Grand Jury to the petty jury, that he might be the more nearly concerned in my death.

Also, I return humble thanks to Almighty God, and the reverend clergy that assisted me in my imprisonment.

Sept. 2, Alice Lisle

On 28 August, probably, the 'Lord Justice General' had proceeded to Salisbury with a full military escort, and thence to Dorchester, where the 'Bloody Assize' was held and some two or three hundred captured rebels were convicted and executed. John Hicks was probably tried at Taunton – he was hanged at Glastonbury – and made one of the longest dying speeches on record. Most of this was on religious matters, but he did admit having joined the rebel army, and made a strange remark about Barter:

I desire God to forgive all my enemies . . . which are many, some mighty, and all most malicious: Particularly Barter of Lisnel, who betrayed me, and proved such a traitor to James Duke of Monmouth his old and intimate friend.

Hicks's brother was the Dean of Worcester, who, when asked to intercede for him, 'savagely replied', 'I cannot speak for a fanatic.'

Richard Nelthorp was also convicted, but he was brought to Newgate and attempts were made to induce him to become an informer, though under the strain he lost his reason. However, he recovered sufficiently to write some letters shortly before his execution on 30 October. His final speech threw little further light on Lady Lisle's trial, but he did say:

I most humbly beg the pardon of all that I have in the least any way injured; and in a special manner humbly ask pardon of the lady Lisle's family and relations, for that being succoured there one night with Mr Hicks, brought that worthy lady to suffer death: I was wholly a stranger to her ladyship, and came with Mr Hicks; neither did she (as I verily believe) know who I was, or my name, till I was taken.

I first read the report of the trial of Alice Lisle under the traditional view that she was an innocent old lady who had allowed genuine refugees into her house out of the kindness of her heart, but when I came to study the case more closely I realized that there were problems that could not easily be resolved; and in particular that Alice Lisle herself must have been involved in some sort of scheme.

There was first the matter of James Dunne. Even after his interrogation by the Lord Chief Justice, questions remained unanswered. It is not to be supposed that 'the little black man' selected Dunne at random from among the tradesmen of Warminster. It is likely that he was a Presbyterian, possibly one who had assisted the rebels or could be blackmailed – perhaps he had baked bread for them. On the other hand, he was not so well known that he would be conspicuous in making a journey of 26 miles to Moyle's Court. And why did they want to go to Moyle's Court? They would not have approached Lady Lisle unless they had been fairly confident of receiving a friendly welcome; this visit was carefully arranged in advance. And what were they going to do when they got there? This was not a social call: how long were they going to stay, and where were they going next? Why did they let their horses loose? Wherever they were going, they were either going on foot or by some other means of transport.

Also, what was the significance of that strange remark about brickmaking? According to the transcript of Barter's evidence, the conversation took place in Lady Lisle's kitchen, and ran as follows:

'What countryman art thou?'

'I am a Wiltshire man.'

'Do'st thou make bricks?'

'No, madam; I cannot, I can help in husbandry work.'

'If thou could'st make bricks, I will give thee ten acres of ground in such a place', and then she went to Dunne, and 'there she was laughing upon me'.

When the Lord Chief Justice came to sum up the case to the jury, he said: 'The prisoner asked him what countryman he was, and whether he was a brick-maker, and promised him so many acres of land in Carolina.'

It is possible that Lady Lisle was planning an extension to Moyle's Court, but unlikely that she would discuss this with a total stranger in her kitchen, or that the work of a brick-maker was to be valued at ten acres of land. It seems to me much more likely that brick-making was a code-word, and that she was really asking: 'Are you one of us?' As for Carolina, perhaps Barter mentioned it while giving evidence and the scribe failed to catch what he said, or maybe the Lord Chief Justice was speaking from an independent source, but the inference is clear – he at least believed that she was in a position to offer someone some land in Carolina. The whole scheme now becomes intelligible: Nonconformists had been persecuted for some years and Moyle's Court appears to have been a 'safe house', conveniently situated some ten miles from the coast, where religious refugees could take ship for Carolina in North America.

There is one further item of evidence supporting this proposition. Did Colonel Penruddock try to arrest Hicks and Nelthorp on the Tuesday evening, or did he deliberately allow them to proceed to Moyle's Court so that the house could be surrounded and Lady Lisle would be caught in the net? This seems a plausible explanation.

This is not the only puzzle in the case: there is the problem of the extraordinary conduct of the prosecution.

It seems to have been the accepted law at the time that an accessory to treason could not be convicted unless or until the principal traitor had been convicted. So why was Hicks not prosecuted first? In those days the rules relating to 'venue' were much stricter than they are today – a person could only be prosecuted for an offence in the county in which the crime (or in the case of treason, at least one overt act) had been committed. There was no evidence that Hicks (or Nelthorp) had committed any overt act in Hampshire, but this difficulty could have been overcome by keeping Lady Lisle in custody until Hicks and/or Nelthorp had been convicted, and dealing with her at a later assize. This departure from standard practice was sufficient to vitiate the whole proceedings.

And that was not all.

Why was Lady Lisle not charged with harbouring Nelthorp as well as Hicks? According to Lady Lisle herself, Nelthorp had been proscribed by proclamation so that she would have had no defence to harbouring him. Also, why was Dunne called as a witness for the prosecution instead of being prosecuted?

The whole thing was bungled – or was it?

There is another possible explanation. In February 1685 Pollexfen had been briefed to defend Richard Baxter on a charge arising out of his religious views. Baxter was tried by Jefferies CJ shortly after his appointment as Lord Chief Justice. While Pollexfen was addressing the jury on behalf of his client, the Lord Chief Justice denounced him in these terms: 'Pollexfen, I know you well. I will set a mark on you. You are the patron of the faction. This is an old rogue, a schismatical knave, a hypocritical villain. He hates the liturgy. He would have nothing but longwinded cant without book.' When Pollexfen reminded him that Charles II had thought that his client deserved a bishopric, he cried: 'And what ailed the old blockhead, then, that he did not take it?'

There were no doubt many stories going round London during that summer of 1685, but one of these is that the king, fearing the excesses of the Lord Chief Justice, deliberately appointed Pollexfen, rather than the Attorney-General, as chief counsel for the Crown – for 'being a known favourer of the presbyterian party, he hoped would moderate the Chief Justice'. On that basis I have formed the opinion that Pollexfen deliberately presented the prosecution of Lady Lisle in such a way as to ensure that she would be acquitted – she would get a good fright and that should have sufficed. However, the Lord Chief Justice overrode him, and took the conduct of the case out of his hands. On this basis, the vituperation of the Lord Chief Justice against the Presbyterians may be seen as being directed, not only against Dunne, but against leading counsel for the Crown.

There is one vital item of evidence supporting this proposition.

Very soon after the Glorious Revolution, Alice Lisle's daughters, Triphena Lloyd and Bridget Usher, presented a petition to parliament:

> Whereas Alicia Lisle . . . by an irregular and undue prosecution, was indicted for entertaining, concealing and comforting John Hicks, clerk, a false traitor, knowing him to be such, though the said John Hicks was not, at the trial of the said Alicia Lisle, attainted or convicted of any such crime: And by a verdict injuriously extorted and procured by the menaces and violences, and other illegal practices of George lord Jefferies, baron of Wem, then Lord Chief Justice of the King's Bench . . . was convicted, attainted, and executed for High Treason: May it therefore please your most excellent majesties . . . That it be declared and enacted by the authority of this present parliament . . . that the said conviction, judgment and attainder of the said Alicia Lisle be, and are hereby repealed, reversed, made and declared null and void . . .

This was done.

Sir Henry Pollexfen was now the Attorney-General under the new regime.

CHAPTER FIVE

The Gordon Riots: the Trial of Lord George Gordon (1781)

After the Reformation many legal disabilities were imposed upon Roman Catholics in England: they were unable to hold any office under the Crown or any commission in the Armed Forces, or to bring any action in the lawcourts, and they were liable to be fined for failing to attend services in the Church of England.

In 1698 a new Act, containing even more stringent measures, was passed: every Catholic priest who exercised any of his functions in England was made liable to perpetual imprisonment, and so was any Catholic who kept a school for the education of youth in their religion, and Catholics were prohibited from inheriting estates from their parents unless they took oaths which by their religion they could not do.

By the middle of the eighteenth century, this Act had become virtually a dead letter. When the Attorney-General opened his case for the Crown against Lord George Gordon, he said that he knew of only one prosecution under the Act, against a man who had said mass, and he was convicted 'and of course doomed by the provisions of this act to perpetual imprisonment'. Nevertheless, Roman Catholics were liable to be subjected to extortionate demands, to which they yielded rather than risk prosecution and the loss of their family property.

It was to repeal this Act of 1698, and this Act alone, that early in 1778 Sir George Savile MP introduced a bill which parliament passed speedily and almost unanimously. Opposition to the bill was, in fact, mainly on the ground that it did not go far enough.

While Sir George Savile's bill was under discussion, a group of Protestants met at Coachmakers' Hall in Foster Lane, Cheapside, and formed themselves into the Protestant Association with the object of opposing 'the growth of Popery' and publishing and distributing literature, and in particular for securing the repeal of Sir George Savile's Act. The association met quarterly, and on 12 November 1779 they wrote to Lord George Gordon inviting him to become their president.

Lord George was born in 1751, the younger son of the Duke of Gordon. While he was still a boy he spent some time in the Navy, and was then elected as MP for Ludgershall, a pocket borough in Wiltshire. Within a few years he acquired a reputation for making outrageous speeches, culminating in May 1780 when he told the House of Commons that he had 160,000 Scotchmen[1] under his command, and if the king did not cut their taxes, they would come and cut off the king's head.

Sir George Savile's Act did not apply to Scotland, but the Scotch were alarmed that a similar repeal would be extended to the Catholics north of the border, and on 5 February 1779 a riot occurred in Edinburgh. Two Catholic chapels were attacked and set on fire, the houses of Catholics were attacked, ransacked and demolished, and, it was said, it was not until the Provost of the City gave an assurance that no Act of Parliament would be applied for respecting Catholics in Scotland that the violence could be brought to an end.

It was, indeed, a time of unrest. For four years the Crown had been conducting a difficult and expensive (and in many eyes, unpopular) war to crush the rebellion in

Lord George Gordon is portrayed standing in St George's Fields on the morning of 2 June 1780. Behind him, the Protestant Association is massed in four divisions: Southwark, London, Westminster and Scotch. Waterloo station was subsequently built on the fields. (British Museum)

the American colonies. France and Spain had joined the war on the side of the rebels and an invasion was expected. Several counties were said to be planning to employ their militia and to be raising volunteers to support their political objectives by force of arms.[2] And then, in June 1780, London was subjected to a degree of violence and destruction unparalleled since the great fire of 1666.[3]

On the morning of Friday 2 June a vast crowd of Protestants assembled in St George's Fields in Southwark in pursuance of a public advertisement, signed by Lord George Gordon as President of the Protestant Association, which had been published in the newspapers and pasted up at street corners and distributed as handbills. The crowd was variously assessed at between 20,000 and 40,000 people, and it was organized in four divisions: the London, Scotch, Westminster and Southwark divisions. They set out to present their petition to parliament. In the reign of Charles II an Act 'against tumultuous assemblies' had been passed which laid down that no more than ten persons should attend the presentation of a petition to parliament. It was argued that this Act had been repealed by the Bill of Rights which declares that subjects have a right to petition parliament, but it was generally accepted that the Act was in full force. This, however, was a relatively minor technicality. Whether legally or not, the petitioners marched to Westminster, all wearing blue cockades in their hats, and the Scotch division was accompanied by a band of bagpipes. They arrived at Westminster at about 1 p.m. and, it was alleged, they (or a rabble which had joined them) besieged the House of Commons, insulted and ill-treated members of both Houses, and filled the lobby shouting 'A repeal! a repeal! No popery.' It was not until 9 or 10 p.m. that the military arrived and dispersed the crowd. The House of Commons then adjourned until the following Tuesday.

On the Friday night attacks were made on the chapels of foreign ministers and they were burnt down, with about a dozen of the rioters being arrested. The Saturday was relatively quiet, although the crowd paraded in different parts of the town. On Sunday

The Protestant Association reaches Westminster on the afternoon of 2 June; Mr Hodgkinson is seen carrying the petition at the head of the procession (British Museum)

they attacked a chapel and private house in Moorfields, bringing out the furniture and setting fire to it, and demolishing the buildings.

On Monday the violence increased. The men who had been arrested were examined at Sir John Fielding's; five of them were committed to Newgate and were, with difficulty, conveyed there by the guard. Attacks were then made on the houses of the men who had helped to arrest them and two others who had given evidence against them, and also upon the house of Sir George Savile.

On the Tuesday, when parliament was to reassemble, the mob returned to Westminster until the House of Commons was obliged to adjourn again. The riot then came to a climax as described by the Attorney-General in opening the case for the Crown against Lord George:

> Upon this their first attack was upon the house of Mr Hyde; the offence given by Mr Hyde, was partly his attendance at the justices upon the Monday at the examination, but principally for his activity as a magistrate in saving the life of a member of the House of Peers, the earl of Sandwich, who, in going to attend his duty, had been violently attacked by the mob. They ransacked and set fire to Mr Hyde's house, and burnt the furniture, and totally demolished every thing they could. In this they were accompanied with their colours, for they appeared again with their flags and with their cockades. Very large parts of the mob marched to Newgate; they set fire to the keeper's house; they attacked the prison; and, in a very short time, they set at large all the prisoners; a place which for its security seemed to be equal to a prison in the centre of the earth. They afterwards attacked and demolished many houses belonging to Roman Catholics, burnt and destroyed the furniture and effects.
>
> Upon the Wednesday they attacked and broke open the other prisons in and about this metropolis, with an exception of the Poultry Compter, and set at liberty all the prisoners; they continued their proceedings without controul or check all that night, and until some time the next morning; in that night various houses in different parts of the town were in flames at the same time; in short nothing was expected less than general conflagration. The next day an attack was meditated upon the Bank, and I believe upon the Pay and Excise office; happily his majesty, by his anxious care, and extraordinary and unremitting exertions, had been able to collect together a force; all the troops within a considerable distance were brought up to the metropolis, and they gave a check to the fury of the mob; this was upon the Thursday, when they were making an attempt upon the Poultry Compter. Every person I believe is convinced, that if a stop had not been then put to the outrages, the whole of this town would have been destroyed in a very short time . . . A bloody war must have taken place; and if an attack upon the houses of Protestants had been provoked, the whole of this town, even before the military could have arrived to our assistance, might have been destroyed.

It was clear by now that the riots went far beyond their original pretext, and the Attorney-General hinted that foreign enemies were involved.

Lord Mansfield, the Chief Justice of the Court of King's Bench, was singled out for attack: his house in Bloomsbury was sacked and his library was destroyed. Some of the rioters walked to Hampstead in order to attack his other home at Caen Wood,[4] but they were diverted into the Spaniards' Tavern and did no further damage there.

Eventually order was restored, and on Friday 9 June Lord George Gordon was arrested on a charge of High Treason and committed to custody in the Tower. A Special Commission under Lord Loughborough, the Chief Justice of the Court of Common Pleas, was then appointed to inquire into the disturbances, and he told the grand jury that riots of the type which had occurred were regarded as levying war within the realm.

At that time the only allegation against Lord George personally was that he was named as President of the Protestant Association on the advertisement for the meeting of 2 June. Therefore, on the first day of the Michaelmas term, he applied by writ of habeas corpus to be either tried or set free. Accordingly, a few days later an indictment was presented to another grand jury for the County of Middlesex and they found a true bill. This alleged that on 2 June 1780 the defendant 'did compass, imagine, and intend to raise and levy war, insurrection, and rebellion' and between 2 June and 10 June, with force of arms and a great multitude of persons 'armed and arrayed in a warlike manner (that is to say) with colours flying, and with swords, bludgeons, staves, and other weapons, as well offensive as defensive . . . did ordain, prepare and levy public war' against the king.

In 1709 parliament had passed an Act laying down that before any person was put on trial for treason, a list of the jurors who were to be summoned (and also a list of the witnesses who were to be called for the prosecution), including sufficient particulars to enable them to be identified, was to be served upon the defendant ten days before the trial. The Act was not to come into force as long as the Old Pretender was still alive, and as he had survived until 1766 this was the first case to which it applied. And so, on 11 November the Attorney-General applied to the Court of King's Bench for a rule directed to the Sheriff of Middlesex to deliver a list of the jurors whom he intended to return on the panel so that this could be given to the prisoner, and the rule was granted.

The prisoner had briefed Thomas Erskine (who had also served in the Navy) to represent him at this preliminary application, and immediately after the court had given its ruling, Erskine applied to the court to assign Lloyd Kenyon and himself to act on behalf of his client at the trial. The practice at the time in cases of treason was for counsel to be assigned by the court, but on the nomination (if he so chose) of the prisoner. The choice was a strange one. Kenyon was a respected member of the bar of long standing, but his work had been confined almost entirely to civil matters and he had had little experience of criminal cases. Erskine had been called to the bar as recently as 1778, and in spite of his dramatic début in the Greenwich Hospital Case, followed by a spate of civil work, he had never yet appeared before a jury.[5]

On 25 January 1781 the prisoner was arraigned in the Court of King's Bench[6] and pleaded Not Guilty. His trial was fixed for Monday 5 February at 8 a.m., and was held in the same court. Lord Mansfield CJ presided, sitting with Willes, Ashhurst and Buller JJ. The Crown was represented by James Wallace A.-G., James Mansfield S.-G.,[7] and Messrs Bearcroft, Lee, Howorth, Dunning and Norton. A large number of jurors was called into court, many of whom were challenged by the prisoner or excused on some other ground. The jurors eventually sworn were:

Thomas Collins, of Berners-street, esq. and surveyor
Henry Hastings, of Queen Ann-street, esq.
Edward Hulse, of Harley-street, esq.
Edward Pomfret, of New North-street, wine merchant
Gedediah Gatfield, of Hackney, esq.
Joseph Pickles, of Homerton, esq.
Edward Gordon, of Bromley, esq. and distiller
Marmaduke Peacock, of Hackney, esq.
Francis Degan, of Hammersmith, esq.
Simon Le Sage, of Hammersmith, esq. and silver-smith
Robert Armitage, of Kensington, esq.
John Rix, of White-chapel, distiller

A great change had come over the conduct of criminal proceedings during the century that had elapsed since the trial of Alice Lisle. Sometime in the middle of the eighteenth century, Thomas Gurney had been appointed the official shorthand writer to the Old Bailey, and a note of the trial of Lord George Gordon was taken by his son, Joseph. It was the transcript of this note that was printed in the *State Trials*, and in most respects the case was conducted as it would be today.

It seems to have been generally assumed that Lord George, by virtue of his presidency of the Protestant Association, must have been the instigator of all that happened in that week in June. In fact, on analysis, the case against him was none too strong.

The Attorney-General's opening speech lasted about an hour. He first explained to the jury that there were two kinds of 'levying war' – the one directly against the person of the king, and the other, known as 'constructive levying of war', against the majesty of the king, as in the case of an insurrection to effect a change in the law or to redress national grievances. It was the latter kind of which the defendant was accused.

The Attorney-General then explained the reason for Sir George Savile's Act and the events in Edinburgh, followed by a dramatic account of the riots themselves. It was only then that he showed how the prisoner was connected with these events. He was the President of the Protestant Association. Lord George had declared that he would not present a petition to parliament unless he was supported by 20,000 people who were to be distinguished by blue cockades, 'that he might know the friends of the petition or the friends of the Protestant cause'. He had directed the petitioners to form into divisions: 'a general could not make a more proper disposition of his army', and they were to march to London in these divisions. He had also reminded the crowd of the firm conduct of the Scotch, a clear reference to the violence which had occurred in Scotland. And he had added that he was willing to go to the gallows for the cause.

The Attorney-General read some of the resolutions that had been passed by the Protestant Association:

> That, as no hall in London could contain 40,000 men, the Association should meet on Friday 2 June in St George's Fields;
>   That they should separate into four divisions, all wearing blue cockades in their hats;
>   That the magistrates of London, Westminster and Southwark be requested to attend, to control any evil-minded persons who might wish to disturb the peace,

upon which the Attorney-General commented:

> What an insult this is to the civil magistrates! . . . For God's sake, who is there that durst look in the face of forty-thousand men! this army wants a protection, and calls upon the magistrates for it; but what magistrates? the London, Westminster and Southwark; of the two first, none can act but in London and Westminster, and in Southwark I believe hardly one magistrate resided, so that none of the magistrates, if called upon to keep the peace, and protect forty-thousand men, could act at all.

Then he described how the march began and alleged that Lord George could at any time have stopped the disorder in the House of Commons: 'he was applied to over and over again to desire them to go out; a word from him would have done it'. Instead, he told them to persevere and reminded them of the conduct of the Scotch, and 'they instantly flew to the chapels of the ambassadors, afterwards to the houses of the Roman Catholics, and of those who had given obstruction to the mob'.

The Attorney-General admitted that he knew nothing of the prisoner from then until the following Tuesday when he appeared again in the House of Commons, still wearing his blue cockade, and he was led off in triumph through the City to the Mansion House. On the Wednesday he sent an 'advertisement' to the papers with the object of having it published on the following day. This document read as follows:

> Lord George Gordon went in person to three different places, where the tumults were subsisting, to harangue the mob, and exhort them to a peaceable and legal deportment; he stood for a considerable time among parties of foot soldiers, accompanied by one of the London sheriffs, but all this was without effect, Lord George Gordon not being able to give them any assurances that the act would be repealed.

This advertisement, said the Attorney-General, meant that the mob could look to some assurances, and that they should continue their depredations until some assurances had been given to them. The prisoner had added that several merchants had requested him to sign papers to show that they were friends of the Protestant cause – so he was holding himself out as the person to be applied to for protections, and one such protection was signed by him that same day.

> Can any body doubt, after this evidence, that the prisoner at the bar was not the author of these disturbances, and that to his encouragement, incitement, and means, they are to be ascribed? . . . If he has turned out upon the public this many headed monster, to ravage and destroy, it will be no excuse to say, I wanted to check its rage and fury! He has designedly given birth to the outrage, and must stand by the consequence. . . .
>
> It is not an accidental assistance, or encouragement, but he is the contriver of the whole. If you are satisfied of this, you will pronounce him guilty, and your verdict will teach the present and future ages this lesson, that no man, however exalted in birth, situation, or

By 7 June 1780 Lord George Gordon had lost control of the situation. While travelling by coach to the Mansion House, the crowd took away his horses and manhandled the coach past Newgate (left). James Jackson, mounted on the cart-horse (right), is depicted directing the insurgents (British Museum)

connexion, can violate the peace, the order, the government, and the laws of his country with impunity.

The Attorney-General concluded by saying that he would call some witnesses: 'not so many, I hope as you may have seen in a list, which, by some means, has been published; it is not the object, I know of delivering lists of witnesses, that they should appear in the public newspapers', and he begged pardon for taking up so much of the jurors' time.

The first witness was William Hay, a printer, who said that he had attended various meetings of the Protestant Association at Greenwood's rooms in the Haymarket, the Old Crown and Rolls in Chancery Lane, the London Tavern in Bishopsgate Street, and St Margaret's Hall in the borough of Southwark. The prisoner was usually present, and at a meeting on 29 May had announced:

> That the Associated Protestants (as they were called) amounted to upward of 40,000 in number; that on Friday the 2nd of June it was resolved, they should meet, at ten o'clock in the morning, in St George's-fields, in four separate divisions, arrayed or dressed in their best clothes.

Kenyon interrupted to ask whether it was 'arrayed' or 'dressed' and the witness went on to say that he thought the prisoner's words were 'to have your best clothes on, with blue cockades in your hats, as he himself should wear a blue cockade, to distinguish them from other people who were Papists or friends to Roman Catholics'. On an earlier occasion, the prisoner had said that by giving his consent to the Act of Parliament tolerating the Roman Catholics in England, the king had broken his Coronation Oath and was in the same situation as James II had been after his abdication.

The witness went on to say that he had gone to St George's Fields and seen a vast multitude with cockades and banners, and Lord George Gordon had been haranguing them. He had followed them to the House of Commons and had stayed there for three hours in the lobby; the crowd was riotous and chiming Lord George Gordon's name – it was their constant chime, he said. The prisoner had come into the gallery and exhorted them to persevere, and said that he hoped that 'they would meet with redress from their mild and gracious sovereign'.

Finally, the witness described how he had been present at the burning of the Fleet Prison and had seen a man there carrying a flag with the words No Popery! on it. He had seen the same man with the same banner in Fleet Street on his way to the House of Commons: 'I saw that very man at Westminster.'

William Hay was evidently the chief witness for the Crown, but within minutes he was badly shaken. Having established at the outset of his cross-examination that Hay had been bankrupt, Kenyon went on to ask him if he was sure that he had seen Lord George Gordon at Greenwood's rooms:

'I think I saw my lord once there . . .'

'I caution you to be upon your guard.'

'I will; it is a very serious matter; I think Lord George Gordon was once at Greenwood's rooms . . .'

'Then you cannot speak with certainty?'

'Unless I look at some notes I cannot tell.'

The court allowed the witness to refresh his memory from his notes, and he went on: 'On 21st of January, Lord George Gordon was not, I find, present at Greenwood's.'

Kenyon then asked him why he had taken notes, and Hay replied that he went purposely to take notes for he had an idea what the consequences of these meetings might be. Kenyon pressed him to say whether it was his regular habit to take notes at meetings, and the witness said that it was, so Kenyon asked him if he had taken notes at any meetings other than those of the Protestant Association. He said he had first made notes in the general assembly of the Church of Scotland, more than twenty years before.

When he addressed the jury the following morning, Erskine commented:

Poor Mr Hay was thunderstruck, the sweat ran down his face, and his countenance bespoke despair, not recollection: 'Sir, I must have an instance; tell me when and where?' Gentlemen, it was now too late; *some* instance he was obliged to give, and, as it was evident to every body that he had one still to choose, I think he might have chosen a better. *He had taken notes of the General Assembly of the Church of Scotland six-and-twenty years before.* What! did he apprehend dangerous consequences from the deliberations of the grave elders of the kirk?

Kenyon then turned to cross-examine Hay on the man with the flag – how did he know that the man he had seen at Westminster was the same as the man he had seen at the Fleet Prison? He was wearing a dress not worth minding, said the witness, a very common dress. He was a coarse-looking man like a brewer's servant in his best clothes – he thought a brewer's servant's breeches, clothes and stockings had something very distinguishing.

Poor Mr Hay – nothing but sweat and confusion again [said Erskine], he knew him to be a brewer's servant, *because there was something particular in the cut of his coat, the cut of his breeches*, AND THE CUT OF HIS STOCKINGS. You see, gentlemen, by what strange means villany is sometimes detected; perhaps he might have escaped from me, but he sunk under that shrewdness and sagacity, which ability, without long habits, does not provide. Gentlemen, you will not, I am sure, forget, whenever you see a man, about whose apparel there is any thing particular, to set him down as a brewer's servant.

Finally, Kenyon elicited that the witness had been acting as a spy for the Roman Catholics and had reported what he had heard to a Mr Butler of Lincoln's Inn, a friend of Kenyon's, who was known to be a Catholic.

William Hay had given a shock to the case for the Crown from which it never really recovered.

William Metcalf, the next witness, gave evidence that he had been at a crowded meeting at Coachmakers' Hall in which Lord George Gordon had said that as the Scotch had succeeded by unanimity, he hoped that the English would do likewise, and that he would not be prepared to present the petition to parliament unless at least 20,000 people assembled in St George's Fields. Lord George had added that he would be prepared to go to the gallows for the cause. When cross-examined by Erskine, Metcalf said he was sure that the word 'gallows' had been used.

John Anstruther, a barrister, said that he had also been at Coachmakers' Hall and confirmed Metcalf's evidence. He had also been in the lobby of the House of Commons on the Friday night and had heard Lord George addressing the crowd from the gallery. When some of the crowd asked Lord George whether he wished them to disperse, he told them that they were the best judges of what they should do.

The Revd Thomas Bowen, the chaplain in the House of Commons, had also been in the lobby. He had heard Lord George tell the crowd to be cool and steady, and he had heard someone say that if Lord George would come and tell them to disperse, they would go. Soon afterwards he went to the eating-room and while he was sitting at a table Lord George came in and threw himself into a chair looking overcome with heat and fatigue. The witness had told him to advise the crowd to disperse. Not long after that, the witness went downstairs and Lord George went up to the gallery and told the crowd to be peaceable and steady, but then had added: 'The Scotch had no redress till they pulled down the mass-houses . . . why should they be better off than you?' Then, taking hold of the witness's gown (Mr Bowen must by now have joined him up in the gallery), he called out: 'This is the clergyman of the House of Commons. I desire you will ask him what his opinion of the Popish Bill is', to which the witness had replied that 'all the consequences which might arise from that night would be entirely owing to his lordship'. In cross-examination, Bowen said that he had seen several Members of Parliament come wearing blue cockades and take their seats in the House.

John Cater MP, and Joseph Pearson and Thomas Baker, the two door-keepers of the House, described the crowd in the lobby. Then Sampson Wright, a justice of the peace, told the court that he had collected some constables and gone to the House: 'there were prodigious crowds there; I never saw such a number of people collected together in my life, except upon one occasion, the coronation', so he had sought the assistance of the military and together they had cleared the House at about 8 p.m.

Sampson Rainforth said that he had been in Palace Yard on 2 June and had seen the procession go past. They were very peaceable and orderly, but later he saw Lord Mansfield and some of the bishops insulted, and had said to a friend, 'Here will be an open insurrection in my opinion before this business is done.' He went on to give evidence of the destruction of the Sardinian ambassador's chapel. Kenyon submitted that this evidence did not affect his client, but the court ruled that it was admissible to show that these people were illegally assembled and committing violence with the intention of forcing a repeal of the Act. So the witness went on to describe how he had fetched troops from Somerset House barracks and had arrested some of the ringleaders, and how his own house had been destroyed on the following day.

Charles Jealous described how he had seen the crowd pull the Bishop of Lincoln from his carriage, pull off his wig, and strike him in the face with it. Patrick Macmanus had been stationed at the Guildhall when a gentleman ran in, pursued by a crowd shouting No Popery. He and Mr Smith, the door-keeper, had collected some broomsticks and tried to shut the door and keep them out, but the crowd ran through the building and broke some windows.

David Miles, a constable, described the attack on Count Haslang's house at Warwick Street, and said that his own house was destroyed a few days later. Thomas Gates, the City marshal, described the destruction of some Roman Catholic houses on the Sunday and Monday. Again, Kenyon objected to this evidence, but the court ruled that the prosecution was entitled to put in evidence anything to show that the mob had a general intent, by terror and violence, to force a repeal of the law, although that did not affect the defendant until he was shown to be privy to it.

However, the judge then added: 'I wonder you don't rather confine your examination to acts of violence at the very time, on the 2nd of June, upon the members of both Houses of Parliament.' Undeterred by this admonition, the Attorney-General examined the witness about the attack on Newgate.

The next witness, William Hyde, a justice of the peace for the county, described the attack on the chapels in Warwick Street and Lincoln's Inn Fields. On Tuesday 6 June he had been informed that the mob had returned to Westminster and there were rumours that Lord Sandwich had been killed, so he had collected some troops and rescued his lordship (his carriage had been broken and he had a cut on his head). Mr Hyde concluded his evidence by saying that his two houses, one in St Martin's Street and one in Islington, were both pulled down. John Lucy had been with Mr Hyde, and he saw one man, whom he identified by name as James Jackson, waving a flag and inciting the crowd to attack Mr Hyde's house – 'To Hyde's house a-hoy'; and later he saw the same man crying 'A-hoy for Newgate.'

Then came Barnard Turner, a sugar refiner and also the commander of the London Military Association, who described his attempts to disperse the mob, some of whom were armed with iron bars and the spokes of wheels and cutlasses.

These witnesses said that some of the mob were wearing blue cockades and carrying No Popery banners, but otherwise their evidence had not the slightest connection with Lord George Gordon and defending counsel did not bother to cross-examine them.

Towards the end the Crown called a witness for a very different purpose. Richard Pond produced a paper which read:

> All true friends to Protestants I hope will particular and do no injury to the property of any true Protestant, as I am well assured the proprietor of this house is a staunch and worthy friend to the cause.
>
> G. Gordon

Pond said that he had heard that his house was likely to be burnt, so he had had this paper signed by a person who, he had been told, was Lord George Gordon, and he identified the defendant in court. He had shown the paper to the mob and it had had the desired effect – his house was not attacked. In cross-examination he said that Lord George was in a coach along with Mr Pugh, the sheriff, when he presented the paper to him, and that this had happened on the Wednesday.

Richard Pond was followed by John Dingwall. Why the Crown called this witness is not clear. Perhaps he was to produce the advertisement which, according to the Attorney-General, Lord George Gordon had sent to the papers on the Wednesday, but which was never produced or exhibited. Whatever Dingwall had told the prosecuting authorities beforehand, they obtained nothing from him in open court, and he denied that he knew the prisoner's writing or had ever seen him write. In cross-examination, however, he said that he had known Lord George from birth. He had seen him just before the meeting in May and was told something 'upon the subject of this business'.

Finally, the Crown called General Skene and three other witnesses from Scotland to give an account of the riots in Edinburgh. Defending counsel strongly objected on the ground that the riots there had nothing to do with the case, but the court ruled that they had been mentioned so it was necessary that the jury should know what the facts were. And so the evidence was admitted.

Kenyon now addressed the jury on behalf of the prisoner. It was unfortunate, he said, that the prisoner should make his defence at a time of day when the attention of the court and of the jury must be, in some measure, exhausted, and he went on to confess that he was very little versed in criminal matters, and had never yet stood as counsel for a person who had so great a stake put in hazard. He accused the Attorney-General of trying, unfairly, to rouse the passions of the jury by referring to the risk that the whole city might have been burnt and that foreign enemies might have been mixed in the business, but further comments upon his opponent read more as if he was apologizing for him rather than criticizing him: 'I wish he had not used some of the phrases which he did use. I wish, when he spoke of the multitude collected together, he had not called them an army.' He did, however, analyse the evidence carefully, dealing in particular with William Hay and asking the jury to decide whether they could believe him. He pointed out that neither the Bishop of Lincoln nor Lord Sandwich had been called to say who had attacked them, and there was no evidence to connect their assailants with the prisoner. He discussed the Attorney-General's assertion that Lord George Gordon was responsible for what had occurred in the same way as a man is responsible for releasing a wild beast, and asserted that there was no authority, either under the law of the land or the law of humanity, for saying that if anyone turned a wild beast out of doors, he was then responsible for the consequences. In any case, was the Protestant Association a wild beast – was a person that led a tame beast in his hand responsible because another person let out a 'tyger or hyaena'?

Finally, he gave the jury a brief outline of the evidence which he proposed to call, and reminded them that 'in this case the facts are to be made out, the guilt to be ascertained beyond all doubt. It is not at hazard that men are to be convicted of such offences.'

It was evening now. In modern times, the court would have adjourned, but in those days it was regarded as essential that a criminal trial should be concluded in a single session, and so the defence called their witnesses.

The first witness was the Revd Erasmus Middleton, a clergyman of the Church of England, a member of the Protestant Association, and the pastor of St Bennet's, Gracechurch Street and St Helen's, Bishopsgate Street. He said that he had been a member of the Protestant Association from the start and he described how it was formed and how it came about that Lord George Gordon was invited to become its president. He added that his lordship always conducted himself in the most loyal affectionate manner, whose only interest was the Protestant cause, and the repeal of the Act by all legal and constitutional means.

The witness then went on to describe the meeting in Coachmakers' Hall on 29 May. His lordship had said that he had been informed that the association was against going up with the petition, and he had asked if this was true, whereupon there was a great shout of 'No my lord' from all parts of the hall. His lordship then read over the resolutions and proposed that they should adjourn to St George's Fields, as no place would contain the number which should assemble. He pointed out that it was easy for a person to write 400 or 500 names to a petition, and therefore it was necessary that they should appear in person. His lordship begged them to dress decently, and to distinguish them from other people, so that no riots might ensue, he proposed they should have a cockade in their hats. Someone objected, Middleton said,

> that by meeting so early they might get to drinking; in answer to which his lordship observed, 'the Protestant Association were not drunken people, and he apprehended no danger on that account.' Some one observed, that he thought such a great number of people being assembled might cause the military to be drawn out, his lordship answered, 'he did not apprehend the military would be drawn out, that they be all peaceable and orderly he did not doubt, he desired them not so much as to take sticks in their hands'.

Lord George begged that if there was any riotous person, then the rest should give him up, and he used the expression, 'if they smite you on the cheek, turn the other also'.

Middleton did not himself go to St George's Fields, and he was cross-examined as to why he had not done so. He had parochial duties to attend to, he said, and when asked what they were, he replied: 'Reading prayers; it was on a Friday . . . at eleven o'clock. I have generally children to baptize, and frequently pensioners to bury, that are buried always immediately after church.'

The next witness was David Viscount Stormont who said that he had been at Buckingham house during the riots when Lord George Gordon had come to see the king:

> I was attending his majesty at the Queen's-house, with several of his majesty's confidential servants, [during the morning of] Wednesday the 7th of June; a page came and scratched at the door, I went out by order, when he said, that the prisoner at the bar was at the gate of the Queen's-house, desiring, I think, to see his majesty; I went out with another noble lord, and gave directions that Lord George Gordon should be brought into a room in the colonade. I then went to him to ask what his lordship desired or wanted; his answer to me was, that 'he desired to see the king, because he could be of essential' or 'material service,' or 'do great service in suppressing the riots.' I went with this message, and delivered it exactly to the king, whom I was then attending . . . and the answer I delivered to his lordship was this: 'It is impossible for the king to see Lord George Gordon until he has given sufficient proofs of his allegiance and loyalty, by employing those means which he says he has in his power, to quell the disturbances, and restore peace to this capital.' . . . His lordship to that answered 'if he might presume to reply, he would say, that his best endeavours should be used,' or 'employed,' or to that purpose, that is, to the best of my remembrance, the whole that passed.

Lord Stormont stressed that he was particularly accurate as to every word he had spoken, and there was no cross-examination.

Thomas Evans, who said he was one of the petitioners, described how he had driven to St George's Fields, where he found the Scotch division formed in a ring with Lord George Gordon in the centre. He had forced his way through and warned his lordship that there would be a riot if more than 30 or 40 people went to Westminster. He had asked whether it was the plan that the whole body should go, and Lord George had replied 'by no means' – it was his intention to go alone, and the petition would follow him to the lobby of the House of Commons and wait there till he came out to receive it. So he, the witness, went to the side of the ring and told the people that they were to stay at St George's Fields as Lord George was intending to go alone. When, later, he saw the whole division on the march, he tried to stop them and warned them that there would be a riot, but they replied that he need not be afraid of that for they were determined to make none. John Spinnage confirmed Mr Evans' evidence and added that the people had no weapons and were in their best clothes.

Mrs Elizabeth Whittingham was also in a coach in St George's Fields, and Lord George Gordon came to her ready to faint and asked if he could get in the coach. Some men then surrounded the coach, begging to attend his lordship, but he said that he would have no help, he was very well. 'Pray let us attend you to the House,' they had said, but his lordship replied 'No, by no means, I shall be greatly obliged to you gentlemen, if you will all go back.' So the coach set off, and set his lordship down at the House of Commons.

Alexander Johnston had also been to St George's Fields, where there was nothing but harmony and peace. He went to Palace Yard at about midday and stayed for a few minutes, then he went with some friends to dinner in the Strand and smoked a pipe

On the evening of 7 June 1780 the insurgents looted the furniture from the house of the Keeper of Newgate. They piled it up against the prison and set it on fire in order to burn down the prison, and released all the felons (British Museum)

until 6 or 7 o'clock when word came that there was a disturbance in Palace Yard. They went there to try to quell the mob, and when they arrived they saw about twenty boys, none of them more than sixteen or eighteen years old, and four or five men stopping the carriages. He took hold of one of them and arrested him, and the rest ran away – they were a set of boys, quite a set of pickpockets.

'Did they appear like those of the Protestant Association you had seen in the morning?' asked Erskine.

'No; not in the least appearance like them; no such thing.'

The witness added, in cross-examination, that when he got hold of the boy, several of the others grabbed his hair and it was a week before he could straighten his neck.

Another witness, Alexander Fraser, said that he had met a crowd of people in Westminster, wearing blue cockades, when he was on his way to St George's Fields early in the morning. When he asked one of them, who seemed to be in liquor, if he was a member of the Protestant Association, he held up a great stick and said: 'No, damn it, this is our Association.'

Sir Philip Jennings Clerke MP then gave evidence. Early in the afternoon of 2 June he had seen a crowd of people both going away from and returning to St George's Fields. They were the better sort of tradesmen, well dressed, orderly and quiet, and very civil to him although they had no reason to be since he was not wearing a blue cockade. Later in the day he went down to the House of Commons and found a great crowd there. In his opinion they were not the same sort of people he had seen earlier, they were a lower kind of people, more a mob of blackguards. He met thousands of people returning from Westminster, and they seemed to be the same sort as he had seen in the morning. He also went into the gallery which looked over the lobby of the House, 'but the stench from the bottom was so bad, nobody would have chosen to have staid long'. In the House, he, the witness, was one of the very few members for entering into the petition, for he thought that a petition signed by 40,000 people did merit some attention from the legislature.

He had had no personal acquaintaince with Lord George, but on the following Tuesday he had met his lordship outside the House. The people began to crowd about them, so he said: 'come, lord George, you must be my protector', but it soon became evident that it was Lord George who needed protection. They reached a tavern with a chariot standing by, and Lord George looked up at the window and saw Mr Wiggons, the owner of the chariot, and said, 'Mr Wiggons, I am in sad distress, will you lend me your chariot?' Mr Wiggons said, 'Yes, with all my heart.' They both stepped in, but at once the crowd closed round the carriage and took off the horses, and it was impossible to get out. 'For God's sake go peacably home and go about your business,' Lord George had said, whenever he could make himself heard, 'whilst you assemble in this tumultuous way, your petition will never be complied with, the House will never consent to it.' Then the witness had asked Lord George: 'can you contrive any way in the world to let me out, for I have a friend waiting for me to dinner at Whitehall?' But the crowd got all over the chariot's braces and dragged them to the far end of the city: 'the carriage went as fast as if we had a pair of very good horses drawing us and it ran over twenty people I suppose'. They made a short stop at Whitehall and another at the Mansion House, and eventually reached Alderman Bull's house where they managed to get inside. However, the mob did not disperse and some of Alderman Bull's family told Lord George that the mob would never go as long as he remained there, so he went back into the carriage.

One of the jury asked the witness if they were the same sort of people as he had seen in St George's Fields on the Friday, to which Sir Philip replied: 'They were so thick and such numbers of them, that I could hardly give any description of them, and to tell you the truth, I had no great pleasure in looking out at the window, I kept pretty snug in the corner of the chariot.'

Other witnesses had been at St George's Fields. John Turner said that he had heard Lord George Gordon ask the people to keep the peace – if anything would add weight to their petition, it would be their peaceable behaviour. John Humphreys had been in the ring of people in St George's Fields – 'those inside sat down, the next kneeled down, and the next stood up' – when a man brought a message from Lord George desiring them to disperse and not on any account go to the House of Commons. Sampson Hotchkinson was also in the ring, and had heard Lord George say that he wished to avoid all offence and wished for a small number to go, but many in the ring had said that they were capable of conducting themselves with peace and order and chose to go in person. John Robinson went in procession from St George's Fields to Westminster. The procession went very quietly, and he went away for two or three hours. When he returned, he found a mob had collected, but he did not think they were members of the association, 'they were seemingly a lower class of people'.

Sir James Lowther was then called to give his account of the events of the evening of Friday 2 June. He had sat in the House of Commons on the bench opposite the Treasury bench, beside Sir George Savile and Sir Philip Clerke. Then Lord George asked the witness if he had a carriage: 'If you have room give me leave to go along with you.' The witness had said that he would stay a little longer, but Lord George wanted to go straight away so they went to his carriage and some of the mob came round asking if the bill was to be repealed. Lord George had replied, 'I do not know, I hope it will, but go home, be quiet, make no riot, nor noise.' The witness had asked Lord George where he wanted to be set down, and he had replied at his own home. The witness had told him that he seemed tired, and he replied: 'Very much so' – Sir James thought he was rather sleepy the whole time he was there. The coach set Sir James down at his own house, and afterwards it went home with Lord George. Mrs Youd, Lord George's housekeeper (who had for a time been under arrest for harbouring her master), was also called and said that he had returned at 10.45 p.m. on 2 June and was at home on the following Saturday, Sunday and Monday.

Erskine then said: 'We are ready, if the Court think it material, to go into evidence to shew where his lordship was every hour and every minute of those days.'

No one took up the challenge, so the defence called their last witness, Alderman Pugh, one of the sheriffs of the City of London. He gave evidence that on Wednesday 7 June he had been in a coach with Lord George when a young man came with a piece of paper – he said his house was in danger of being destroyed, and asked his lordship to sign the paper. The witness could not remember whether the prisoner had asked for his opinion, but he did sign it.

It was midnight. The defence had many more witnesses to call – their statements, 'immense piles of papers', were scattered over the floor under the front row of counsel's benches – but they decided to close their case. And so Erskine rose to address the court:

> Gentlemen of the jury; Mr Kenyon having informed the Court that we propose to call no other witnesses, it is now my duty to address myself to you, as counsel for the noble prisoner at the bar, the whole evidence being closed;– I use the word closed, because it is certainly not finished, since I have been obliged to leave the place in which I sat, to disentangle myself from the volumes of men's names, which lay there under my feet, whose testimony, had it been necessary for the defence, would have confirmed all the facts which are already in evidence before you.

When a collection of Erskine's speeches was published many years later, a writer in the *Edinburgh Review*[8] had this comment to make on his speech in defence of Lord George Gordon:

> We are unable to extract any passages which can give a just notion of its character and high merits; for these consist, not in dazzling sentences, nor in particular bursts of eloquence, but in the close texture of the whole argument, both where Mr Erskine lays down the principles of treason-law . . . and where he more particularly and directly makes the application of those doctrines to the charges against Lord George Gordon. The whole speech must be read, and even carefully studied, before a just sense of the talents displayed in it can be entertained, or a conjecture formed of its great effects upon the audience who heard it, and the tribunal to which it was addressed.

This is indeed true: a summary or précis of this speech, which occupies some thirty pages in the *State Trials* and must have taken two hours or more to deliver, is very difficult to achieve.

After the opening paragraph, Erskine echoed the words of his leader:

If Mr Kenyon has such feelings, think what mine must be? – Alas!, gentlemen, who am I? – a young man of little experience, unused to the bar of criminal courts, and sinking under the dreadful consciousness of my defects. I have however this consolation, that no ignorance nor inattention on my part, can possibly prevent you from seeing, under the direction of the judges, that the crown has established no case of treason.

He criticized the Attorney-General for having failed to explain the law properly, and then embarked on a detailed account of the Act in which the wisdom and justice of our law were so strongly manifested in the *'rigid, accurate, cautious, explicit, unequivocal* definition of what shall constitute this high offence', for if treason were left to the judgment of ministers without any boundaries

there could be no public freedom,– and the condition of an Englishman would be no better that a slave's at the foot of a sultan; since there is little difference whether a man dies by the stroke of a sabre, without the forms of a trial, or by the most pompous ceremonies of justice, if the crime could be made at pleasure by the state to fit the fact that was to be tried.

He then proceeded to comment at some length on the meaning of the phrase 'levying war' and the situation in which a riot could be said to amount to 'constructive levying of war'. It is well known that, after the trial, Dr Johnson observed: 'I am glad that Lord George Gordon has escaped, rather than a precedent should be established of hanging a man for constructive treason.'[9] But in fact Erskine conceded that if the evidence had shown that his client had directed the multitude in their attack on the bank, in breaking open the prisons, and in setting fire to London, it would have been impossible to defend him. The leading case of constructive levying of war was that of Dammaree where the crowd was attacking the meeting houses of the dissenters, but there Dammaree had been caught *in flagrante delicto*, with a torch in his hand, in the very act of destroying one and inviting his followers to destroy the rest. However, it had never been argued 'that a multitude, – armed with nothing, – threatening nothing, – and doing nothing, was an army levying war'.

The vital issue for the jury to decide was: 'with what intention did they meet?' Undoubtedly, an immense multitude was assembled, but the guilt of his client depended wholly on the evidence of his purpose in assembling them, and it was for the jury to decide whether he assembled them in hostile array to take the law into their own hands and to dissolve the constitution of the government unless his petition should be heard by parliament.

Erskine then analysed the evidence for the prosecution, word by word. Some of his comments on Mr Hay have already been quoted. On Mr Anstruther's evidence that Lord George Gordon had recommended 'temperance and firmness', he asked: 'Is it to be presumed, without proof, that a man means *one* thing because he says *another*? . . . Is it possible, with decency, to say in a court of justice, that the recommendation of temperance is the excitation to villany and frenzy?'

No evidence of the destruction of the house of the presiding judge had been placed before the court, but it was a matter of common knowledge, and Erskine turned it to his client's advantage:

Can any man living . . . believe that Lord George Gordon could possibly have excited the mob to destroy the house of that great and venerable magistrate, who has presided so long in this high tribunal, that the oldest of us do not remember him with any other impression, than the awful form and figure of justice:– a magistrate who had always been a friend of the

Protestant Dissenters, against the ill-timed jealousies of the establishment. . . . No, Gentlemen, it is not credible, that a man of noble birth, and liberal education . . . could possibly consent to the burning of the house of Lord Mansfield.

Turning to the evidence that had been called for the defence, he stressed that the crowd which had assembled in St George's Fields, so far from being assembled in a warlike array, were all in their best clothes, and not a man among them had a weapon. And if, as the Crown alleged, the defendant should have foreseen that the crowd would turn into a hostile array, why did the government do nothing about it?

If a peaceable multitude, with a petition in their hands, be an army, – and if the noise and confusion inseparable from numbers, though without violence or the purpose of violence, constitute war, – what shall be said of that GOVERNMENT, which remained from Tuesday to Friday, knowing that an army was collecting to levy war by public advertisement, yet had not a single soldier, – no, not even a constable to protect the state?

Gentlemen, I come forth to do that for government, which its own servant, the Attorney-General, has not done. – I come forth to rescue it from the eternal infamy, which would fall upon its head, if the language of its own advocate were to be believed. But government has an unanswerable defence. It neither *did* nor *could possibly* enter into the head of any man in authority to prophesy – human wisdom could not divine, that wicked and desperate men, taking advantage of the occasion, which, perhaps, an imprudent zeal for religion had produced, would dishonour the cause of all religions, by the disgraceful acts which followed.

Erskine then alleged – again, it had not been given in evidence, but seems to have been a matter of common knowledge – that the government had compiled a book containing the names of all those who had signed the petition, to ensure that none of them was summoned to sit on the jury – and

NOT ONE CRIMINAL, OR EVEN A SUSPECTED NAME, IS TO BE FOUND AMONGST THIS DEFAMED HOST OF PETITIONERS. After this, Gentlemen, I think the crown ought in decency to be silent. [If he was wrong,] why did not the Attorney-General produce the record of some convictions, and compare it with the list? – I thank them, therefore, for the precious compilation, which, though they did not produce, they cannot stand up and deny. Solomon says, '*O that my adversary would write a book!*' – so say I.

Lord George Gordon had gone to Buckingham house and asked to see the king, saying, 'he might be of great use in quelling the riots; and can there be on earth a greater proof of conscious innocence?'

Lord George's language was simply this: 'The multitude pretend to be perpetrating these acts, under the authority of the Protestant petition; I assure your Majesty they are not the Protestant Association, and I shall be glad to be of any service in suppressing them.' I say, by God, that a man is a ruffian, who shall, after this, presume to build upon such honest, artless conduct as an evidence of guilt.

This remark seems to have been regarded as the climax of the speech, as related thirty years later in the *Edinburgh Review*:

The sensation produced by these words, and by the magic of the voice, the eye, the face, the figure, and all we call the manner, with which they were uttered, is related, by those present on this great occasion, to have been quite electrical, and to baffle all power of description.

As for the supposed 'protection' which the prisoner had signed, he did so in the presence of Sheriff Pugh, whom he was assisting to keep the peace – and yet it was given in evidence against him.

As his speech drew to a close, Erskine asked the jury 'whether you can say, that this

After the destruction of Newgate and an abortive attack upon the Bank of England, the insurgents
proceeded to Broad Street and set fire to a house at the corner of Wormwood Street. On the left, looters
can be seen throwing furniture out of windows to be set on fire; in the centre, William Blizzard, surgeon to
the London Hospital, is attending to an injured man; on the right, James Jackson's horse is caparisoned
with chains pilfered from Newgate. The insurgents were now confronted by troops (British Museum)

noble and unfortunate youth – [he was actually a year older than Erskine himself] – is
a wicked and deliberate traitor, who deserves by your verdict to suffer a shameful and
ignominious death, which will stain the ancient honours of his house for ever'. To
support such a charge, the most incontrovertible proof would be required, but the
only evidence offered by the Crown were a few broken, disjointed words, heard by the
witnesses in the midst of tumult and confusion and uttered by the defendant in
agitation and heat:

> Which of us all, gentlemen, would be safe, standing at the bar of God, or man, if we were
> not to be judged by the regular current of our lives and conversations, but by detached and
> unguarded expressions, picked out by malice, and recorded, without context or
> circumstances, against us?

He went on to point out that in the prosecutions which had arisen out of the riots,
no fact had appeared which showed any plan, or object, or leader:

> Since out of 44,000 persons who signed the Petition of the Protestants, *not one* was to be
> found among those who were convicted,[10] tried, or even apprehended on suspicion; – and
> since out of all the felons, who were let loose from prisons, and who assisted in the

destruction of our property, not a single wretch was to be found, who could even attempt to save his own life by the plausible promise of giving evidence to-day.

And so he asked the jury to 'restore my innocent client to liberty, and me to that peace of mind, which, since the protection of that innocence in any part depended upon me, I have never known.'

Most of those present in court that night may have been electrified by Erskine's speech, but one man was not. James Mansfield, the Solicitor-General, opened his reply on behalf of the Crown by an outright attack upon his opponent, and castigated him because he had 'boldly, adventurously and licentiously inveighed against every man who has had any thing to do in the conduct of this cause'. He had never known greater provocation by counsel for a prisoner given to the advocates for a prosecution, and thus much he could not help observing, but the invective and censure, the calumny and slander, that had been so freely spread, and so often repeated, had not influenced him in any way and would make no impression upon him: 'and though a learned gentleman at the bar shall tell me ten times, to my face, that I am a ruffian, I shall not think I deserve it because he says so; nor will any such abuse frighten me from doing the duty of an English advocate'.

Having got this off his chest, the Solicitor-General reviewed the law: 'the question which you will have to decide upon the noble lord, will be . . . whether he has been a partaker, a promoter, and inciter of an insurrection, made against the government of this country, to repeal by force the law that you have heard of?' He repeated the evidence of the outrages which the mob had committed and the evidence which suggested that Lord George had been responsible, not only for assembling the petitioners in the first place, but for inciting them to violence. He reminded the jury that Lord George had compared the king with James II when he had abdicated the throne – 'If one meant to sound rebellion through the land, in terms the loudest, the strongest, and most effectual, does language furnish one with expresssions that would better answer the purpose?' – and had told his audience that he would go to the gallows for the cause. And on the Tuesday Lord George Gordon had returned to the House of Commons still wearing his blue cockade, had been carried in triumph by the mob, and had encouraged them to follow the example of the Scotch. He went on in the same vein at considerable length, and concluded by asking the jury to do their duty, however painful the task might be.

At about 3.30 a.m. on the morning of Tuesday 6 February Lord Mansfield CJ summed up the case to the jury. In his biography of Lord Erskine, Lord Campbell described the summing-up as 'hostile' to the defence, although the text does not give this impression. His lordship directed the jury on the law: he explained the law relating to the Roman Catholics and the purpose of Sir George Savile's Act, and commented on the Act on Tumultuous Assemblies and its supposed repeal by the Bill of Rights. Then he left two questions to the jury:

First, Whether this multitude did assemble and commit acts of violence with intent to terrify and compel the legislature to repeal the act called Sir George Savile's? – If upon this point your opinion should be in the negative, that makes an end of the whole, and the prisoner ought to be acquitted: but if your opinion should be, that the intent of the multitude, and the violence they committed, was to force a repeal, there arises a second point –

Whether the prisoner at the bar incited, encouraged, promoted, or assisted in raising this insurrection, and the terror they carried with them, with the intent of forcing a repeal of this law?

Upon these two points, which you will call your attention to, depends the fate of this trial; for if either the multitude had no such intent, or supposing they had, if the prisoner was no cause, did not excite, and took no part in conducting, counselling, or fomenting the insurrection, the prisoner ought to be acquitted; and there is no pretence that he personally concurred in any act of violence.

The judge then reviewed the evidence. He had observed that the jurors had been taking notes, so he refrained from making any comments on the evidence and left it to them. He repeated the two questions which he had left to them, and concluded by saying: 'If the scale should hang doubtful, and you are not fully satisfied that he is guilty, you ought to lean on the favourable side and acquit him.'

The jury retired at 4.45 a.m. and returned half an hour later with a verdict of Not Guilty.

Following his acquittal, Lord George spent some time in France, and on his return he wrote an outspoken attack upon the queen of France; at about the same time, he wrote a libellous account of conditions in Newgate. As a result he was prosecuted and convicted, but before he could be sentenced he absconded. It was at this time that he converted to Judaism, and went to live in a Jewish community in Birmingham. He was found there, brought back to court and sentenced to three years imprisonment. He was also fined, and required to find £10,000 as security for his good behaviour – a sum which was impossible for him to raise, so that in effect his sentence was for life. He was sent to Newgate, where he seems to have lived in some style, entertaining his friends and fellow-prisoners, and it was there that he died in 1793.

CHAPTER SIX

The Trial of Francis Henry de la Motte (1781)

London was only just recovering from the effects of the Gordon Riots when the government received information of a very different kind of conspiracy.

Stephen Ratcliffe, a seaman, lived at Folkestone and owned a cutter. During the early part of 1780 he was employed by one Isaac Roger, a Frenchman, then resident at No. 28 Greek Street, Soho, to carry packets to Boulogne, for which he was paid £20 a trip, and a bonus for speedy delivery. The packets were addressed to the commissary of marines at Boulogne. On one occasion, Ratcliffe delivered the packet to the commissary in person, but usually he gave them to the wife of a merchant with whom he was dealing, and she passed them on to their destination.

It may seem strange that enemy aliens could live openly in this country, and even carry on foreign trade, but, as Wallace A.-G. explained in his opening address to the jury in the case against de la Motte, it was not then the custom to drive out subjects of the enemy who were resident here, or even to prevent others coming on business or curiosity: 'But it has ever been understood, that, whilst they are here under the protection of the laws and government, they do nothing detrimental to the state, and that they owe the same allegiance to the king, during the time they stay, as any natural-born subject whatever.'

The circumstances in which Ratcliffe was employed to carry these packages to France raised the suspicion that they contained intelligence designed to assist the enemy. He therefore consulted Joseph Stewart, a merchant at Sandwich, and they agreed that one of these packets should be handed to Stewart who would take it to the office of Lord Hillsborough, the Secretary of State.

And so, on 4 July, Stewart took a packet to the house of Sir Stanyer Porten, one of Lord Hillsborough's staff, in St James's Place. The packet weighed about three-quarters of a pound, measured 4 inches by 9 inches, and was wrapped up in white paper and tied with string. It was addressed 'Mr Smith, negociant, at Boulogne'.

It was 6.00 a.m. when he arrived in St James's Place, and Sir Stanyer was still in bed, but he said that the packet must be opened. This was done, and inside was found a letter dated 30 June 1780 and addressed to M. Sartine, the marine minister of the Court of France. It started by referring to some earlier correspondence, and continued with an account of the East India affairs and the India ships preparing to sail, the troops that were going there, the ships expected home, and a great deal of information respecting the India possessions. The letter then went on:

> We[1] have no news from Admiral Rodney: we know he is at Barbadoes with fourteen ships of the line, and that Rowley keeps at sea with seven, and that the others are under repair at St Lucia . . . We receive very frequent accounts from admiral Geary, who cruizes [sic] between the Scilly islands and Ushant, and preserves his communication with the channel. We are getting ready several vessels with provisions for his fleet. The Marlborough sailed last Tuesday from Spithead to join him. With regard to the other ships in our ports, we are getting them in readiness, but want men to fit them out. The Nonesuch of 64, Jupiter of 50, five frigates, and two fire-ships, continue off Cherbourg, of which you must needs be well informed. By my next letters, I shall send you the state of our ports, and of the fleets of merchant ships to come in, those of which, from Jamaica and the Leeward islands, cannot arrive before the end of June.

Also in this packet was a letter addressed to M. Baudovin, another minister employed in the French court, asking him not to send any intelligence by the post: 'In the name of God, write no more by the post to me . . . For God's sake, take care to preserve life.'

Sir Stanyer copied these two letters himself, and a third, which appeared to relate to private matters, was copied by someone else. The packet was then sealed up again and handed back to Stewart, who had to wait until about 1 o'clock before it was ready. He took it back to Folkestone and gave it to Ratcliffe who took it across to Boulogne.

On 16 July Stewart received another packet. This time he sent it by post-office express to Mr Stephens at the Admiralty. An Admiralty messenger brought it back to his home at Canterbury at midnight on 17/18 July. He was in bed at the time, but he arranged for it to be forwarded to a Mr Wilson, a builder at Sandwich, who presumably knew what to do with it. There is no record of the contents of this packet.

On 2 August Ratcliffe and Stewart met each other on Westminster Bridge. Ratcliffe stepped down from the diligence in which he was travelling and got into Stewart's chaise where he handed over another packet. Stewart took the packet to Sir Stanyer who had the contents copied before returning it for transmission to France. This packet contained a letter addressed to M. Baudovin:

> I have the honour to send you herewith a very exact state of the naval forces, armed and to be armed this year; though observing in this dispatch my monthly custom (as for eight days the public papers give us a very imperfect account of the naval forces.) I desire you to observe, that the particulars of this state, from the accuracy of my accounts, are always of two and three months before their execution.

Westminster Bridge was built in 1750, the second bridge across the Thames (the first was the old London Bridge); part of the Protestant Association marched across this bridge on its way to Parliament on 2 June 1780, and Ratcliffe and Stewart met each other here on 2 August (British Museum)

Then, after giving some information about the ships which were at sea, he set out a list of the naval forces, and their stations, destinations and crews as at 1 August: 'The naval force under the command of admiral Geary, on the 26th of July, off the bay of Ushant; longitude, E. of London, 11 deg. 12 min. lat. 49 deg. wind E.N.E. changeable.'

Other documents in the packet included a list concluding: 'Total 26 ships of the line, nine frigates, five cutters, and three fire-ships', and a list of ships and frigates which had recently sailed or were about to sail and their expected times of departure: 'It is to be observed, that the ships above described, are all that we can arm this year; therefore I make no mention of those on the stocks, to the number of nine, which cannot be finished before about the month of March 1781.' The letter concluded with a recapitulation of all the ships which were in port or were cruising in their respective squadrons.

On 10 August Stewart received another packet at Canterbury. This packet contained two letters dated 9 August. One of these was addressed to M. Sartine, and contained a copy of a letter of Admiral Geary, stating his condition and the situation of his ships. The letter then set out that five ships were being prepared to join Admiral Geary, and that a fleet of merchantmen was being detained at Spithead until they received news from America. 'Our' fleets, ready to start at a moment's notice, consisted of one for New York, with 3,000 German troops and from 60 to 80 merchantmen, another fleet of 36 vessels, with provisions and ammunition, ready to sail from Cork to New York, and a fleet of 20 sail for Charleston and Savannah. There were 300 sail expected home from the Windward Islands, and others from the East Indies, Lisbon and Oporto, and the Baltic.

Also in the same packet was a letter to the commissary of the marine at Boulogne, in which the writer complained that he had not been receiving the commission to which he was entitled.

During the autumn and winter several other packets were intercepted and their contents copied before being returned for transmission to France, but no details of these documents were disclosed at the trial.

Although it was now clear that this was a case of espionage, no one could discover who was the spy,[2] so a plan was made to find out. Ratcliffe complained to Roger that he had not been paid the gratuity for despatch that he had been promised, so he pretended to quarrel with Roger and insisted on seeing his principal. Roger himself, apparently, was not suspect. He was a 'toy-man', that is to say he manufactured tooth-pick cases, smelling-bottles and snuffboxes, and dealt in 'Birmingham goods' and prints, some of which were sent abroad to Mr Barwens at Ostend.

Sometime in the previous year Roger had been approached by M. Waltrond, a Frenchman who had come to England a couple of years before, and asked to arrange for packets to be despatched to the Continent. For a time Waltrond was living in lodgings in the Temple and was involved in smuggling contraband goods. He was in partnership with de la Motte, and when Waltrond returned to Paris, de la Motte continued to supply packets for delivery abroad. Roger was paid 8 guineas a month for acting as an agent for Waltrond and de la Motte.

And so it was arranged that Ratcliffe should go to town and be introduced to de la Motte. Ratcliffe went to Roger's house, and Roger went out and returned with de la Motte. Ratcliffe made his complaint. De la Motte told him that the first three or four despatches had gone with all the expedition he desired, but later ones had been delayed, so that news had reached France before them by other channels: 'The gentleman complained, over on the other side,' said de la Motte, 'that I did not carry them quick enough, and he could not pay me the money then, unless I could make satisfaction, and carry them quicker.' De la Motte went on to tell Ratcliffe that he would, in future, pay him £20 a trip and in addition, in the New Year, a present of 100 guineas if the despatches were carried expeditiously. He then sent Rogers upstairs to fetch some more papers, which he handed to Ratcliffe with a £20 note, and also two trunks. One of these contained a model gun. Roger put some maps and prints in the other, de la Motte recommended that they should put some oilcloths round it, and Ratcliffe took a padlock from his own pocket and locked it.

Ratcliffe and de la Motte were together in a little room in Roger's house for a few minutes only; de la Motte left, and Ratcliffe spent the rest of the day with Roger and dined with him.

Francis Henry de la Motte was, his counsel told the jury at his trial, by birth, education and profession, a gentleman. During the previous war he had served France with honour and had become the colonel of the regiment of Soubise. When the war ended the regiment was broke, and he retired to his estate in Alsace, from which he derived the title of Baron D'Akerman. There he lived beyond his means and became so much in debt that, although not ruined, he found it expedient to retire to England in order to arrange his affairs. He came to this country as Baron D'Akerman, and after his estate had been sold and his creditors paid off, he was able to live here in comfort and some degree of affluence. He dropped his title, resumed his family name of de la Motte, and resided in the house of Mr Richard Otley in Bond Street.

This was the house to which, on the morning of 4 January 1781, went Charles Jellous, a king's messenger, and Mr Prothero, a constable. They arrived between 10 and 11 a.m., and de la Motte's servant told them that his master was not at home. So they waited all that day and all the next until between 7 and 8 p.m. when there was a double rap on the door. 'I believe that is my master,' said the servant, 'I will go downstairs.'

'No,' said Jellous, 'do not go down by yourself.'

Prothero went with him, and the servant opened the door and let de la Motte into the house. When he reached the stairs the servant said something to him, and de la Motte immediately turned round as if he was going out again. However, Prothero and Jellous got hold of him, and he took some papers out of his pocket and threw them on the stairs. They took him upstairs and said they wanted to search his pockets. When he refused to allow them to do so, Prothero took hold of his collar and tripped him up by the heels and held him down, while Jellous searched him, and found more papers in his pockets. These included the following:

(i) A list of forty ships stationed at Spithead with details of their state of readiness, expected destination, etc., e.g. 'Britannia, Victory, Prince George, Ocean, Queen – Completing provision for six months, and will be ready for sea in ten days . . . Solebay – Fitted for foreign service. Vestal – Fitted for Channel service.'

(ii) A similar list of thirty-seven ships in Portsmouth Harbour, e.g. 'Lionness, Mars – Hospital ships to receive recovered men from the hospitals. . . . Courageux, Valiant – On a cruize. Marlborough, Bellona – In the Downs. . . . Foudroyant, Bienfaisant – At Plymouth.'

(iii) Lists of three ships missing and given up for lost, three others known to have been lost, six ships cruising near Jamaica, and four stationed at Jamaica.

(iv) A note that eighteen sail of the line, with six months' provisions, were to be despatched to Gibraltar.

(v) A note headed 'Commodore Johnston's Squadron, naming ten ships victualled for eight months, to sail with two regiments of 1,000 men each, and to take artillery: 'but when they sail and on what service, is a profound secret'. The note also included references to various other ships, including some which had been damaged: e.g. 'Ruby, Grafton – All their quarter-deck guns thrown overboard. . . . Hector – All her guns thrown overboard except two. . . . Trident – None, or little damaged. . . . Bristol – All her quarter-deck guns thrown overboard.'

(vi) A copy of a weekly return of Haslar Hospital, consisting of a schedule listing the number of seamen and marines respectively in the hospital – very ill, not dangerously ill, on recovery – and discharged, and 'The most reigning Distempers at this Time – Fevers and Consumptions, lame, hurt, and weak in the Scurvy'.

(vii) Two letters addressed to a Mr John Theed, and signed by Henry Lutterloh, from Wickham.

(viii) A bill for entertainment at the Bush Inn, Farnham, and a bank note for £10 which was returned to de la Motte.

Steps were now taken to arrest Lutterloh. On the very same day as de la Motte was arrested, a king's messenger, Matthew Slater, was sent to Wickham, a village near Portsmouth, with a warrant signed by Lord Hillsborough. Lutterloh was apprehended and brought back to London. No papers of any consequence were found upon him, but under examination by Lord Hillsborough he acknowledged that the papers which had been found were in his handwriting, and that he was in de la Motte's employment to procure information relating to the fleet at Spithead and in Portsmouth harbour. He also said that he was being paid 50 guineas a month by de la Motte, besides additional presents, which had enabled him to corrupt a clerk in the office at Portsmouth to furnish him with intelligence, and that he had buried other documents in his garden.

So on 16 January Slater returned to Wickham and dug in the garden where Lutterloh had directed and a bundle of documents was found there. These included the following:

(i)

INSTRUCTIONS

When commodore Johnston shall sail from Spithead, you will order your two smugglers to go straight to Ushant, or to Brest, and to deliver the letter which you shall give him; and on the receipt of it, he shall give the hour and the day that he shall have received it. If the wind, or other circumstances, will not permit the said smuggler to go straight to Ushant, or Brest, he will do his utmost to carry the letter to St Maloe's; but Ushant, or Brest, are the port which he shall endeavour to make, and not think of St Maloe's but upon a very extraordinary circumstance. The smuggler who shall go to Cadiz, will deliver the letter to the commandant of the marine at Cadiz, and shall take a receipt, from the said commandant, of the hour and the day the letter shall be delivered. If the wind, or circumstances, shall hinder positively the said smuggler from going to Cadiz, he will do his utmost to make Ferrol, or Lisbon. If the said smuggler shall make Ferrol, he will deliver his letter to the commandant of the marine, and will take a receipt. If the said smuggler shall make Lisbon, he will go and carry the letter to Monsieur the ambassador of France, and will take a receipt; but it is to be observed positively, that the principal object is to go directly to Cadiz, and that Ferrol and Lisbon are only on the impossibility of going to Cadiz.

A late eighteenth-century view of Portsmouth, Spithead, the Isle of Wight, Gosport and Porchester Castle, from Portsdown Hill (From the collection of the Royal Naval Museum, Portsmouth)

(ii) An incomplete letter which read:

Sir; This —— day, —— month, —— hour, set sail from St Helen's, Portsmouth, commodore Johnston, with the following vessels [there followed eight blanks] the wind being ——.

There are no other vessels ordered to follow him. I desire you to give a receipt, to the bearer, of the hour and of the day.

When he gave evidence at the trial, Lutterloh explained that he was to fill in the blanks before sending off the letter.

(iii) A note which read:

I promise to pay to Mr Henry Lutterloh, on the 25th day of the present month, the sum of £121 sterling, for the liquidation of the account between us, at London, this 14th June, 1780.

Lutterloh explained this as a note for £121 from de la Motte, paid to Lutterloh's banker, for the business which he was transacting.

(iv) A note which read:

Four thousand guineas, ready money.
For a man of war of 50 guns, 2,000 guin.
For a man of war of 64 guns, 3,000 guin.
For a man of war of 74 guns, 4,000 guin.
For a man of war of 90 guns, 4,000 guin.
For me you must ask [sic]

Lutterloh explained at the trial that he and de la Motte had met in the latter's house in Bond Street, and had worked out the terms which they would put to the minister of France for the capture of Commodore Johnston's fleet, and the price of individual ships captured. It seems to have been arranged that Lutterloh would go to M. Sartine in Paris to arrange the terms. The phrase 'for me you must ask' referred to an additional bonus to be paid to de la Motte.

(v) A series of letters, bearing different apparent signatures, referring to a variety of financial and 'family' matters, but believed to have been coded references to the fleet and in particular to Admiral Hood. Evidence was given at the trial (although this was disputed) that these letters were in the handwriting of de la Motte.

(vi) Two letters, addressed to M. Grolay, Richelieu-street, Paris, No. 64, which had been intercepted by the Post Office. These were also said to be in the handwriting of de la Motte.

The first of these was an unusually long letter, dated London, 11 January 1780. The opening paragraph was on personal matters – best wishes to his wife and children – and this was followed by a note to say that the writer was awaiting news from all parts of the world. Then the letter went on:

> As to our home concern, we are engaged in rendezvousing at Portsmouth the seven East Indiamen, which are to sail from that port between the 26th and 30th instant; three of which are already gone round from Gravesend to Portsmouth completely laden and equipt, and the remaining four are to sail likewise from Gravesend within six or eight days at farthest. We are also busied in assembling the four regiments, making four battalions, of Tottenham, St Leger, Ackland, and Chewton, consisting of 2,200 men, which are part of the troops newly raised by the duke of Ancaster and lord Harrington. These four battalions are destined for the West Indies, and are the last of the troops intended for that country; and when gone, will complete the number of 8,871 men destined to operate in the West Indies, Georgia, and Africa.
>
> We are preparing for our convoys, which are to sail the beginning of March, for North America and Canada, consisting of 10,000 effective men, whereof a part is to be made up of new levies, recruits, and Germans.
>
> As our convoy from Cork is to sail between the 15th and 18th instant, under escort of only two 28 gun frigates; there will remain but the two above-mentioned to be sent out at the appointed time.

The letter then stated that there was some anxiety as to the return of ships from the East Indies and New York, which would add to the strength of the home fleet. At the time there were no more than eight ships fit for sailing to guard the entrances to the Channel, and the force was being supplemented by cutters and frigates. Finally he turned to deal with the domestic situation:

> The object of the association now forming becomes more and more important, and the cause of uneasiness to administration, because the heads of the association aim at disposing of the militia and the new levies of volunteers. The counties of York, Cumberland, Hants, Sussex, Surry [*sic*], and Middlesex, have declared themselves, and the leaders multiply daily. Wilkes is the firebrand, and points out the means. I shall acquaint you with the sequel of this affair, which we apprehend may become of consequence.
>
> The association of the Protestants against the Catholics is not so dangerous; but they are a burthen on our minds, and shackles to our operations.

The second letter dealt, on the face of it, with a commercial transaction relating to the sale of some prints (but it may have been in code), and bore the signature 'J. Wandermeek', but then there was a postscript:

> Sir Samuel Hood sailed Thursday the 29th with eight ships of the line, ten frigates, and three cutters, and every thing wanting for our West India islands. We have insured, at 50 per

cent. the seventeen vessels sent on private account to Gibraltar: as they sail with admiral Hood unto a certain latitude, we only fear their entrance into the straits; – but this insurance does not concern you.

These two letters were read in translation at the trial.

Following his arrest, de la Motte was confined in the Tower for seven months. For the first four months he was kept in solitary confinement without sight of any human being except his keeper, and without the use of pen, ink or paper. After that, he was allowed access to his legal advisers.

On Friday 13 July he was brought from the Tower to Newgate, but in view of the ruinous state of the prison which had been destroyed in the Gordon Riots and had not yet been fully restored, the sheriffs on their own responsibility took him to a commodious apartment in the New Prison at Clerkenwell. On the same day he was brought to the bar at the Old Bailey, where he pleaded Not Guilty to the indictment, and counsel, Dunning and Peckham, were assigned to him by the court on his own nomination. Peckham applied to the court that his client should be remanded to the New Prison, and the court, although doubting whether it had power to order his detention anywhere other than in Newgate, made an order accordingly. Two under-sheriffs sat in his bedchamber with him all night and brought him back to court on the Saturday morning.[3]

The court consisted of Sir Watkin Lewes (Lord Mayor), Buller J. (who was in effect the presiding judge), Heath J.,[4] Serjeant Adair (Recorder of London), and other justices. The indictment alleged in the first count that de la Motte had compassed the death of the king,[5] and in the second count that he had adhered to the enemy. The overt acts, in respect of the letters which had been intercepted, were set out separately and repeated under each count. Wallace A.-G. (who appeared for the Crown with Mansfield S.-G., and Messrs Howorth and Norton, instructed by William Chamberlayne, the Treasury Solicitor) opened the case for the prosecution and the evidence was called. Defending counsel argued that there was no evidence to link their client with the letters which had been intercepted by Ratcliffe and Stewart and copied by Sir Stanyer Porten and his staff, and the court ruled that these were inadmissible. It also transpired in cross-examination that Sir Stanyer had lost the cover of the letter which, he said, had been addressed to M. Grolay in Paris.

'You have delivered a letter without any address to it?' asked Peckham.

'There was a cover to it.'

'How came that cover to be lost?'

'I really cannot say. . . .'

'How happened it you lost that cover?'

'I have lost it, I don't know how.'

However, this attack upon one of the leading witnesses for the prosecution made little impression, and it was only when Lutterloh was cross-examined that the defence began to make any serious inroads into the case for the Crown.

The prosecution had presented Lutterloh without, as it were, any introduction, but his background was extracted from him by Dunning under cross-examination. He said that he had been born in Brunswick and had come to England fifteen or sixteen years previously to see an uncle 'in the character of an ambassador here'. He went to Winchester where he was taught English by a Mr Taylor, and married his daughter – 'and by doing so, I disobliged all my relations, who would know nothing of me, by marrying a woman without fortune or family'. He had spent 'what little money I had' and went to live for a year with a Captain Phillips in Charing Cross, and when Captain Phillips was taken ill, he went to live with Mr Wildman in Lincoln's Inn Fields. He lodged with him for some months until Mr Wildman said one morning: 'I want a livery servant; I suppose that will not suit you.' Lutterloh told him that he could not think of wearing a livery, so Mr Wildman had said, 'I should be glad if you would find another place.' Mr Wildman sent him £15 and his father also assisted him, so he set up a small shop in Castle Street, Leicester Fields, where he sold tea and sugar. Then his uncle 'took me into his hands', and made him sign and accept a great many bills so he lost a lot of money and returned to Germany where he recruited for the government.

On coming back to England, he applied to the Court of King's Bench to be cleared of the debts which he had contracted, and then went abroad again, this time to recruit for the Prince of Orange, 'by which I gained a pretty little sum'. Then again, sometime in the late 1770s, probably, he returned to England. His uncle was going to America and he was intending to follow him, but he was taken ill and could not go. When he recovered, he went to Portsmouth. The king was visiting Portsmouth, so he applied to a Mr Fielding, who kept the George, and said he wanted some employment while waiting to sail to America, and Mr Fielding employed him to receive his money and keep his accounts during the king's visit. He was still planning to go to America on government service – 'a man that speaks different languages, perhaps, is more valuable than a mere carbineer' – when he became involved in an 'imaginary' plan to procure arms for America. There were 'several officers at Hamburgh that sent all kinds of effects to America, and got a great deal of money; and that a great deal of money might be got by buying arms and sending them to America'. However, nothing came of this scheme.

The circumstances in which Lutterloh and de la Motte became acquainted were never properly explained, although Peckham, in his closing speech to the jury, hinted that Lutterloh had approached de la Motte with a view to sending intelligence to France under cover of de la Motte's genuine commercial transactions. However, from about 1778, said Lutterloh, he was regularly visiting de la Motte in the latter's lodgings, first in Wardour Street, then in Hampstead, then at No. 1 Old Burlington Street, and finally at Mr Otley's in Bond Street. Lutterloh told the court that de la Motte said that he wanted to procure intelligence for transmitting to France, and paid him 8 guineas a month, a salary which was later increased to 50 guineas 'besides many valuable presents'. Lutterloh now resided in Wickham and sent intelligence 'by post, or the diligence', but 'if there was anything extraordinary, I came post to town', and sometimes de la Motte came to visit him at Wickham. Lutterloh was evidently a trusted agent now, and in August 1780 he went to Paris on de la Motte's behalf.

Lutterloh said that he and de la Motte had made an agreement not to discuss their arrangements with anyone, but Lutterloh disclosed what was going on to Sir Hugh Palliser (although without mentioning de la Motte's name).

'When did you impart this to Sir Hugh Palliser?' asked Dunning.

'After I had settled the plan with the ministry of France. I went to Paris; the ministry of France wished to take commodore Johnstone's squadron; I laid them the plan how to take it; they agreed in every respect. I asked 3,000 guineas for a friend of mine, who would procure me all necessary intelligence, as likewise the third part of every ship that should be taken; that was done by M. de la Motte's desire. The French ministry would not agree a third part; they agreed to give me £3,000 and £2,000 a year to my friend, which I said I had in the Admiralty.'

'Who was this friend in the Admiralty; not Sir Hugh Palliser, I hope?'

'It was an imaginary friend; it was a plan of my own making.'

'You are a dexterous hand at making plans, I perceive. Then you made a plan, and invented a lord of the Admiralty, and went to the French ministry? Be so good as to tell me which of the French ministers had the honour of your conversation.'

Lutterloh then gave an account of what had happened. He said that de la Motte had often asked him if there was any possibility of getting at the private signals and taking the fleet, and he (Lutterloh) thought that there was. So de la Motte gave him a letter which he took to the 'prime secretary of the ministry at France', and de la Motte later went to France himself and settled a plan for the French to give £3,000 and an eighth part of every ship to be shared between de la Motte, himself, and his friends. But he now regretted that he had become involved so he went to Sir Hugh Palliser, and told him of the whole transaction, 'and made him a plan, that instead of the French taking the English fleet, the English should take the French fleet'.

'See if I understand you,' said Dunning, 'you first settled a plan with de la Motte, by which commodore Johnstone and his fleet were to be taken; and, when they were taken, they were to be divided between you, de la Motte, and your friend?'

'Not divided; only an eighth part of it divided.'

'Then you were to have an eighth part for yourself, for de la Motte, and for your friend? Be so good as to tell me who this friend was. You said, this moment, that it was an imaginary thing?'

'So it is.'

'Then the meaning is, you are to settle a plan with M. de la Motte, and cheat him out of a partition of the plunder you were to have, for your imaginary friend? Was it but one imaginary friend you had?'

'Only one that I employed in that business,' said Lutterloh.

'How many imaginary friends were there to have shared in the plunder?'

'Only we three.'

'That makes five of you: you, M. de la Motte, and three imaginary friends.'

'If you can make five out of three, I cannot. I wished to give up this business in which I was employed: I wished likewise to render myself serviceable to England. . . .'

'I want England to know her benefactors. You entered into this conspiracy with a view to destroy England and enrich yourself. Having enriched yourself, be so good as to tell us what was the plan you and Sir Hugh Palliser had concerted to serve England?'

So Lutterloh explained that he had gone to Sir Hugh Palliser and told him that he had arranged with the French to take the English fleet, and suggested that the English fleet should instead take the French fleet.

'Which of the fleets of France was it that was to be destroyed by this conjunction between you and Sir Hugh Palliser?'

'Sir Hugh Palliser was to go to the minister, and inform him of my plan; which he has done.'

'Then you, Sir Hugh Palliser, and the minister, are all together. I only want to know what it was you were to do for the annoyance of France. I understand that a recollection of your opulence, and a little qualm of conscience, carried you to Sir Hugh Palliser, for the sake of turning the tables upon the French; and, instead of doing them a service, you meant to do them a mischief?'

'Yes.'

'What was the mischief you intended?'

'To take the fleet of France.'

'What! all of them?'

'No, the fleet that was to come to take governor Johnstone were to be taken, by sending out more men of war in a secret manner.'

'I hope it was done?'

'It was not, I wish it had; there happened to be a mistake; I went out of town, and Sir Stanyer Porten was sent by Lord Hillsborough to converse with me upon this subject.'

'When so many wise heads get together, I wonder how this scheme failed!'

'If you had been there, it might have been better perhaps.'

Lutterloh was also the witness on whom the Crown principally relied for proving de la Motte's handwriting on the documents which had been found in the garden at Wickham and those intercepted on their way to M. Grolay, and he was strictly cross-examined on this issue. It was also put to him that he had said that he would ensure that the grand jury had sufficient evidence to return a true bill against de la Motte, and that he would gain financially as a result, but he denied this.

The Crown also called two witnesses who had seen de la Motte write, and who corroborated Lutterloh's evidence that the documents were in his hand, and closed its case sometime in the evening.

Dunning was taken ill, so it fell to Peckham, his junior, to address the jury on behalf of their client. It was a formidable task for him, but he handled it with great skill.

Peckham opened his speech by referring to Dunning: 'Were my learned friend to make the defence which now devolves upon me, he would easily convince you of the innocence of M. de la Motte, and repel the accusation with infamy on his accusers,' and he went on to make some flattering observations about the reputation of English juries in times of war. He had noticed that, in civil actions, between enemy aliens and English insurers, the jurors of the City of London always acted with the utmost impartiality as between the foreigner and the native, and he had the right to expect that a Middlesex jury would be at least as attentive to the life of an unhappy fellow creature. Then he endeavoured to attack, as best he could, the case for the Crown. He alleged that de la Motte had been carrying on a perfectly legitimate trade until he was approached by Lutterloh who suggested a scheme for carrying false information to France:

> Lutterloh insisted, that the scheme was plausible. 'I am, for instance,' says he, 'a very good friend of Sir Hugh Palliser' (whether Sir Hugh feels it as a compliment is not for me to determine): 'I can, through his means, get a passport of lord Sandwich; and, under the ostensible idea of conveying false intelligence to France, we shall then get a passport; our vessels will go in safety; and we will tell the French ministry that we will give them true intelligence, but, in fact, will give them false.'

Peckham suggested that Lutterloh might have placed incriminating papers in de la Motte's pockets when he knew that he was about to be arrested, and that the papers which, it had been alleged, de la Motte threw down on the stairs, had been planted there by the men who arrested him (although this had never been put to them in cross-examination). He attacked the character of Lutterloh:

> But who is this Lutterloh? If you credit the picture of his own drawing, he is a monster, not a man; and his whole life has been a satire on the vices of human nature. The unblushing miscreant on his oath confesses, that he has been guilty of treason to France, who employed

him, and to England, who protected him: he has been guilty of treachery to Sir Hugh Palliser, (who honoured him with his friendship) and now thirsts for the blood of his benefactor, whose unbounded liberality has raised him from beggary to affluence. What a tale he has told. He was a foreign officer: he came here to see his uncle, who was an ambassador that never existed, from a country as yet unknown. This ambassador uncle puts his hopeful nephew to school at Winchester, to learn the language of Mr Taylor, a clergyman: that in the acquiring the language, he likewise obtained the daughter of his preceptor in marriage: that this uncle ambassador was so exasperated at his nephew for contaminating the purity of his blood, and for degrading himself by marrying the innocent daughter of a respectable English clergyman, that he turned him out of doors, dismissed him from his presence; and all streams of liberality were at once shut from this worthy nephew, who before had been the favourite object of his tenderness and care.

Peckham analysed the evidence relating to the handwriting to show that it was impossible to be sure that de la Motte had written the letters which had been found and produced in evidence. He also scoffed at Sir Stanyer Porten for losing the cover addressed to M. Grolay: 'It is astonishing to me, that with all his ability, care and assiduity, he should have lost that which is alone material in this indictment; for that great man has lost the cover, without which this letter cannot be admitted in evidence.' And he contended that, even if his client had written the letters, their contents were matters of common knowledge which were reported in the newspapers.

At the conclusion of his speech, Peckham called two print-sellers, Pictor Picot and William Faden, who gave evidence that they had sold prints to de la Motte during 1779 and 1780. Roger was recalled and described a conversation with Lutterloh after the latter had given evidence to the grand jury. Lutterloh had told him that he would swear to anything, and to the writing too, and he had said, 'I know very well I could work better than him; I should be glad he would be hanged, because I could work by myself a great deal better than we do together.'

Another witness, Jasper Lappel, described Lutterloh's plans for purchasing arms from Germany: 'He made a kind of proposal to go to France, as he said there was a prince in Germany (I have forgot his name) that wanted money, and that he had several thousand stand of arms, and he would endeavour to sell them for him to the American Congress, and would advise with Dr Franklin about it: he was to write to Dr Franklin, to see if they could agree for them for the Americans.'

Mr Wildman was also called. The defence seem to have believed that he would say that he had dismissed Lutterloh for breaking into his bureau, but he referred to this simply as an accident, and could cast no imputation upon Lutterloh for being involved.

There was no closing speech on behalf of the defendant, and there is no record that he was asked if he wished to say anything for himself. So the Solicitor-General replied on behalf of the Crown and reviewed the evidence. He did his best to rehabilitate Lutterloh. He was the nephew of the agent (although he called him the ambassador) of the duke of Brunswick. He had been called a monster and a traitor – but if that was true, he had done his best to make some recompense for his crimes by endeavouring to bring the principal offender to justice. Attempts had been made to blacken his character by supposing that Mr Wildman had detected him in a crime, but Mr Wildman himself had cleared him beyond all possible suspicion. As for de la Motte:

> I have heard of men having been driven by their distresses from this country, and going to live in France, on account of the cheapness of the country; but I never before heard of a baron, an officer of a regiment in France, coming here because he could not support himself

in France; and I never heard of a baron coming here to deal in prints. The whole of that is so extremely ridiculous, that if you read it in a romance you would laugh at it, as being too absurd for that species of composition.

And he added, improperly and in the absence of any evidence:

I have no doubt but he employed other instruments, and gained other intelligence, than by the means of Lutterloh. Lutterloh's district was Portsmouth. I have no doubt but that the scheme extended to Plymouth, and every part of the kingdom where any intelligence was to be obtained. . . . And sorry I am to say, that one unfortunate fact has occurred, that the secret signals which should be known only to the officers of a fleet at sea, have, either by de la Motte or some other, been communicated to France.[6] I do not say that is proved upon de la Motte: I only say that such a thing has happened; and it is obvious that such intelligence must be extremely important to the enemies of this country, and infinitely detrimental to it.

Buller J. summed up. He dealt briefly with the law, explaining that sending intelligence to the enemy was an overt act both of compassing the death of the king and of adhering to the enemy. He reviewed the evidence, and he told the jury that if they were satisfied that the defendant had been sending intelligence to the enemy, they should convict him.

The jury retired at 10.35 p.m. and returned eight minutes later with a verdict of Guilty.

Buller J., in his capacity as the senior judge, addressed the defendant. He stressed that the offence of which he had been convicted was so enormous that it would be a waste of time to enlarge upon it:

It is an offence of which every state under the sun has agreed in inflicting the most exemplary punishment.

There is no other nation, no other government under heaven, which would allow to a traitor of your description the same privileges, and the same indulgences, which you have experienced, during the course of your trial, at this bar. You have had a long, a full, and patient trial: you have had the assistance of such of the advocates at the British bar, as you yourself approved: you have had a long previous information of the names of those who were to decide upon your guilt, or innocence; and you have had information, of equal length, of those who were to be adduced as witnesses against you. These are indulgences which are allowed in no country but in England; and you, though a foreigner, though a native of that country which has harboured an old inveterate hatred against this kingdom, and which is now at war with it, have yet received every indulgence which a British subject could enjoy.

The judge reminded de la Motte that, while residing in England, he had enjoyed the protection of the laws of the land which he had betrayed and abused, and he had corrupted others to join him to become traitors and to endeavour to ruin the constitution, and subject England to the sway of its inveterate foe.

Buller J. then pronounced sentence in the usual terms. De la Motte received the awful doom with great composure, although he 'inveighed against Mr Lutterloh in warm terms'.

In the meantime the defendant's counsel had already submitted an application, requesting that, in the event of de la Motte's conviction, he should not be imprisoned in Newgate, but should be returned to the Tower. This request was granted. And so, immediately after de la Motte had been convicted, an under-sheriff was despatched to Lord Hillsborough's office for an order addressed to the Lieutenant of the Tower that he should receive the prisoner. At midnight he was conveyed there, accompanied by Mr Akerman, who said that he never saw a man in such a situation behave with such becoming firmness and fortitude, and that he only expressed the wish that His Majesty should grant that he should be beheaded. Throughout the whole proceedings, indeed, he had exhibited a combination of manliness, steadiness, and presence of mind – as if he 'felt a conscious innocence within his own breast, that he had devoted his life to the service of his country'.

On arriving at the Tower, there was a delay of a quarter of an hour until the gates were opened. Mr Sheriff Crichton then handed his prisoner over, and de la Motte thanked him and his colleague, Mr Sheriff Sainsbury, for the way in which thay had attended upon him while he was in custody, and particularly for the trouble they had taken in arranging for him to be sent back to the Tower.

The *State Trials* usually record the fate of those who were convicted of serious criminal offences, but the report of this case stops at this point. Croly, in his *Life of George IV*, states that de la Motte was in fact executed, but I have found no other details. Presumably he was hanged at Tyburn, one of the last to have suffered there before the 'usual place of execution' was transferred to Newgate.

CHAPTER SEVEN

The Pop Gun Conspiracy: the Trial of Robert Thomas Crossfield (1796)

In May 1794 Thomas Hardy, John Horne Tooke, and other members of the London Corresponding Society and the Society for Constitutional Information had been arrested, and they spent the summer in the Tower awaiting trial on suspicion of treason. In August, in Scotland, David Downie and Robert Watt had been convicted of treason on the basis that they were conspiring to overthrow the constitution. By the end of September they were awaiting execution.[1]

This was the state of affairs when, on Friday 12 September, Thomas Upton, a member of the London Corresponding Society who had recently quarrelled with other members of the society, reported to Robert Ward, a barrister, that there was a plot on foot for the assassination of the king. Ward waited upon the Prime Minister on the next day, although he did not see Mr Pitt until the Wednesday. Shortly afterwards, three men – George Higgins, Paul Thomas le Maitre and John Smith – were arrested. Robert Crossfield may have been under suspicion at this stage, but he was not arrested.

The evidence which emerged, and which was later given at the trial, was that on 8 September three men had gone to a brass-founder's shop, owned by Mr Penton, at No. 32 New Street Square. One was Upton, who was lame, one was Peregrine Palmer, an attorney in practice at Barnard's Inn, Holborn, and the third, it was believed, was Robert Crossfield, a surgeon. They spoke to the clerk in the counting-house and he fetched John Dowding, for Mr Penton himself was out at the time. Dowding came down and one of the three men asked him if he could make them a tube: three feet long, an eighth of an inch thick, five-eighths of an inch inside the bore, with the inside a smooth cylinder. They asked what the price would be, but Dowding could not tell them because it would be an out-of-the-way job and he would have to make tools on purpose to make it. He asked what the tube was to be used for, and said that he could be a better judge of how to make it if he knew, but Upton said it was a secret and the other two agreed with him. It appears that the three men had had previous dealings with this firm, for they then produced a piece of tube which they had purchased there and returned it, and the clerk refunded 10d.

Joseph Flint was another brass-founder who worked in Cock Lane, Snow Hill. On the same day, after dinner, the same three men came into his shop and sent his apprentice, James Hubbard, to fetch him. They asked him for a long pistol-barrel so he showed them a musketoon-barrel. Then they explained that they wanted a straight cylinder, five-eighths of an inch in the bore and one-eighth thick, and Flint told them that he could not cast it unless they brought him a pattern. That was the end of the conversation, and the three men went away.

Thomas Bland was also a brass-founder; his shop was at No. 40 Shoe Lane. On the same day two men came to his shop and asked for a tube or barrel, but he said it was not in his line of business – if they wanted a barrel they should apply to the clock-makers, if they wanted a tube they should apply to the tube drawers. They went away and shortly afterwards Palmer came and asked for them.

Some time early in September David Cuthbert, a maker of mathematical instruments who lived in Graham Court, Arundel Street, had called on Upton to subscribe some money for the wives and children of the men who were in prison in the Tower. He invited Upton to come and look at an engine of his which he thought would be a treat for him. A few days later Upton arrived, accompanied by another man, and he noticed an air pump lying in the shop and Cuthbert explained it to him and showed him an airgun. The gentleman who had come with Upton said that he was very fond of shooting and had lost some of his fingers in an explosion. He handled the gun and said it was a handsome one. For some reason Cuthbert was angry with Upton and remained seated at his table while this conversation was proceeding, but just as Upton and his friend were leaving Upton asked him if he wanted a job. Cuthbert replied that he had more business than he could do.

The three men who had been visiting the brass-founders also went to John Hill, a wood turner in Batholomew Close. Upton asked him if he could turn in wood, and he said that he could so Upton asked him to do a job for him. Hill could not understand what they had in mind, so asked Upton to draw a sketch. There was a piece of paper lying about with the words 'This house to let, inquire within' written on it, but the other side was blank so Hill provided a pen and ink and Upton drew a sketch of what he had in mind. Part of it was a straight piece like a round ruler, and Upton said it was something in the way of an electrifying machine and as a model for a piece of brass-work. About three days later, Hill took the model round to Upton's house and gave it to him.

At about this time a quarrel broke out in the branch of the London Corresponding Society of which Upton was then a member. He was accused of having set fire to his own house to cheat his insurers. When this issue arose at a committee meeting at which Upton was present, a fellow-member said he ought to be expelled. Upton then 'threw the whole assembly into a very great degree of agitation . . . and broke out in a strain of abuse, and used all those epithets which men in the habit of abuse are accustomed to use'. It appears that the general committee of the society met later that same evening and a vote of censure upon Upton was moved. He evidently wanted to avoid the vote being passed upon him, so he moved towards the door, whereupon George Higgins, a fellow-member, said to the chairman: 'if you are about to pass a vote of censure upon Upton, you must be quick, for he seems to be hopping off'. Upton was extremely angry at this and replied: 'You wretch, that is a reflexion upon my natural infirmity.'

It was almost immediately after this that Upton went to see Ward.

Crossfield was not, apparently, a suspect at this stage and in October 1794 he and Peregrine Palmer went to Bristol. Crossfield was ill and taking opium and he wanted to see if the waters of Bath and Bristol might be of help to him, and he was also considering whether to set up in practice there as a physician. Palmer usually went to the West Country at that time of the year, and he stayed with Crossfield for a short time before returning to London. Crossfield also returned to London, but went to Portsmouth at the end of January where he joined the *Pomona*, a South Sea whaler, as the ship's doctor.

The *Pomona* sailed to Falmouth and left there on 13 February, bound for the southern fisheries round Cape Horn, but two days later she was seized by a French corvette, *la Vengeance*, and taken to Brest. Some months afterwards, the crew of the *Pomona* were repatriated, and on 31 August 1795 Crossfield was arrested at Fowey in Cornwall.

In the meantime, on 22 February, Upton gave his wife the seal with which he usually sealed his letters, and left home. The next morning a watchman found the hat that he had been wearing and took it back to Mrs Upton. Upton himself was never seen again.

On 11 May 1796 Robert Crossfield appeared at the Old Bailey before Sir James Eyre, Grose J. and the Recorder of London.[2] He was charged with conspiracy, along with Paul Thomas le Maitre, John Smith and George Higgins, to compass the death of the king by procuring the manufacture of an instrument for the discharge of a poisoned dart at His Majesty. The Crown was represented by Sir John Scott A.-G., Sir John Mitford S.-G., and Messrs Law, Garrow, Wood, Fielding and Abbott; the prisoner by Messrs Adam, Gurney, Moore and Mackintosh. A large number of jurors were called, and many were challenged by one side or the other, or were excused on various grounds. Eventually the following were sworn:

John Greenside, corn factor
Francis Barstow Nixon, merchant
William Walker, sugar baker
Alexander Black, merchant
William Shone, wine merchant
Arthur Windus, coachmaker
William Norris, mason
William Gosling, carpenter
Daniel Pinder, mason
Benjamin White, bookseller
John Reid, distiller
John Coe, taylor

The Attorney-General opened the case for the prosecution and explained the law and the evidence which he proposed to place before the court. The Crown then called the brass-founders, John Dowding, Joseph Flint and Thomas Bland, and the instrument-maker, David Cuthbert. None of these witnesses was able to identify Crossfield as one of the men who had come into their shops.

The Crown then called Peregrine Palmer. It seems clear that they hoped that he would implicate Crossfield in the conspiracy. The two men had known each other for fifteen or sixteen years, and they were both members of the London Corresponding Society. The witness had gone with Upton and Crossfield to the various brass-founders, but, he said, he had always stayed outside and knew nothing of what had passed inside the shops. He was examined on behalf of the prosecution by Garrow, who soon became exasperated at the witness's attitude:

'What passed at the brass-founder's when you were so in [Upton and Crossfield's] company?'

'I know nothing of what passed; Upton had some business there as I understood.'

'I am asking what passed at the brass-founder's when you were present making one of the company, and I desire you to state it on your oath?'

'I have no recollection of any thing that passed there.'

'Attend to what you are about, and speak the truth.'

'I know what I am about, and shall speak nothing but the truth . . .'

'Do you know what a tube is?'

'Yes; certainly any man must know what a tube is.'

'Was there any conversation there about a brass tube and its dimensions?'

'I have no recollection of any thing of that kind.'

'Recollect that you are upon your oath?'

'I know that perfectly well; and therefore I shall say nothing but the truth.'

A few minutes later, Garrow tried to persuade the witness to identify Crossfield's handwriting:

'Look at this paper and tell me whose hand-writing you believe that to be.'

'I cannot swear to this hand-writing.'

'Do you mean to swear that you have no belief upon the subject?'

'I have not. . . .'

'Now open this paper and look at it. Have you ever seen it before?'

'I do not know upon my word.'

'I am sorry to be obliged so often to admonish you, that you are upon your oath?'

'You might save yourself all that trouble – I know it very well.'

Eventually Adam, for the defence, objected to this line of examination, and Eyre CJ declared:

> The whole course of this species of examination is not regular. This is a witness for the crown; if he disgraces himself, which it is the tendency of this examination to make him do, they lose the benefit of his testimony. The idea of extracting truth from a witness for the crown, who disgraces himself, is in my apprehension, and always has been, a thing perfectly impracticable, for the moment he has gone to the length of discrediting his testimony, by the manner in which he shuffles with your examination, there is an end of all credit to him.

So Garrow gave up and passed on to the visit to Mr Hill, and Palmer remembered that Upton had given instructions for something – 'I think the word model was made use of, but I am not a mechanic myself; the word model or pattern or something of that nature was mentioned' – and he thought he remembered Upton producing a drawing, but beyond that he remembered nothing.

Under cross-examination by Adam, Palmer said that Crossfield was in poor health, and was taking opium.

The defendant's visits to the brass-founders were not, however, the only evidence relied on by the Crown, who now called a series of sailors who had served as prisoners with him.

The first of these was John le Breton, the boat steerer of the *Pomona*. He described how Crossfield had joined the ship where he was known as 'the doctor'. When the *Pomona* was captured, the defendant was transferred to *la Vengeance*, and as he went over the side, said the witness, Crossfield said that 'he was happy he was going to France, he would sooner go there than to England'. Part of the crew stayed on the *Pomona*, but later they were put on board *la Vengeance* and taken to Brest, and there he heard the defendant make some remarkable assertions. 'I heard him say, he was one of those who invented the air-gun, to *assignate* [sic] his majesty – to shoot his majesty . . . He told me the arrow was to go through a kind of tube by the force of inflammable air . . . He described it like one of our harpoons, which we kill whales with.' The witness said that he stayed in Brest all the time they were prisoners, until a cartel[3] came from the West Indies and they were all transferred to it to be taken back to England. The defendant, said le Breton, stood at the gangway taking a list of the prisoners, and he wrote his own name down as 'H. Wilson of the *Hope*.'

In his cross-examination Adam asked the witness some questions designed to show that his client had been behaving in a perfectly normal manner while the *Pomona* was at Portsmouth preparing for the journey, and had gone ashore with other members of the crew. There was some discussion about loading the ship with casks of water and provisions for the voyage, and the captain's 'private trade': jewellery, trinkets and watches. The witness said that he himself had two dozen pairs of stockings.

Le Breton was then asked about the voyage and their capture by the French, and agreed that they had all, including Captain Clarke and the defendant, organized a scheme to capture *la Vengeance*, but the scheme had failed because some 'outlandish' prisoners from other ships were disheartened. When they reached Brest, they were transferred to a prison ship the *Elizabeth*, and other prisoners were on board, and also nearby on *l'Achille* and the *Normandy*. Later he was transferred to the *Peggy* which was lashed alongside the *Active Increase*, and it seems that the prisoners were constantly on the move from one ship to another. If a prisoner was seriously ill he was moved ashore to hospital, but 'they let them be pretty bad first, and then they were taken on shore'. The prisoners also managed to move their 'private trade' to the prison ships and there was some suggestion that they were sold, but when le Breton was asked specifically if he had heard Crossfield warn the prisoners that he would tell the insurer that their goods had never been captured, he said he never had.

The next witness was the mate of the *Pomona*, Thomas Dennis. He said that, the night after they had sailed from Falmouth, the defendant said to him: 'If Pitt knew where he was, he would send a frigate after him;' moreover, 'that Pitt would have been shot, only he crossed some bridge in the room of Westminster bridge, the bridge I have forgot'. On being asked if he had heard Crossfield say anything about His Majesty, the witness replied: 'Yes, I heard him say, "his majesty was to be assassinated at the playhouse with a dart blown through a tube, and that he knew how the dart was to be constructed".'

After they were captured, the witness went on, Crossfield had said that he was glad he was going to France. All the time he was a prisoner, he had gone under the name of Crossfield, but on the day he was to return to England, he had himself listed as 'H. Wilson, being captured in the *Hope* brig' instead of the *Pomona*.

In cross-examination by Gurney, the witness agreed that he and Crossfield and Captain Clarke had all meant to rise against the French and seize *la Vengeance*, and then he went on to put to the witness that they were all selling their 'private trade'. 'I ask you whether Mr Crossfield did not expressly charge you and Captain Clarke with defrauding the underwriters, by the sale of these articles.' The witness denied this, but admitted that he knew that Crossfield had been accusing him, behind his back, of negligence by not making sail, so that it had been his fault that the *Pomona* had been taken.

Then the cross-examination took a different turn. The witness agreed that Crossfield had spent most of his time with Captain Clarke and the captains of the other ships. The questions continued.

'You were miserably off in these prison-ships for want of provisions?'

'No, I cannot say I ever wanted provisions while I was there.'

'Had you never any bad provision there?'

'Yes.'

'Bad provision and confinement were not very pleasant to you I suppose?'

'No.'

'Did you ever take any steps whatever for getting your liberty?'

'No.'

'Did you ever state to the French, either directly or through the medium of Mr Crossfield, that you were an American?'

'Yes.'

The witness then described how he had thought of obtaining a certificate from the American consul, purporting to show that he was an American, and that the defendant had said that he was a naturalized Hollander because he held a diploma from Leyden University. Then the cross-examination continued:

'Was Mr Crossfield a man of the most grave and serious deportment imaginable?'

'No.'

'I believe he was very much to the contrary?'

'He was a man that drank very much.'

'I mean he was a man of grave deportment, or of a good deal of levity?'

'Very much levity in talking.'

'Talking and rattling a good deal?'

'Yes.'

'You hardly knew sometimes whether he was in jest or earnest?'

'Indeed, I did not pay much attention to him.'

Before Dennis left the witness box, Eyre CJ asked him whether the defendant could have stayed in France, but he could not say. The judge asked whether the crew were obliged to stay on the cartel ships if they had expressed any inclination to stay, and he replied that he had never heard anybody say they had an inclination to stay.

The next witness was James Winter, the Captain of the *Susanna* which had been captured during a journey from Newfoundland to Spain. He had spent some time on a prison ship in Brest, he said, before being transferred to Brest Castle. On 20 March he had been taken up the river Landernau where the three British cartels were lashed together, and he was put on board one of them – the *Revolution* brig, under Captain Yellowley. The latter introduced the defendant to him, and said 'his name was not Crossfield but Tom Paine', and laughed. Later, said the witness, Crossfield had told him that he had 'shot at his majesty, but unluckily missed him', and this was 'between

The attack on George III, 25 October 1795; this is the incident referred to on page xvi (Museum of London)

the palace and Buckingham House'. Some time later when they were walking together on the quarterdeck, the witness said he had asked Crossfield where it was he had shot at his majesty, and Crossfield had hesitated and said 'between Buckingham House and the Palace'. It was his constant subject every day after dinner and after supper: 'I dined and supped with him every day, sometimes on board one ship, sometimes another, for five months together.'

When asked if Crossfield described the weapon with which he had shot at his majesty, Winter replied: 'He showed me in what manner they were made, with his finger in some wet upon the table; he stroked with his finger as if there were hairs in it; he said "they opened when it struck, and something flew out and let the poison in."'

'When the arrow penetrated the poison came out?' asked counsel.

'As soon as the arrow struck, the poison came out of the dart.'

'Had you any conversation about where he got the poison?'

'He said, "he prescribed it;" but I do not know the place where it was bought; he said, "he was the very person that ordered it to be made up."'

This was Crossfield's constant topic of conversation for the five months they were together, and he had said that 'he hoped he should live to see the day when the streets of London should be up to his ancles [sic] in the blood of the king and his party'. On that occasion Captain Yellowley interrupted and said: 'God forbid, matters may be done more easily.' On another occasion Captain Collins, another prisoner, said he would be happy to have the cutting off of the head of both the king, Pitt and parliament, and Crossfield had replied: 'Have patience, have patience, I hope to have the cutting off some of them by-and-by myself.' He and Crossfield had sailed back to England on the *Revolution*, and immediately he landed at Mevagissey he, the witness, had inquired at a public house for a justice of the peace. The landlord told him there was one three miles away, so he went there at once – he was not ashore five minutes before going to the justice's. When he arrived the justice was out, but he saw him later and laid an information against Crossfield. The justice granted a warrant for his arrest, but by the time they came down to Mevagissey the next morning, the ship had sailed again, so they followed it to Fowey and arrested him there.

In cross-examination Winter agreed that he and Crossfield had messed with Captain Alexander, Captain Collins, Captain Yellowley, Captain Lambton, William Byron and Richard Taylor, and they had all lived together as a family until Crossfield started to sing seditious songs, when he withdrew at once to his own ship. They had all gone back to England together on the *Revolution*, though the others had not gone to the justice at Mevagissey, but had stayed on the ship until it reached Fowey. Then Adam asked an apparently strange question:

'Do you remember anything about the story of a hare . . . that used to entertain the company very much, about a hare jumping into your lap?'

'No, only into my arm,' replied the witness.

'What was that story?'

'I was coming through Uplime to Lime, in my way from Axminster; just as I got to a wall, I stopped to make water; as I was buttoning up the fall of my breeches, a hare came through my arm; I catched him by the leg and turned him round; it was about twelve o'clock at night; I threw him in over the gate, in among a parcel of dogs, and he remained there that night; and the next day, just as the parson was going away to church, the hare got out, and the dogs followed it all through Lime; there they catched the hare, and it was carried up.'

The witness elaborated on this story, and said that anyone in Lime would vouch for him. Counsel asked him what he took the hare to be:

'The gentleman asks you what you took the hare for,' said Eyre CJ. 'I suppose he means to ask you whether you took her for a witch?'

'They say the place is troubled; now I took her to be an old hare.'

'Did you not use to tell those gentlemen,' asked Adam, 'in the course of conversation, that you took this hare to be a witch, or the devil in the shape of a hare?'

'No; it was an old hare that had been hunted many times by the dogs, and they never could catch him; if you want a voucher for it, if you send to Lime, you may get vouchers.'

'Where did you throw this hare into?' asked Eyre CJ.

'Over a place seven feet high, among a kennel of hounds, and it was twelve o'clock at night.'

After this curious digression, Winter said that he had been on a grand jury in Newfoundland for twenty-five years, and in re-examination by the Attorney-General he said he had raised a corps of fifty during the American war and sixty-nine in the present war: 'I supported fifty men myself during the whole American war.'

Richard Penny said that he was master-at-arms on his majesty's ship *Active*. After her capture he was put on board the *Elizabeth* where he met Crossfield and heard him sing a song: 'Damnation to the King'. When asked What king? Crossfield had replied 'the King of England' and had added that he was one of the men who had tried to blow a dart at His Majesty in Covent Garden. Just before they reached Mevagissey, Crossfield had said to the witness, 'Young man, was not you on board the *Elizabeth*?' and he desired 'I would take no notice of what was said on board the *Elizabeth*.' But when he, the witness, arrived at Portsmouth, he reported all this to Mr Cheetham, the king's solicitor there.

The Crown then called Edward Stocker, one of the constables of Fowey, and Walter Colmer, also of Fowey, who had arrested Crossfield on board the ship there. At about 9 p.m. they had set off in a chaise to take him to Bodmin gaol, about twelve miles away, and both these gentlemen said that their prisoner tried to bribe them to let him go. He said 'he would give us a guinea to let him go, and take the irons from his hands; that we should only have a few shillings for carrying him to Bodmin, and he would give us a guinea each to let him go'. When the witnesses asked him what he would do with the driver, he said that if they let him have one of the pistols he would pop at him and soon settle that business. They said, in cross-examination, that they thought the defendant was not drunk, although Mr Stocker agreed that he fell asleep halfway to Bodmin.

Elizabeth Upton was called to give evidence of her husband's disappearance, and she was followed by George Steers who 'did unfortunately attend one meeting' of the London Corresponding Society, although he was not a member. He noticed Upton holding something in his hand which he thought was a walking-stick until he realised that it was made of brass. William Pusey was at the same meeting and saw Upton holding a brass tube under his coat: 'I saw a bit of it sticking out from under his coat; he pulled it farther out that I could perceive it better.' When he asked what it was, Upton shook his head.

Towards the end, the Crown called Harvey Walklate Mortimer, who had been in business as a gunsmith in Fleet Street for more than thirty years, and was experienced in the construction of airguns – he had once sold one to the king who had sent it as a present to the Dey of Algiers. At one time he had sold them as walking-sticks, but had stopped as he thought they were too dangerous. One of the advantages of an airgun was that it made little noise: 'If it is discharged where the air passes briskly by, you cannot hear it yourself; but if it is in a confined room, where the external air does not pass freely, it makes a noise like that,' and he clapped his hands. He agreed that it would make less noise in a theatre than in a small room. Another advantage was that it had a small recoil: 'if you were to hold it against your face with a glass upon your eye, you would not perceive it injure the glass.' It was so accurate that 'I have shot with it so as to hit a nail twice out of thrice upon the head, and drive it through a board; I have used it when a gentleman has desired to hold a small thing between his finger and thumb while I have shot at it.'

The witness agreed that it could be used to discharge an arrow, and he was shown a drawing of two arrows, one barbed, the other unbarbed, and he explained that a barbed arrow could easily be inserted into a gun and would keep closed until it struck a solid body, when it would open and release whatever was inside: 'I think it would be a dreadful instrument, if it was projected from an air-gun. . . . I could with a tube which I take in my hand blow without any condensed air whatever, I could with my mouth blow an arrow of that sort, if within six or eight yards, with sufficient force to do a mortal injury to any man living: my men are frequently trying little experiments.'

Here Eyre CJ interrupted him: 'Be content just to answer the questions.' The following afternoon, in his summing-up, he explained that he had not encouraged the witness to go farther, because he did not wish the world to be informed of that which it was better the world should not know.

The witness then examined the pieces of wood and the drawings of the tube and said that one of the pieces of wood must have been designed as the piston to condense the air, but it must have been disconnected from the gun, and only to have been screwed on when required for condensing it: 'This wood,' he added, 'might be a model for making a piston to contain air enough in a brass tube to have expelled three or four times without re-charging such an instrument of death.' The drawings, he said, were not well done, but with verbal explanations he could have made an airgun from them: 'Taking the tube and the models together, I am satisfied they were for an air-gun.'

Finally, the Crown called Robert Ward who gave evidence that Upton had come to see him, and said that he had seen the wooden models and the drawing of the barbed arrow in Upton's possession. Peregrine Palmer was re-called to answer one question – the defendant was heavily in debt: 'His whole property was assigned over for the benefit of his creditors.'

It was now 11 p.m. and Adam informed the court that there was no way in which he could conclude his case in a single sitting. Accordingly the court adjourned, and the jury was accommodated in the London Coffee House.

Adam addressed the jury when the court sat again at 8 a.m. the following morning. There was little he could say on the law, but he stressed that this was a time ripe for false informers and spies to 'bring their inventions into action'. As for the brass tube, there was really no evidence as to the purpose for which it was designed. Dowding had said that the men who had come to his shop had been haggling over the price: 'Need I ask you . . . whether . . . persons carrying on such a plot as this – a plot founded, necessarily, in an extensive plan of revolution – . . . could be influenced by the price of a small metal tube? or that a few shillings one way, or a few shillings the other, could be at all an object?' It was clear that the conspirators knew nothing of compressed air – they were ignorant of the very principles of the machine which they were to use.

The Old Bailey in session (*c.* 1800). Note the position of counsel's table below the bench; the dock, with the mirror over the prisoner's head so that his expression could be observed; and the desks, presumably for the shorthand writers, opposite the witness box (Museum of London)

As for Crossfield himself, he had assumed no feigned name. He had gone to Bristol, a port from whence he could have embarked for anywhere in the world had he wished to escape. He had then gone to Portsmouth, the most frequented seaport in the country, and a town where there was, 'to the honour of the chief magistrate let it be spoken, the best regulated police that exists in any town in the kingdom'. He had gone ashore at Falmouth, a small town with only one street, where no one can conceal himself, but the resort of the king's messengers: 'the very persons sent to apprehend those accused of treason'.

Adam still had to deal with the declarations that his client was alleged to have made while he was a prisoner, and he prefaced this part of his address with a quotation from Blackstone:

> But hasty, unguarded confessions, made to persons having no authority, ought not to be *admitted* under [the Treason Act]; and indeed, even in cases of felony, at the common law, they are the weakest and most suspicious of all testimony – ever liable to be obtained by artifice, false hopes, and promises of favour, or menaces – seldom remembered accurately or reported with due precision, and incapable in their nature of being disproved by other negative evidence.[4]

So he commented on Winter, the old man who had come to give testimony to these grave declarations, where soundness of judgment, and accuracy of memory, constituted a most important quality, 'who told you as a matter of his firm belief the incredible story of the hare having lived amidst the dogs, without being touched by them'.

And so he entreated the jury to acquit his client.

The defence first called four members of the London Corresponding Society to describe the quarrel that had developed between Upton and his fellow-members: James Parkinson, a surgeon and apothecary of Hoxton Square; John Bone, a muslin cleaner of No. 8 Western Street, Southwark; John Huttley, a spring-maker of Great Sutton Street, Clerkenwell; and William Brown. Parkinson started to tell the court that the society had instituted an inquiry to ascertain the truth of a report that Upton had set his house in Coldbath Fields on fire, but Eyre CJ would have none of this: 'You do not mean, I hope, to detail to this Court the proceedings of such a committee upon a charge which ought to be heard here and not there.'

Bone described a violent quarrel on 4 September when a letter from Upton was read which 'threw the whole assembly into a very great degree of agitation'. This was the occasion when Upton broke out into a stream of abuse and Higgins told the chairman that he must be quick as Upton was hopping off. And Messrs Huttley and Brown described Upton as a dishonest and very dangerous man.

It is not clear whether the defence intended to call any more witnesses on this issue, but the Attorney-General called a halt: 'I have no objection to any of these orators; I am ready to admit that Upton is what he stated himself to be, when he brought forward such a charge in which he was an accomplice; that he was as bad a man as you please; and I have no objection to your taking his motive to be as malicious as you please.'

The next witnesses had been prisoners with the defendant at Brest. John Cleverton was an agent for a house in St John Street and had been going out to the Canaries 'for wines for government' when he was captured. He had been on the same ship as Crossfield from 19 February to 18 or 19 May when he was taken ill and transferred to hospital until July. He and Crossfield had been in the same mess along with Captain Clarke, Captain Bligh, Mr Denton (who was Bligh's mate), and Mr Widdiman, the mate of his own ship. The defendant was very jolly and drank hard and often sung republican songs, but he never said anything about any plot – in the mess, they always called him Doctor. It was in cross-examination that the Attorney-General elicited that the 'republican song' was 'The Tree of Liberty',[5] and this was then read by Mr Skelton, the Clerk of Arraigns:

> See, Britons, see that rising beam,
> The Eastern skies adorning;
> 'Tis freedom's sun begins to gleam,
> And wakes a glorious morning.
> Now despotism from France is chas'd,
> And church illusions vanish'd,
> Ne'er let them in our isle be plac'd,
> But far from Britain banish'd.
>
> CHORUS:
>
> Plant, plant the tree, fair freedom's tree,
> Midst danger, wounds, and slaughter;
> Each patriot's breast its soil shall be,
> And tyrant's blood its water.

They come, they come, see myriads come,
From Gallia to invade us;
Seize, seize the pike, beat, beat the drum,
They come, my friends, to aid us.
Let trembling despots fly the land,
To shun impending danger;
We'll stretch forth a fraternal hand,
To hail each glorious stranger.

Chorus: Plant, plant the tree, etc.

That palace which for ages past,
To despots was appointed;
The sovereign people claim at last,
For they're the Lord's anointed.
The useless Crown which long adorn'd,
The brows of Royal Ninnies;
To nobler purposes is turn'd,
Coin'd into useful guineas.

Chorus: Plant, plant the tree, etc.

Those high nicknames Lord, Duke, and Earl,
Which set the croud a gazing;
Are priz'd as hogs esteem a pearl,
Their patents set a blazing.
No more they vote away our wealth,
To please a King or Queen, Sir;
Now glad to pack away by stealth,
To 'scape the Guillotine, Sir.

Chorus: Plant, plant the tree, etc.

Our Commons too who say forsooth,
They represent the nation;
Must scamper East, West, North, and South,
To 'scape our indignation.
Their Speaker's mace to current coin,
We presently shall alter;
And ribbands late so gay and fine,
We'll change for each an halter.

Chorus: Plant, plant the tree, etc.

On holy mummeries our boys,
Contemptuously shall trample;
And yonder dome that props the sky,
Shall turn to Reason's temple.
Then cá ira, each corps shall sing,
To chear the broken hearted;
And Priestcrafts bells no more shall ring,
To thund'ring guns converted.

Chorus: Plant, plant the tree, etc.

Behold the Bank its specious trash,
Unworthy our regarding;
Mere paper wealth, ideal cash,
Whole pounds not worth a farthing.
The Stocks like vapours on the hills,
Shall vanish from our sight, Sir;
And Abraham Newland's swindling bills,[6]
May cover paper kites, Sir.

Chorus: Plant, plant the tree, etc.

Those Lawyers see, with face of brass,
And wigs replete with learning;
Whose far-fetch'd apophthegms surpass,
Republicans discerning.
For them to ancient forms be stanch,
To suit such worthy fellows;
Oh, spare for them one legal branch,
I mean, reserve the gallows.

Chorus: Plant, plant the tree, etc.

'Tis done, the glorious work is done,
Rejoice with one another;
To plowshares beat the sword and gun,
For each man is his brother.
Detested war shall ever cease,
In kind fraternization;
For all is harmony and peace,
And all the world one nation.

Chorus: Plant, plant the tree, etc.

Anthony Collins, the next witness, had commanded one of the prison ships at Brest. He told the court that when he heard there was a doctor on one of the other ships, he asked the commandant's permission to invite him on board his own to take care of the sick prisoners, which he did with great skill and saved fifty or sixty lives. However, he agreed that they drank a good deal – 'Did the glass go pretty freely round?' – 'Our situation was such, that for want of better employment it did so.' Crossfield never mentioned any plots against His Majesty or the government, but he did remember Winter's stories.

'Oh yes, a number of silly foolish things he used to tell . . . one was, of his catching the devil in the shape of a hare, and such ridiculous nonsense as that.'

'Did he say, that he took this hare for the devil?'

'He certainly did; and was very much displeased when we contradicted him.'

'. . . He was, in short, a man who dealt in the marvellous?'

'He did; and he was the common laughing stock of the whole of the ship's crew. . . . I have known him myself, walking the deck, and talking to himself the whole night . . .'

In cross-examination by Law, the witness said that he had no recollection of Crossfield singing 'The Tree of Liberty', or for that matter 'God Save the King', but they used to sing 'Rule Britannia'. In re-examination he told the court that the prison commandant had ordered Crossfield to stay in France to superintend the hospital at Landernau, but he had refused to comply as he wished to return to England.

Towards the close of the case, Adam called five witnesses as to the character of his client. Elizabeth Watson, of Dyer's Buildings, said that the defendant had lodged with her for two months from 26 July 1794 – he passed under his own name and had nothing locked away while he was in her house. Margaret Beasley had known him intimately for four years – he was a humane, good-natured man. Mr Wyld, a surgeon from the Kent Road, had known him for three years – he was a man of good character. Simon Wilson, a surveyor from Dorset, had known him 'ever since I remember anything . . . I always thought him an exceedingly good man . . . I never thought he would commit the least crime'. Mr Hepburn, another surgeon who lived in Great Hermitage Street, had known him for four years and attended the family where he lodged – he was a very good-natured man.

In the autumn of 1794 John Gurney, the son of Joseph Gurney the shorthand writer, had been briefed as assistant counsel for the defence at the trials of Hardy and Horne Tooke. He had taken no active part in the proceedings, no doubt busily engaged in taking a note of evidence to assist his father as well as his client. He was now the junior counsel for Crossfield, and he addressed the court in a speech which lasted about an hour and a half, and in substance repeated the arguments which his leader had employed earlier that day.

At the end of his speech Eyre CJ asked the defendant whether he wished to say anything himself, to which he replied: 'My lord and gentlemen of the jury, I have nothing to add to what has been already stated by my counsel, except, that however, occasionally, I may have appeared imprudent in words or in actions, I am totally incapable of the atrocious crime laid to my charge. Farther I say not, but rest my case satisfied with my own innocence and the justice of an English jury.'

The Attorney-General had opened the case for the Crown, and he now replied on behalf of the Crown. The gist of his argument was that the plan to make a brass tube was an overt act, and the defendant's intention was demonstrated by what he had said to his fellow-prisoners. He stressed that Crossfield could not have had any information relating to the tube and the plan to assassinate the king, except from his own knowledge. Immediately he closed his speech, however, Adam stood up to state that his learned junior had pointed out to him an explanation for their client's knowledge of the airgun and of the conspiracy: 'immediately upon the apprehension of Smith, Higgins, and le Maitre, all the circumstances to which Upton had deposed were published in the newspapers'. The Attorney-General conceded, 'I do not know the fact; but it is very probable,' and Grose J. added, 'I dare say they were.'

Eyre CJ now summed up. After a brief reference to the law, he repeated at length all the evidence of the witnesses, mostly, at this stage, without comment, although he did remark upon Winter's story of the hare: 'he gave us some particulars of that story, and that certainly raises a considerable degree of doubt whether this man is perfectly and entirely to be depended upon, in respect of his capacity, the story was certainly a foolish one, though not absolutely impossible to be true . . . even though there should be no reason to doubt but that he means to speak the truth'. His evidence, if it stood alone, would hardly suffice for a verdict of Guilty.

When he mentioned the song, 'The Tree of Liberty', he commented: 'it were better that such songs should have no circulation; a more flagrant seditious song, aiming more directly at the whole constitution of the government of this country . . . could not have been composed: it was truly said by Mr Attorney-General, that it was an epitome of every thing that could be imagined to be sedition'.

When he came to comment on the case as a whole, the judge was clearly arguing for a conviction. There could really be no doubt that it was Crossfield who had gone with Upton to the brass-founders and Hill, the wood turner, and had participated in their conversations. Also, because of what he had said when he was a prisoner, it was difficult to avoid inferring that Crossfield was a party to the conspiracy. 'A man may have a bad habit of talking very wildly and extravagantly, but to account for these declarations without imputing guilt, there must be an impression upon the mind of the prisoner almost to insanity.' Then there was the evidence of his attempt to bribe the officers who were taking him to gaol – his conduct appeared difficult to be reconciled with his innocence.

Eyre CJ reminded the jury that the defence had called many witnesses to the prisoner's good character. He was good-natured and humane, and he had devoted himself to the care of his fellow prisoners:

> I can only say with respect to this, that in some cases good habits, manners, and principles are tainted and corrupted by circumstances; and I am afraid that nothing has done more towards corrupting them than the effusion of modern political principles, which have unsettled men's minds, and have prepared them to conceive that new duties belong to them . . . whether any such circumstances have entered into this business or no I do not know; this man was in a situation, certainly, to be deeply tinctured with republican notions: and they could not be carried into the excess into which they are carried in that song – that execrable composition, which was laid before you – without a dereliction of all principle, without a man's having by degrees prepared himself to become, from a humane, tender, good-hearted man, capable of doing friendly offices and bearing his part in the society in which he lives – to become a downright monster – not a citizen, not a man, but, I repeat, a downright monster.

Nevertheless, it was not for him, said the judge, to interfere in the province of the jury, and he left it to them to decide whether the evidence was sufficient to satisfy them of its truth.

The jury withdrew at 6 p.m.; they returned at 7.40 p.m. with a verdict of Not Guilty and the prisoner was immediately discharged. No further proceedings were taken against the other members of the conspiracy.

CHAPTER EIGHT

The Cato Street Conspiracy: the Trial of Arthur Thistlewood (1820)

Many strange tales have been told in the Old Bailey, but few are as strange as the story which was unfolded there one morning in April 1820.

The number of men who were actively involved in the Cato Street Conspiracy fluctuated from time to time, but there seems to have been a hard core of about twenty, of whom eleven were put on trial.

Arthur Thistlewood was regarded as the ringleader. He had been born in 1774; he had for a time been a lieutenant in the army, but was a radical and a revolutionary, and was often in debt. In 1816 he had organized a mass meeting at Spa Fields in connection with a plan to seize the Tower and the Bank of England, and as a result he was prosecuted for treason; the principal witness for the Crown was a man called Castle, a government spy, and it was probably owing to the jury's disgust at the spy rather than the weakness of the evidence that Thistlewood was acquitted.

An Accurate View of the Inside of the Court of King's Bench, Westminster,
WITH THE PRISONERS,
WATSON, PRESTON, THISTLEWOOD, and HOOPER,
At the Bar, at the time of their Trial.

The first trial of Arthur Thistlewood, 1816; Thistlewood and the three other men named here were put on trial for treason and acquitted (Westminster City Archives)

James Ings had been a butcher in Portsmouth; his business flourished during the Napoleonic War, but afterwards it failed and he left his wife and four children there and came to London and opened a coffee shop; but this too failed, and he became destitute. William Davidson, a negro – a 'man of colour', as he was described – was the son of the Attorney-General of Jamaica, and had for a time been a law student at Edinburgh University; he fell in love with a wealthy sixteen year old girl, but her father sent her to a distant part of the country where she married another man; after that, his career went steadily downhill, and he acquired a reputation for indecently assaulting girls; in 1820 he was employed as a cabinet-maker.

The others included John Brunt and Richard Tidd, who were both shoemakers; John Harrison, who had been in the army; and James Wilson, Richard Bradburn, John Strange, James Gilchrist and Charles Cooper.

Two other men must be mentioned. One was Robert Adams; he was a member of the conspiracy but gave evidence for the Crown, and most of what is known of the scheme came from him. The other was George Edwards, who was undoubtedly a government spy and an *agent provocateur*.

Thistlewood lived in Stanhope Street, Clare Market, and Brunt in Fox Court, Gray's Inn Lane. The latter was lodging in a house kept by Mr and Mrs Rogers, who lived on the first floor with their niece and children. Brunt himself lived with his wife and an apprentice, Joseph Hale, on the second floor. Sometime in January 1820 Ings also hired a room in Fox Court, but it was never furnished and he never slept there.

Adams, who lived at No. 4 Hole-in-the-wall Passage, Brook's Market, joined the conspiracy in January 1820. He had at one time served in the Horse Guards and had met Brunt in France in 1816. It appears that Brunt and Ings invited him to meet Thistlewood in Stanhope Street early in 1820. As soon as they met, Thistlewood said, 'I presume you are a good swordsman,' to which Adams replied that he was out of practice. Thereupon Thistlewood started to condemn the 'genteel people' of the country, and 'as to the shopkeepers of London', they were a set of aristocrats altogether and were all working under one system of government, and he should glory to see the day when all the shops were shut up and plundered.

During the next few weeks Adams attended various meetings in a public house, the White Hart in Brook's Market, but towards the end of January it was decided that it would be safer to meet in Fox Court. It soon became clear to Adams that the conspirators were planning to assassinate the entire cabinet, preferably when they were all together at a cabinet dinner. However, after the death of George III on 29 January, a new proposal was put forward, namely to make an insurrection on the day of his funeral. Most of the troops would be in Windsor for the ceremony, and it would be a very suitable opportunity to 'kick up a row'. They would take two pieces of cannon from Gray's Inn Lane and six others from the Artillery Ground. They would set up a cannon in Hyde Park to prevent any message being sent to Windsor, and if the troops did return to London they would be too tired to do anything. They would also set up a provisional government, and send down to the seaports – Dover, Ramsgate, Margate, Brighton – to prevent anyone from leaving the country without a passport from the provisional government. As for the new king: 'we cannot think of his ever wearing the crown, the present family have inherited the crown long enough'. After some discussion, however, it was decided that they did not have enough men to put this plan into effect.

Adams did not attend a meeting again until Saturday 19 February. Several conspirators were present, and they seemed depressed and decided that they could not wait any longer. Thistlewood told Brunt to go round and collect his men for a meeting on the following morning and to tell them to bring their arms with them in case any officers should come on the scene, to which Brunt replied: 'Damn my eyes, if any officers was to come into this room I would run them through, and murder them, and take care after I had done it, I should never be found out.'

There was a heavy snowfall and thick fog the following day, Sunday, and it was so dark in the room at Fox Court that when Adams arrived he could hardly see who was there. After they had been talking a while, Thistlewood said it was time to begin the business. There were twelve present and Thistlewood said that was enough to form a committee; Richard Tidd was elected chairman, and he sat with a pike in his hand, with Thistlewood and Brunt standing on either side of him. They then decided that if there was no cabinet dinner before Wednesday, they would try to murder the ministers separately in their own homes, and content themselves with getting three or four. They would fetch the cannon from Gray's Inn and the Artillery Ground, take the Mansion House as the seat of the provisional government and attempt to take the Bank of England and set fire to some buildings. A man called Palin seems to have been regarded as the expert in raising fires, and when he came in later he was asked to go to see if he could set fire to Furnival's Inn, which was close by. So he and Brunt went out and returned about ten minutes later, saying it was very easily done and would make a 'damned good fire'.

Then Thistlewood said that he would like to give the men a treat on the Tuesday or Wednesday, but they were so poor that he did not know how this could be done. Brunt said he had a pound note and would spend it on the men, and they discussed

An early nineteenth-century picture of Grosvenor Square, which was to have been the scene of an assassination by the Cato Street conspirators of the entire cabinet at a dinner-party (Museum of London)

hiring a room below stairs at the White Hart, but nothing seems to have come of this proposal.

Now it so happened that the Earl of Harrowby, the Lord President of the Council, decided to hold a cabinet dinner at his house in Grosvenor Square on the evening of Wednesday 23 February.[1] It was the first cabinet dinner since the death of George III, and he sent invitations to the entire cabinet: Lord Liverpool (Prime Minister and First Lord of the Treasury), Lord Eldon (Lord Chancellor), Mr Vansittart (Chancellor of the Exchequer), Earl Bathurst (Secretary of State for the Colonial Department), Lord Sidmouth (Secretary of State for the Home Department), Lord Castlereagh (Secretary of State for the Foreign Department), the Earl of Westmoreland (Lord Privy Seal), Lord Melville (First Lord of the Admiralty), the Duke of Wellington (Master General of the Ordnance), Mr Canning (First Commissioner of the India Board), Mr Robinson (President of the Board of Trade), Mr Bathurst (Chancellor of the Duchy of Lancaster), Mr Wellesley Pole (Master of the Mint), and the Earl of Mulgrave.

An announcement of this dinner was published in the press, and on the Tuesday Edwards came to the Fox Court meeting and told Thistlewood that there was to be a cabinet dinner on the following day. Thistlewood said he did not believe this could be true, so he sent out for a newspaper, and the announcement was read out, upon which Brunt exclaimed: 'Now I will be damned, if I do not believe there is a God; I have often prayed that those thieves may be collected all together, in order to give us a good opportunity to destroy them, and now God has answered my prayer.' Thistlewood immediately proposed that a committee should be set up to form a fresh plan for the assassination.

They arranged to set a watch on Lord Harrowby's house, two men at a time throughout the evening to see if any soldiers went there. Then Thistlewood outlined the plan for the attack, which he had evidently thought up within a matter of minutes. He himself would go to the door on the pretext of having a note for his lordship. When the door was opened his men would rush in and take command of the stairs, others would go into the room where the cabinet were at dinner and fling in hand-grenades, and others were to be stationed nearby, to throw in another grenade if anyone attempted to retreat from the lower part of the house.

Ings now intervened, saying that he would go in, supported by two swordsmen, with a brace of pistols, a cutlass and a knife to cut off every head in the room. He would call out: 'Well my lords, I have got as good men here as the Manchester Yeomanry,' – a clear reference to the 'Manchester Massacre'[2] – and he would bring away the heads of Lord Castlereagh and Lord Sidmouth in two bags which he would provide for the purpose. Thistlewood appointed Harrison as one of the swordsmen, and asked Adams if he would be the other. On seeing no chance of escape, and knowing his own life would be in danger if he refused, Adams agreed.

On leaving Grosvenor Square Harrison was to go to the King Street Barracks. He knew the premises well and would be able to gain accesss through a window at the back, which led to a loft where straw and hay were kept. He was to set this on fire to cause consternation among the troops and prevent them from getting themselves and their horses accoutred. The cannon from Gray's Inn Lane and the Artillery Ground were to be taken to the Mansion House, and if the Mansion House did not surrender at once they would fire upon it from both sides. They would attack the Bank of England and plunder it – but they would keep the books to enable them 'to see further into the villainy that had been practised in the country for some years past'.

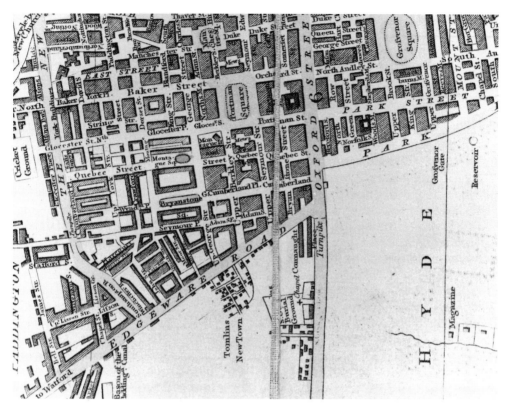

An early nineteenth-century map showing Grosvenor Square and Cato Street, near the Edgeware Road, between John Street and Queen Street. After the conspiracy, Cato Street was for a time renamed Horace Street, but then reverted to its original name, by which it is still known (Museum of London)

The meeting was on the point of dispersing when Harrison thought they should have a password, which was to be 'button'. If anyone was accosted, he was to say the letters 'b, u, t' to which the other person, if one of the conspirators, would reply 't, o, n'. This arrangement seems to have been accepted.

The conspirators had managed to acquire a considerable quantity of arms and ammunition (believed to have been financed by Edwards), which was stored at Tidd's home next door to Adams. Thistlewood called it his depot, and as this was some distance from Grosvenor Square they decided to try to find somewhere nearer for their rendezvous, and they were able to secure a building in Cato Street. Although called a street, it was more of an alley or mews, between John Steet and Queen Street, which both led off from the Edgeware Road. It was accessible to a horse and carriage at one end, through an archway, and there were posts at the other end to prevent access to anyone other than pedestrians.

The first building on the right, as one entered Cato Street from John Street, was a stable, opposite a small public house called the Horse and Groom. It was owned by General Watson, and had been occupied by a man called Firth who had kept five cows there, but he had recently let it to Harrison. The ground floor consisted of three stalls and a small room for a cart. A ladder led up into a loft, the main part being fifteen feet five inches long and ten feet ten inches wide, with two small side rooms over the carthouse.

Throughout the Tuesday and Wednesday, the conspirators were completing their preparations.

When Adams went back to Fox Court on the Tuesday evening, he noticed a strange smell and found Ings and two other men making fuses for hand-grenades, and dipping yarn into an iron pot containing tar for making 'illumination balls' or fire-balls. These were incendiary devices to be thrown into buildings. The hand-grenades were made by enclosing three or four ounces of powder in a tin case, to which a tube was attached for the fuse. Round the tin was tied a quantity of tow, to which was fastened, as tight as may be, sharp pieces of iron, so that when the tin exploded the pieces of iron would be scattered in all directions. The intention was that when the attacking party entered the dining-room at Lord Harrowby's house, the fuses would be lighted and the grenades thrown at the ministers.

Adams went back again on the Wednesday and saw Brunt with two pistols, and he and Strange were fitting the flints in them. He also saw several blunderbusses and cutlasses. Thistlewood asked him how he was, and he said that he was in very low spirits, so Thistlewood asked him if he wanted something to drink and sent for some beer for him. Then Thistlewood said that he wanted to write out a notice, and Brunt gave Joseph Hale, his apprentice, a shilling and sent him out to buy some paper. When he returned, Thistlewood said that he would write out three bills to stick on the buildings which were to be set on fire so that the public should know what they were doing, and he wrote out the following: 'Your tyrants are destroyed. The friends of liberty are called upon to come forward. The provisional government is now sitting. James Ings, secretary, 23 February, 1820.' By the time he had written out these three bills, Thistlewood was extremely agitated and tired, and was unable to write any more.

Ings was preparing himself to enter the room where the ministers would be dining: he put a black belt round his waist for a brace of pistols, another black belt to hang a cutlass to his shoulder, and two large bags, like soldiers' haversacks, one from each shoulder. Then he viewed himself and exclaimed: 'Damn my eyes! I am not complete now. I have forgot my steel!' He produced a large, broad-bladed knife, about twelve inches long; the handle was bound with a wax-end,[3] and he said 'in doing the thing his hand should not slip'. Some of the others were arming themselves, and putting cutlasses into slings, to hang by their wrists. Brunt said that they should all take something to drink with them, but one man said: 'I hope you are not going to drunkenness, because drunkenness in a thing like this was of no good; because a man drunk the only service he is of is to run himself into the hands of his enemies.' Adams also saw some hand-grenades and flannel bags for cartridges for the cannon, and there were poles ready to receive pikes, and bayonets.

They brought their arms and weapons to Cato Street. In addition to the grenades and fire-balls, they had collected some 1,200 ball cartridges, and cartridges for loading cannon, made of flannel bags each containing about a pound of powder. They had no cannon-balls, but were planning to smash up some iron railings and fire the fragments instead.

One man who had been a conspirator for a short time was a cowman called Thomas Hiden. He had met James Wilson in the street sometime in the middle of February, and Wilson put a proposition to him – he asked him if he would come forward to destroy His Majesty's ministers. Wilson gave him some details of the plan, and he agreed to join. Instead, however, he approached Lord Harrowby when he was riding in the park and gave him a message to be passed on to Lord Castlereagh.

Cato Street in 1820. The street has since been largely rebuilt but No. 1a has been preserved and now has a plaque stating: 'Cato Street conspirators discovered here; 23 February 1820.' (Westminster City Archives)

On the afternoon of 23 February Hiden was walking home, holding the hand of his little daughter, when he met Wilson again who said that there was going to be a cabinet dinner that night, and told him to go to the Horse and Groom in Cato Street by about 6 o'clock that evening. Wilson said that there would be other 'parties' in the borough and Gray's Inn Lane, and another in Gee's Court where there was a colony of Irishmen. Hiden went to Cato Street at about 7 o'clock, saw Wilson and Davidson, and they told him that they would be setting out for Grosvenor Square at about eight. Hiden, however, said that he had to go for some cream. Before he left, they told him to come back to Cato Street, but if he was too late, to go straight to Grosvenor Square.

It was also alleged that the conspirators had tried to involve the Irish.

Thomas Dwyer lived at No. 15 Gee's Court, near Oxford Street. Sometime in the second week of February he had met Davidson who introduced him to Thistlewood, who commented that Ireland was in a disturbed state at that time. No more was said on that occasion, but on the morning of 23 February Davidson came to Dwyer's house and took him to Fox Court, where Harrison showed him a grenade and various other weapons. Thistlewood was also there and said that a grenade was to be thrown into the horse barracks and into Lord Harrowby's, and they told Dwyer about the cabinet dinner. Thistlewood asked Dwyer how many of his countrymen he could muster, and he said about twenty-five or twenty-six. He was told to assemble them at the Horse and Groom, but he himself was to be at the Pomfret Castle at the end of Barrat's Court at six o'clock. This was a house frequented by Irishmen, especially on Saturday nights when they went there for a pint of porter. Thistlewood then told him to take some of the best of his men to the Foundling Hospital, knock at the porter's lodge and put a pistol to his breast. There, just beside the lodge, he would find a stand of firearms. However, soon after Dwyer left Fox Court, he consulted a Major James, who advised him to go to the Secretary of State, which he did at about 1.30 p.m.

The government had had their suspicions for some time that something was afoot, and now the dinner was cancelled. The preparations for it continued, however, until about eight in the evening in order to make it appear that nothing had been discovered. In the meantime, the police and the army were instructed to take the necessary steps to deal with the conspiracy.

Sometime in the evening Adams started out from Fox Court, armed with a blunderbuss; Brunt went with him with a broomstick ready prepared to receive a bayonet. Somewhere on the way to Cato Street they became separated, and Adams turned round to go home, but he met Brunt again and, finding no excuse to leave him, walked with him towards the Edgeware Road where they met Thistlewood.

On arriving at Cato Street, Adams saw Davidson and Harrison in the stable, and when he climbed up the ladder to the loft he found Thistlewood, Brunt and Ings, and several other men he did not know. He thought there were about twenty altogether. In the loft was a carpenter's bench, on which were candles and some beer, and by the window there was a chest or trunk. Tidd was also there and asked whether any of the ministers had gone to Lord Harrowby's house. Thistlewood left the loft and after a time Adams heard talking downstairs, so he went down the ladder, and they were 'all in a bustle' and said what good news they had. When Adams asked them what the news was, Thistlewood replied that the carriages were getting there as fast as they could, no less than six or seven carriages, he said, had already arrived. (In fact, the Archbishop of York, who had a house next door to Lord Harrowby, was also entertaining guests that night, and no doubt it was their carriages that had been seen.) Brunt exclaimed: 'Damn my eyes! what a haul we shall have amongst them.'

Strange though it may appear, the conspirators seem to have been so carried away with their enthusiasm that hardly anyone questioned the feasibility of their enterprise. It appeared, however, that Tidd was becoming anxious, but Ings said: 'Do not think of dropping it now; if you do, I shall hang myself, I shall go mad.' Thistlewood counted the men – there were eighteen in the loft and two downstairs – and he said there were plenty: fourteen would be sufficient to go into the room, and the other six to take care of the servants. He then picked fourteen men to one side of the room, and Brunt pulled a bottle of gin out of his pocket and said: 'Now I conceive this number of men is quite sufficient.' Thistlewood said: 'Supposing Lord Harrowby should have sixteen servants; they are not prepared, we are; we can go and do what we have to do and off, in ten minutes time.'

It was at that moment that the police arrived.

Soon after 8 o'clock that evening Lieutenant Fitzclarence[4] of the Coldstream Guards took up a position with a picket of men at the John Street end of Cato Street. At the same time, George Ruthven, a couple of 'conductors'[5] and several other constables from the public office at Bow Street, about a dozen altogether, also arrived on the scene. They assembled at the Horse and Groom, and while they were sitting there, Cooper and Gilchrist came in with a broomstick. They left it behind, but the boy of the inn, who had noticed that it was cut at one end as if to receive a pike, removed it, so it had gone when they came back to fetch it.

The murder of police officer Richard Smithers by Thistlewood in the loft over the stable in Cato Street; from a painting by Cruikshank, who was taken to the scene a few days after the event
(British Museum)

When all the officers were there, at about 8.30 p.m., Ruthven led them into the stable. Seeing a man with a gun on his shoulder, he told his constables to secure him. James Ellis, one of the conductors, took hold of his collar, and saw that he was Davidson, a 'man of colour'; evidently, however, he released him. Ruthven himself climbed up the ladder, immediately followed by Ellis, Luke Nixon and Richard Smithers. On reaching the loft and looking inside, Ruthven saw, he thought, about twenty-five men, and he immediately called out: 'We are officers,' and then, to his own men: 'Seize their arms!' He recognized Thistlewood: he had known Thistlewood since the previous trial in 1817, and had been keeping him under observation for five or six weeks. Thistlewood was standing by the bench, and when he saw Ruthven he seized a sword and backed towards one of the side rooms leading off from the loft. Ellis held out his staff to him and, when he threatened him with his sword, held up his pistol and said he would fire. At that moment Smithers rushed towards Thistlewood who thrust his sword at him, and Smithers collapsed saying, 'Oh my God, I am done for!' and died instantly.

At this there was confusion. The candles were put out; somebody called: 'Kill the b——s [*sic*], throw them downstairs!' and Ruthven heard a rush towards the ladder and cries of 'kill them'. Another conductor, William Westcoatt, who had stayed at the bottom of the ladder, saw Ings and took him by the collar. They were struggling against a wall and Westcoatt hit Ings on the head. While he was getting a pair of handcuffs ready, a crowd came tumbling down the ladder. Thistlewood was one of them and he presented a pistol to Westcoatt's head, who put a hand up to defend himself, but Thistlewood fired, very close to his head. He was a very lucky man: the ball grazed his hand and made three holes in his hat – he showed it to the jury at the trial. Westcoatt was then struck on the head and fell down. He saw Thistlewood trying to strike him with a sword, then Thistlewood fled, and by the time Westcoatt could follow, he had disappeared. Ings also ran away. Nixon fell backwards down the ladder and injured his leg and his head, but he recovered sufficiently to pursue Ings.

Constable John Wright had started to climb the ladder when he was knocked back, but he turned round and saw a man, presumably Ings, who had something shining under his coat. Wright was able to take it and found it was a sword, but Ings also had his butcher's knife with the handle tied round with wax-end. At that moment Wright was knocked down and stabbed in the side. He was able to get up again, but when he reached the stable door, some soldiers, who had now arrived on the scene, stopped him, but he persuaded Lieutenant Fitzclarence that he was an officer, and they went into the stable and arrested Wilson and Bradburn.

Ings managed to run as far as John Street, where he was accosted by William Brooks, another constable. Brooks said, 'You scoundrel,' and Ings said, 'I will shoot you.' Ings had a pistol in his hand and Brooks tried to snatch it when Ings fired. Brooks was another lucky man: the shot passed through his coat and his waistcoat, bruised his shoulder, and went out by the back of his neck. Brooks staggered back, but was able to pursue Ings, and now Giles Moay, a nightwatchman who was on his beat in the Edgeware Road, joined in and struck at him with his stick and helped to arrest him. When they searched him they found he had two haversacks, one slung over his shoulder, the other over his arm, but hidden by his greatcoat. He also had two brace of pistols still on his belt, and a tin full of powder.

In the meantime Ruthven had managed to climb down the ladder. He ran to John Street where he met the soldiers, and they went back together to the stable while shots were being fired all round. He saw Tidd, caught his right arm, and fell with him into a dung heap and some soldiers came and secured him. They took him to the Horse and Groom and searched him and found that he was wearing a leather belt, and had two ball cartridges in his pocket. Bradburn was brought in and also searched: he had some string round his waist to serve as a belt and six ball cartridges. Davidson was brought in, damning and swearing against anyone who would not die in the cause of liberty, and he started to sing: 'Scots wha' ha' wi' Wallace bled.'

While this was going on, Adams had retreated into one of the side rooms by the loft, and when he saw the coast was clear he climbed down the ladder and through the stable – 'as unquashed as if nothing had been the matter' – and went home.

Lieutenant Fitzclarence and his picket were now on the scene. After securing some of the men in the stable, he called a file of grenadiers to follow him up the ladder. Immediately he reached the top he fell against the body of poor Smithers, and he arrested four or five more men without a struggle. Ruthven also returned to the loft to search it, and found two swords and a bag containing ten hand-grenades with their fuses in.

Brunt had managed to escape, but on the following morning Samuel Taunton from Bow Street went to Fox Court with a warrant for his arrest. He arrested Brunt and searched his rooms, but found nothing of significance there. He then searched the back room which had been occupied by Ings, and there he found an iron pot with remains of tar in it and two rush baskets, one of which was tied up in an apron. In the baskets he found some papers with rope yarn and tar, and some steel filings, and he also found four grenades, and two one-pound bags of powder.

He then proceeded to Tidd's house in the Hole-in-the-wall, where he found a large box full of cartridges, 965 of them, another 171 cartridges and about three pounds of powder in a haversack, ten grenades and eleven one-pound bags of powder wrapped in coarse canvas cloth, ten empty flannel bags, and various other weapons.

Thistlewood had escaped from Cato Street and did not return home, but on the following morning, between 10 and 11 a.m., Daniel Bishop, another Bow Street officer, accompanied by Stephen Lavender, found him at No. 8, White Street, Little Moorfields. Bishop obtained the key to a ground-floor room from the landlady and opened the door. The room was in darkness, but light was coming in through some holes in the shutters and he saw Thistlewood in bed. Bishop, with a pistol in one hand and his staff in the other, told Thistlewood that he had a warrant for his arrest, and immediately threw himself upon the bed, whereupon Thistlewood said that he would make no resistance. Bishop and Lavender searched his coat and waistcoat, which were lying beside the bed, and found a belt with places to hold pistols, and some balls and flint.

Within a few weeks a Special Commission was appointed to inquire into the events of 23 February 1820. The commission consisted of Sir Charles Abbott (Chief Justice of the Court of King's Bench), Sir Robert Dallas (Chief Justice of the Court of Common Pleas), Sir Richard Richards (Chief Baron of the Court of Exchequer), Mr Justice Richardson, and the Common Serjeant. The proceedings opened before a grand jury on 27 March, and on the following day they found a true bill for High Treason against Thistlewood and ten other men. On the following day, on separate indictments, Thistlewood and many of the others were charged with the murder of Richard Smithers, and with shooting at the police officers.

On Saturday 15 April, at the Old Bailey, the prisoners were arraigned. All the prisoners pleaded Not Guilty to all the charges (except for Wilson, who claimed that he had been wrongly named in the indictment, which was subsequently amended). When asked how he would be tried, Ings, instead of answering in the usual form – 'By God and my country' – said, 'By the laws of Reason.' When the governor of Newgate (who was presumably standing near the dock) remonstrated with him, he said, 'By God and my country – the laws of reason are the laws of my country.' Ings also intimated that he wished to be tried separately, and the Attorney-General said that he also desired separate trials, and that he proposed first to proceed against Thistlewood. Counsel, who had been nominated by the accused, were then formally assigned to represent them, and the case was adjourned until 9 a.m. on Monday 17 April.

At the trial of Thistlewood,[6] the Crown was represented by Sir Robert Gifford A.-G., Sir John Copley S.-G. (the son of John Copley, the American artist), and Messrs Gurney, Littledale, Reynolds and Bolland, instructed by George Maule, the Treasury Solicitor. The defence was represented by Messrs Curwood and Adolphus, instructed by James Harmer. The sheriff had summoned about 150 jurors, many of whom were found to be ineligible on the ground that they were not freeholders to the amount of £10 a year. Many others were excused on the grounds of illness, deafness or age, or were challenged by the Crown or by the prisoner. Eventually, the following were sworn in:

Alexander Barclay, gentleman and grocer
Thomas Goodchild, esq.
T. Suffield Aldersey, esq.
James Herbert, carpenter
John Shuter, gentleman
Samuel Granger, lighterman
George Dickenson, builder
John Edward Shephard, gentleman
John Fowler, iron-plate-worker
William Gibbs Robert, cooper
John Dobson, esq.
William Cooper, gentleman

The trial of Thistlewood now commenced. Although he was being tried alone, all the other conspirators were kept in the dock so that they could be identified by the witnesses.

The Attorney-General spoke for about an hour and a half.[7] He explained the terms of the indictment: on count 1 Thistlewood was charged with compassing and imagining the deposition of the king, contrary to the Act of 1795 (which was still in force at the time, although due to expire at the end of the first session of parliament in the new reign). Count 2 was for compassing the death of the king, contrary to the Act of 1351, count 3 was for conspiring to levy war in order to compel the king to change his measures, contrary to the Act of 1795, and count 4 for levying war in the realm, contrary to the Act of 1351.

After he had outlined the facts which were to be proved against the defendant, the Attorney-General asked the jury to note two points. Firstly, he said that they were not to inquire whether the scheme was practicable, or whether it could ever have entered the minds of rational men. If they were satisfied that a plan had been formed for the purposes set out in the indictment, however wild and visionary it might appear, and if they were convinced that the defendants had taken any steps towards its accomplishment, then a verdict of Guilty would be justified. Secondly, he warned the jury to treat the testimony of Adams, an accomplice, with great caution, but added that it would be amply supported by other evidence.

Adams spent the rest of the first day of the trial in the witness box, and recounted the story which has already been set out.

Curwood started his cross-examination by asking Adams whether he had set out to Cato Street with the full intention of assassinating his majesty's ministers.

'No, I did not: I deny that.'

'What carried you there?'

'My legs.'

'Look at the jury will you. Your legs carried you there?'

'Yes.'

'What intention carried you there?'

'What intention? I certainly cannot say, but I went there under that pretension to every outward appearance.' But he added that his inward intention was against them.

Curwood extracted from Adams an admission that he had originally joined the conspiracy with the intention of assassinating the ministers, and also that he had gone to France in 1816 (where he met Brunt) because he was in debt in England.

He put it to the witness that he had decided to give evidence to save himself: 'You did not like to be hanged?'

'I do not know who would.'

'And you would rather thirteen men should be hanged on your evidence than that you should be hung yourself?'

'I only came here to give the truth; if it is against the prisoner I cannot help it.'

Adams also admitted that, although he had intended to give himself up to an officer after escaping from the Cato Street loft, he had found no one to whom he could surrender, so he went home.

At the end of the day, Adams may have appeared a rather shady character, but the evidence which he had given remained intact and unchallenged. It was now evening, and it was clear that the case could not be completed in a single day, so the court was adjourned until the following morning.

The fact that Adams had agreed to give evidence for the Crown made the prosecution case much easier, but there was much else besides.

There were the Monument brothers, John and Thomas. John was another accomplice. Towards the end of 1819 he had met Thistlewood who had told him: 'Great events are at hand, the people are every where ready for a change,' and on 23 February Brunt had come for him and taken him to Cato Street. Thomas was not an accomplice, but confirmed that Thistlewood had had a conversation with his brother.

John Morison was a cutler, and had ground a couple of swords for Ings during the winter.

Mary Rogers, Brunt's landlady at Fox Court, and her niece Eleanor Walker explained how a back room had been let to Ings, and Joseph Hale, Brunt's apprentice, gave much more detailed evidence about this.

Hale said that a number of persons came to Ings's room every evening and used to stay for two hours, and he was able to identify Ings, Thistlewood, Davidson and Tidd among others. There was no furniture in the room, so they took chairs from Brunt's own room. Although he did not normally enter the room himself, Hale heard hammering going on there, and once when the door was open he saw about twenty long poles. On 23 February some of the men came into his workshop with pistols and flints and started to put the flints in, but Brunt said that people would see them from across the road, and told them to go back to Ings's room. Hale confirmed that he had been sent out to buy some paper, and later that same evening, at teatime, Mrs Brunt asked for her table (which had also been taken into the back room) and when he went to fetch it for her, he noticed four or five men in the room. Mrs Brunt also showed him a pike and a sword in a cupboard in her own room.

According to Hale, Brunt himself came home at about 9 p.m. that night, dirty and confused. He told his wife that 'it was all up', then another man came in and Brunt asked him if he knew who had informed. The other man said that he had received a dreadful blow on the side. Later that evening, Brunt and Hale went into Ings's room and they wrapped up some grenades and other items into two baskets, and covered one of them with Mrs Brunt's blue apron, which had previously been used as a curtain on the window in the back room. The following morning Brunt asked Hale to take the baskets to somebody in the borough, but before he could set out two officers arrived and took his master into custody.

In cross-examination, Hale said that he was sure he had seen twenty poles in Ings's room, and that only one was left on the Wednesday morning.

There was also ample evidence of the activities of the conspirators in Cato Street. George Caylock, of No. 2 Cato Street, saw Harrison at the stable door. He had known him previously, and asked him what he was doing. Harrison said he had taken the stable and was cleaning it out. In the evening the witness saw several other men going in and out of the stable. Richard Mundy, of No. 3, knew Davidson, who had visited Firth when he kept his cows there. He had gone to the Horse and Groom for some beer when he saw Davidson get a light from a woman there, and then open the door. As he did so he stooped down and the witness noticed that he had a belt with two pistols in, and a sword which was sticking out under his coat. He went home and said to his wife, 'In the name of God——', but counsel told him he was not allowed to repeat what he had said to his wife. He too had seen several men going in and out of the stable, and a piece of sacking across the window of the loft. Elizabeth Weston lived at No. 1, and she had been watching her boys playing in the street when she saw someone unlock the stable door and go inside. Later she passed a 'man of colour' in the street, and when she had gone inside her house, Davidson came and knocked at her door and asked for a light for his candles.

At the end of the case for the Crown, after Samuel Taunton had produced all the weapons and ammunition that had been found, Sergeant Hanson of the Royal Artillery was called. He explained how the grenades had been made and said that if one exploded in a room full of people it would do a great deal of damage: 'it would be very destructive' and the pieces of iron would fly about like bullets. Mr Aldersey, one of the jurors, asked to have a grenade dismantled, and this was done. He asked Sgt. Hanson if he considered the gunpowder good by its granulations. Sgt. Hanson said that it was and also explained the composition of the fire-balls, which had been made of oakum, tar and stone-brimstone pounded, and maybe rosin. Mr Aldersey asked if there was no killicrankie and refuse of rosin, and Sgt. Hanson said that there was, and added that if a fire-ball was thrown into a building it would be sure to set it on fire. It would burn for three or four minutes, and nothing would put it out.

Curwood opened his speech for the defence as follows:

> Gentlemen of the jury; – Had it been permitted to me, consistently with my own sense of moral and professional duty, to have declined the arduous task which is now before me, I had not stood here to address you upon the present momentous occasion. But, perhaps it is one of the brightest attributes of our profession, and which we the members of that profession think redounds to our greatest credit, that we are not at liberty to refuse our assistance to persons in the situation of the unfortunate man at the bar.

And a few minutes later he added:

> The weight of this duty both to my learned friend and myself is not a little increased by the lateness of the moment at which we were called upon to execute it. Not until Thursday night was it that I received instructions in this case, or knew that I was to be called upon to defend the prisoner.

He had had to prepare to meet the 'first talents at the bar', who had all the support of the wealth, the power and the influence that the government could give them. As to the facts of the case, there was really very little that any counsel could say, and he fell back upon reciting the law, and stressing the need to have the case clearly proved, and how absurd it was to suppose that the conspirators could have hoped to set up a provisional government.

The defence first called Tidd's daughter, Mary Barker, who had been living with her father. She gave some rather dubious evidence that the items found in Tidd's house on the morning of 24 February had been brought there that morning, after her father had been arrested, possibly by Adams or Edwards, but even if this was true it had no bearing on the case against Thistlewood. They then called Edward Huckleston for the sole purpose of stating that Dwyer, the Irishman, was not fit to be believed upon his oath, and Dwyer was later recalled to deal with this allegation. They also called some newspaper reporters to give evidence relating to the announcement of Lord Harrowby's dinner party, in order to establish that the notice had been published in only one paper, whereas genuine announcements were normally published in several. Adolphus then asked if the court could be adjourned until the morning to enable him to prepare his speech, and his application was granted.

John Adolphus[8] was the son of a German immigrant. He had spent part of his youth in St Kitts, and had often visited the island court and had formed an ambition to go to the Bar. On his return to England, he found himself unable to afford this, but he qualified instead as an attorney. He hardly practised, however, and spent the 1790s writing books on France and commencing his *History of the Reign of George III*, and was employed as a salaried adviser to the Prime Minister. It was not until 1807 that he fulfilled his ambition of being called to the Bar, and rapidly became established as a criminal advocate at the Old Bailey. It was a matter of common knowledge that he was a Tory, and it was a great tribute to his integrity as well as his professional skill that such extreme radicals as Thistlewood and Ings chose him as their counsel.

It was 4 o'clock in the morning before Adolphus had finished composing his speech, and he was in court again at 9 a.m. on Wednesday 19 April.

He was faced with a task which must have few parallels in our legal history, and he commenced by asking the jury for sympathy for his client and for himself:

> The prisoner is, of all the men I remember tried before a jury for the crime of high treason, the most unhappy, and I may say, without meaning to alter the case of guilt, if guilt shall appear against him, the most unfortunate. I have known many trials in the course of my life on these subjects, but never saw one where a prisoner was so absolutely denuded of all countenance and support – so much thrown on the mercy and charity of those who would undertake his case, as the prisoner on the present occasion.

As for himself, he had not heard of the case until the previous Thursday, he had been out of town on Friday, and had only received his instructions on Saturday night.

He went on to say that 'the line of defence which I shall have to pursue on behalf of this unhappy man, is one more difficult than ever I knew to fall to the lot of an advocate', and he now conceded that there was no defence to the central issue of the case, namely that his client had intended to assassinate the cabinet. This was not treason in itself, he argued, and that to make it treason it was necessary to establish that the actions of the conspirators were aimed at the king. There was no evidence of such an intention except in the testimony of Adams, and this was so outrageous and absurd that it could not be true, and must have been invented by Adams for the purpose of securing the conviction of the accused.

And so, item by item, he dealt with Adams's extraordinary assertions. Both he and Harrison had been in the army: how did they suppose that twenty-five men with eight cannon could secure possession of London? Did they really believe that the troops, if they had to march back from Windsor, would be too exhausted to rescue the metropolis from a handful of desperate ruffians? Was it possible to suppose that any man, unless he were too insane to come before a jury, would invent such a plan:

> That any seven or eight men, two of them soldiers, should have met to act on so ridiculous a proposal, exceeds all human credulity. If this can be credited, there is nothing in oriental

fiction – nothing in ancient or modern poetry – nothing in the legends of the fathers, or the lives of the saints, but may be received as history and credited as truth.

They were to send to the ports ('Very fine indeed! I wonder they omitted Harwich'); who were to go there? They were to seize the Mansion House ('The Mansion House! – twenty-five men would have been completely lost in the passages; they might as well have gone to take the Tower of Babel'). They were going to set up a provisional government – of whom was it to be composed? Palin was to wander about, setting fire to buildings for his amusement. As for Furnival's Inn, it had recently been rebuilt with party walls to comply with the Building Act[9] and to prevent the spread of a fire – perhaps Palin was confusing it with the old Furnival's Inn, or one of the wooden buildings nearby. There was the question of the conspirators' funds: they had a few shillings and a one pound note. It was generally supposed that a printing-press is one of the first requirements of a revolutionary movement – but when Thistlewood wanted to produce a notice, he sent out for paper and wrote it out by hand.

And so Adolphus demolished Adams's evidence, and portrayed him as a man who had deliberately thought up these tales to betray his colleagues. It is true that this had never been put to him in cross-examination, but Adolphus explained this by saying that Adams had so carefully contrived his story that, if challenged, he would have embroidered it still further.

Adolphus spoke for some three hours. Considering the contraints imposed by the facts of the case, and of the time available to him to prepare his address, it is difficult indeed to know what more he could have said.

After he had concluded, Abbott CJ asked Thistlewood if he had anything to say, and Thistlewood replied that he wished to call two witnesses to further discredit Dwyer, but he was told that it was now too late to call any more evidence, so Thistlewood simply said, 'I am quite satisfied, my lord.'

The Solicitor-General now replied on behalf of the Crown, asserting that there was ample evidence to support Adams's testimony, including at least some to support his assertion that the conspiracy was not limited to the murder of the cabinet. In any case:

> If they formed the design of murdering the ministers of the Crown, it is impossible to suppose that this was intended to be effected with any other than an insurrectionary view. . . . Such a blow could [not] have been intended with any other view than to form the basis of an insurrection, in which it was hoped and expected that the great body of the people would instantly join.

Abbott CJ summed the case up during the afternoon. He dealt briefly with the law and advised the jury to concentrate on the charges under the Act of 1795 rather than under the Act of 1351. He then reviewed the evidence in detail, repeating practically everything that the witnesses had said. Towards the end, he repeated, in effect, what the Solicitor-General had said. The conspirators were unconnected with the persons who conducted the affairs of His Majesty's government, and the jury would have to consider whether they planned their assassination as part of a general insurrection, or simply to gratify their lust for human blood. He directed the jury to pay attention to the quantity and type of weapons which had been assembled – far more than would be required or used in the projected attack upon Lord Harrowby's house. The hand-grenades might well have been used there, but not the fire-balls.

> If, upon the whole of this evidence, you shall feel satisfied that a conspiracy to levy war against his majesty, or to depose him, is made out by the evidence laid before you – if your

The Cato Street conspirators: (clockwise from top left) Arthur Thistlewood, James Ings, William Davidson, John Brunt (British Musem)

consciences are satisfied of that, you will discharge the painful duty imposed upon you by pronouncing the prisoner guilty.'

The jury retired at 4.45 p.m., and returned five minutes later to ask for a copy of the Act of 1795. Abbott CJ agreed, but a juryman said it would suffice if his lordship read it, which he proceeded to do. The jury retired again, and after a quarter of an hour returned with verdicts of Guilty on counts 3 and 4. The court was then adjourned.

During the week which followed Ings, Brunt, Davidson and Tidd were put on trial and convicted. The evidence followed much the same pattern as in the trial of Thistlewood, but more and more attention was devoted to Edwards. He had been named on the warrant for the arrest of the conspirators – but he was never arrested; his name appeared on the list of prosecution witnesses – but he was never called; his address was given as 166 Fleet Street – but the defence were unable to find him. Repeated demands that he should be called were ignored, and it became increasingly clear that he was, in some way, deeply involved in the case.

On 27 April Thistlewood, Ings, Brunt, Davidson and Wilson all wrote a series of 'dying words' for their counsel, John Adolphus, who left these autographs to his daughter, and they emerged, more than a century later, in a second-hand bookshop in Edinburgh where John Stanhope found them in the winter of 1940–1.

Following the conviction of the five principal conspirators, the others agreed to plead Guilty, on the understanding that they would not be sentenced to death, and on Friday 28 April they were all brought back into court and asked why sentence should not be passed upon them. They all addressed the court, some at considerable length. They contended, firstly, that the ministers deserved all that had been prepared for them, as revenge for the Manchester Massacre; and secondly, that they had all been inveigled into the conspiracy by Edwards, who was described as a villain of the deepest atrocity. They also alleged that practically all the witnesses called by the Crown were government informants.

Abbott CJ then pronounced sentence in the usual terms, adding to those who had pleaded Guilty:

> If any of you shall have your life spared, which as to some of you I trust may be the case, I hope you will always bear in your minds, that you owe that life to the benignity of your sovereign – to his merciful disposition, aided and seconded by the merciful disposition also, of those very persons whom you had doomed to a violent and sudden death.

Tidd then said, 'the irons I have got are so heavy, that I cannot step; my legs are very tender, they have been very bad for some time', and Abbott CJ replied, 'I have no doubt the keeper of Newgate will do everything in his power to contribute to your ease, so far as it can be done with safety.'

At the close of the proceedings, the Attorney-General called upon the proprietor of the *Observer* to explain why he had published an account of the trials of Thistlewood and Ings in defiance of an order from the court that no account should be published. He was fined £500 for contempt of court.

The execution was fixed for 1 May, and it proved to be the most gruesome episode.

The 'usual place of execution' had been transferred in 1783 from Tyburn to Newgate, and it was the practice to erect a platform on 'hanging days' outside the Debtors' Door of the prison. On this occasion, the platform was larger than usual, so that all five men could be despatched together. The authorities were expecting

The Cato Street autographs of Thistlewood and Ings (left) and Brunt, Davidson, Tidd and Wilson. In the winter of 1940 Mr John Stanhope, a veteran of Spain and Finland, was touring the country giving lectures to the Home Guard on guerilla warfare; while waiting to deliver a lecture in Edinburgh, he was in a second-hand bookseller's shop, where he was offered the manuscript (for 7s 6d) and a facsimile of the autograph notes written for John Adolphus by the convicted men trouble, and the troops were stationed at each end of the Old Bailey. At about 7 a.m. the condemned men were brought, one by one, on to the platform. When Thistlewood was brought out, a man from the crowd managed to address him, and, in spite of protests from the sheriff, asked him when he first became acquainted with Edwards.

'About June last.'

'Where did you become acquainted with him?'

'At Preston's.'

'At Preston in Lancashire?'

'No, at Preston's, the shoemaker.'

'Did he give you any money?'

'Yes, I had a little from him, a pound note at a time.'

It was observed that the stranger was making a careful note of this conversation.

And then, one by one, the five man were strung to the gallows and the drop was released so that they all died simultaneously. The old ritual of disembowelling and quartering was no longer practised, but it was still necessary that the heads of the convicted traitors should be displayed to the public. Previously, the decapitation had been performed by an axeman, but on this occasion a man was employed to cut off the victims' heads with a surgeon's knife, a method which horrified and disgusted even those who were hardened to the sight of executions. The executioner wore a mask and could not be identified; it was thought at the time that he was a surgeon, and if he had been found he might well have been lynched, but Stanhope believed

The execution of the Cato Street conspirators at Newgate, on 1 May 1820 (Westminster City Archives)

that he was Tom Parker, a 'resurrection man' (*i.e.* a grave robber), who was later employed as a 'dead-house' assistant at St Thomas's Hospital.

The man who had spoken to Thistlewood on the platform was Alderman Wood MP, a notorious thorn in the flesh of the government. In an attempt to find out the truth about Edwards he had written to Lord Sidmouth on 26 April, after the convictions but before the executions, requiring him to institute criminal proceedings against Edwards on the grounds that he was one of the conspirators; he received an evasive reply. He raised the matter in the House of Commons on 2 May, and again a week later, but received no satisfaction; and he seems to have been instrumental in securing from the Grand Jury of Middlesex a true bill of indictment against Edwards on a charge of treason; but by this time, no doubt with offical help, Edwards had absconded, and was last heard of in Guernsey, although it was later rumoured that he went to live in South Africa.

And there the matter rested for more than a century, until Stanhope carried out his researches into the papers in the Public Records Office. These not only confirmed that Edwards was indeed a government spy and an *agent provocateur* but that he had been deliberately instigated to act in this capacity by Lord Sidmouth himself, the Home Secretary.

CHAPTER NINE

The Chartist Rebellion: the Trial of John Frost
(1839–40)

In what used to be the county of Monmouth (now part of Gwent) there is a district of high hills intersected by deep glens and fast-flowing streams. To the north, there is Ebbw Vale and Nantyglo, to the east, Blaenavon and Pontypool, to the west, Blackwood and Risca, and to the south there is Newport, some twenty miles from Ebbw Vale and Nantyglo, and about ten miles from Pontypool. Newport itself was an important town, and was the port from which iron and coal were exported. There was a tramway from there to Nantyglo on which ran horse-drawn trams and steam engines. This is the area which was, on the night of 3/4 November 1839, the scene of the last 'levying of war' in the realm.

At the end of the eighteenth century this area was almost uninhabited, having only a few shepherds' huts scattered up and down, but by the 1830s it had become, as Campbell A.-G. put it in his opening address to the jury, 'the seat of a dense population, estimated, I think, at above 40,000', who were employed in the iron and coal mines, and in supplying the wants of the workmen, and, he went on:[1]

> I am afraid that this population, which has suddenly sprung up, is, in many instances, not of the most peaceable description. I am afraid, gentlemen, that ignorance prevails there to an extent very much to be deplored, and that many of the persons who live in this district are subject to be practised upon by designing men. It would appear that this population has been organized by the establishment of affiliated societies, so that upon any occasion a command might be issued and circulated among the population, and speedily obeyed.

This was a reference to the Chartist movement.

Ever since the end of the eighteenth century, the working classes of Great Britain had been advocating major parliamentary reforms. They had supported the Great Reform Act, confident that the Parliament elected under the new rules would give effect to their proposals; but all further reforms were blocked.

Betrayed, deceived and bitterly resentful, the working classes established their own associations to redress their grievances, and submitted a draft bill to Parliament, the provisions of which were summarized in a Charter containing Six Points: universal manhood suffrage; annual parliaments; vote by ballot; no property qualification for Members of Parliament; the payment of Members; and equal voting districts.

Support for the Charter grew rapidly. Radical newspapers sprang up, notably the *Northern Star* in Leeds which was founded by Feargus O'Connor, who claimed to be descended from the kings of Ireland. During the summer of 1838, processions and meetings, with 10,000–20,000 people, paraded with bands playing and banners flying; in the major industrial centres the numbers ran to 100,000 or 200,000. Leading Chartists came to address these meetings, notably Henry Vincent, who, almost alone at that time, was also advocating votes for women; delegates were elected for a forthcoming Convention of Working Men; and subscriptions were raised. Nor were the demonstrations restricted to men in industrial towns – the women of Trowbridge gave Vincent a silk scarf as a token of their affection.

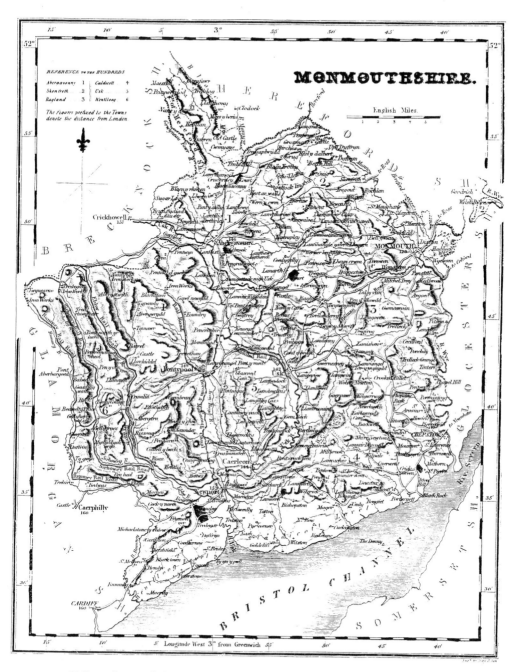

Fullarton's map of Monmouthshire, 1840 (Gwent County Council Record Office)

The more respectable and responsible Chartists advocated reform by legal and constitutional means, but some of the more outspoken leaders, and O'Connor in particular, were threatening the use of armed force.

When Vincent, who was about twenty-five at the time, visited Newport he was entertained by John Frost.

Frost was born in 1784, the son of an innkeeper in Newport. He was for a time apprenticed to a draper in Bristol, and spent a year or two in London. On returning to Newport in the early 1800s, he set up as a draper, and married Mary Geach, a widow; she had a son William and a daughter Mary by her first marriage, and eight children by her second, most of whom survived into adulthood.

It was at about this time that Frost began to form his political views, based on a burning indignation at the lavish wealth of the aristocracy, and at the impoverished distress of the working classes. There were at least three interwoven strands for his resentment: a purely personal one, derived from the fact (or the belief) that he and his wife had been cheated out of an inheritance by a fabricated will; a local one, bound up with the intricate local government of Newport; and a national hatred of the aristocracy. And these were personalized into a long-drawn out vendetta with one Thomas Prothero, the town clerk of Newport and the agent of Sir Charles Morgan of Tredegar, the local landowner. In 1821 Frost wrote and published a vitriolic letter about Prothero which was certainly defamatory, and delighted the inhabitants of Newport. Prothero was left with no alternative but to institute proceedings for libel, and, although the contents of the letter were probably true, Frost was ordered to pay £1,000 damages, and was imprisoned for six months in the Cold Bath Fields prison in London. It was at about this time that Prothero took on an articled clerk called Thomas Phillips, who later became his partner and another target for Frost's displeasure.

Frost now had to devote his energies to building up his drapery business and providing for his growing family; but the vendetta simmered on. In 1835 the Municipal Corporations Act was passed, and Newport was required to elect eighteen councillors; Frost was one of them, but Prothero managed to secure that his own nominee was elected mayor; in the following year, however, Frost became mayor, and he was named on the Commission of the Peace as a magistrate for the borough.

In the spring of 1839, a General Convention of Working Men met in London; Frost was the delegate for Newport, and it was on account of a speech which he made at a Convention dinner that the Home Secretary, Lord Russell, removed his name from the Commission of the Peace; from that time, Lord Russell became another of Frost's enemies. It was while the Convention was in session that a petition with over 125,000 names on it was presented to the House of Commons; a motion in favour of the petition was then debated, and was rejected by 237 votes to 48.

There followed increased tension throughout the country. There were confrontations between the demonstrators and the police in Birmingham and elsewhere, particularly in Wales; the Chartists took over Llanidloes and ruled it for a week. Many Chartist leaders were placed under arrest. Vincent was arrested at Newport and sentenced at Monmouth to twelve months' imprisonment, along with three other men, Messrs Edwards, Dickenson and Townsend. These three received lesser sentences, which they served in Monmouth Gaol.

The Convention was now making plans for calling a general strike on 12 August. However, the delegates seemed to lose their nerve, and many ceased to attend. The strike was called off, and on 6 September a motion was put that the Convention be dissolved; Frost was the chairman that day; eleven delegates voted for, and eleven against, the resolution; Frost gave his casting vote for dissolution.

And there the matter appeared to rest.

Although Frost was at times very outspoken, there was nothing in his career until then to suggest that he might become the leader of a major insurrection.

It was said that during the last week of October 1839 Frost was in consultation with two other men to prepare a general rising; these were Zephaniah Williams, a collier and an innkeeper at Coalbrookvale near Nantyglo, and William Jones, a watchmaker from Pontypool. They met in the Coach and Horses at Blackwood, and formed a plan to march in three divisions – Frost from Blackwood, Williams from Nantyglo and Jones from Pontypool – and to meet at Risca, about five miles north-west of Newport, at midnight on 3/4 November, with a view to attacking Newport at 2 a.m.; they would attack the troops who were known to be stationed there, seize the town and break down the bridge across the Usk. They would then stop the mail, and this, said the Attorney-General:

> was to be a signal by which the success of the scheme was to be announced; the mail bag from Newport not arriving at Birmingham in an hour and a half, it would be known by those who were in concert with them . . . that this scheme had succeeded. There was to be a general rising through Lancashire and throughout the kingdom, and Charter law universally and instantly established.

The optimism of the insurgents was not well founded. There had evidently been some fear of trouble, and a company of soldiers under the command of Captain Stack had been in Newport for some time, quartered in a workhouse which had been converted into barracks on the outskirts of the town. On the Sunday information came to Thomas Phillips, who was now the mayor of Newport, that there was some 'movement in the hills'. About a dozen Chartists were taken into custody, some of them being detained in the Westgate Hotel, others in the same workhouse as the troops. He took steps to guard against an attack and stationed some special constables, armed with staves, at three inns – the Westgate, the King's Head, and the Parrot. The Westgate was considered the most important, and the mayor himself and other magistrates sat up there all night, sending out patrols for further information and taking such steps as they could to preserve the peace and defend the town. At about 10 p.m. they sent Thomas Walker to find out what was happening. Walker went to Risca, where he met about a dozen men. One of them stabbed him in the thigh, but he was able to return, badly injured, into Newport and report what had happened.

The mayor now decided to send for military aid, and Captain Stack despatched about thirty men, under the command of Lieutenant Gray and two sergeants, to the Westgate Inn. The inn faced north and had two main rooms: on the east side was a room with a bay window facing the street,[2] which was where the troops were stationed, on the west side there was a similar room where the magistrates were assembled. There was a corridor between the two. The special constables were placed in front of the door of the Inn.

In the meantime the insurgents' plan had miscarried. It was a wet and stormy night, one of the worst in memory. Frost's division crossed from Blackwood to Newbridge and marched down to Risca and the Welch Oak, a public house nearby, but

The attack by the Chartists on the Westgate Hotel, Newport, from a lithograph by J.F. Mullock. It probably gives a realistic picture of the attack (Newport Museum and Art Gallery)

Williams's and Jones's divisions were delayed and failed to reach Risca at the time agreed.

So Frost decided to march on Newport with his own division of about 5,000 men, many of them armed with guns and pistols, and others with spears and pikes, mandrels (pickaxes used in the coal mines: 'a very dangerous and deadly weapon if used as a weapon of offence'), scythes, roasting spits, bludgeons and sticks. They marched in military order, five abreast, and came down to Tredegar Park, the seat of Sir Charles Morgan. From there they marched on, by the Waterloo public house, to Court-y-bella where there was a weighing machine at the side of the road, about half a mile from Newport.

It was at Court-y-bella, at about a quarter to nine, that two young lads met them – John Rees and James Coles (when the latter was asked how old he was, he replied: 'I am sixteen; I cannot say exactly the month, but about three months; I am sixteen and three months.') Frost, who was known to them, asked whether there were soldiers in the town, and Coles said that some had gone down to the Westgate. Frost, they said, was wearing a red handkerchief or cravat round his neck.

Frost now ordered his men to start marching again, and they marched down Stowe Hill, with Frost, still wearing his red handkerchief, at their head. Near a Catholic chapel at the back of Westgate Street, they tried to gain admission into the inn through a carriage entrance into the courtyard, but the gates were shut. Frost is alleged to have said 'Turn around and show your appearance at the front', although his exact words were in dispute. They wheeled round in front of the inn and, according to prosecution witnesses, asked the special constables, who were still in front of the door, to surrender, but they said: 'No, never.' The defence, on the other

TO THE
Working Men
OF
Monmouthshire.

COUNTRYMEN,

The scene which Newport yesterday presented to our view must, to every honest man, have been painful in the extreme. Numbers of men, of the working classes, with broken heads, and these wounds inflicted by Special Constables, sworn to preserve the Peace. Many of them Drunk, and under the command of a Drunken Magistrate. Numbers of Tradesmen of Newport, either aiding in assaulting Men, Women and Children, or silently witnessing, without any attempt to prevent those attacks on their unoffending neighbours. Is this the way in which the Mayor and the Magistrates of Newport preserve the peace? Was it to sanction actions of this description that the Soldiers were sent for to Newport? Will conduct of this sort produce no desire for revenge in those who suffer by it? Men of Monmouthshire, be cool, be patient; if justice be set aside: if Club Law is to be the order of the day, those who play at that game may find it a losing one.

My advice to you, working men of Monmouthshire is, be cool, but firm. We seek for nothing but our rights as members of a civil community. We have sought them peaceably; we still seek them peaceably. It is the object of our enemies to drive us to some outbreak in order to destroy us. This is the state in which our country is now placed. The people ask for bread, and the answer is the bludgeon or the sword. Let not the desire of the enemy be gratified.]

Faithfully, your obedient Servant,

JOHN FROST.

John Partridge, Printer, Newport.

This broadsheet, although undated, appears to have been issued after the attack on the Westgate Hotel. It was printed by John Partridge, in whose house John Frost was arrested (Newport Museum and Art Gallery) hand, asserted that the words used were 'Surrender us our prisoners' or 'We want our prisoners', on the ground that they had come to secure the release of the prisoners in the inn, or alternatively to demand the release of Messrs Vincent and others from Monmouth gaol. Be that as it may, it was said that the command 'Fire' was given and Frost's men started firing at the bay window of the room where the troops were stationed. Simultaneously, the insurgents attempted to break down the front door of the inn, using their pikes for this purpose. One man levelled a gun at Thomas Oliver, a special constable, but he managed to swing the door against it and it went off a few inches from his head. They succeeded in breaking down the door, and stormed inside – Frost, it was said, shouting 'In my boys' from the steps.

The bay window in the room where the troops were had three sides, the glass reaching down almost to the floor. The shutters were closed, but when the shots were fired, the glass was shattered. However, the soldiers could not fire back as long as the shutters were closed. Lieutenant Gray now gave the order to load, and he, the mayor and Sergeant Daily opened the shutters. Immediately the mayor was shot and wounded in the shoulder and hip, and Sergeant Daily in the head. Lieutenant Gray then gave the order to fire. The troops fired into the street, several of the insurgents were wounded and fell, and the rest fled in different directions. The troops also fired at the insurgents who had gained access to the passage inside the inn, and several fell there. The whole incident was said to have lasted about ten minutes, and the soldiers fired an average of three rounds each.

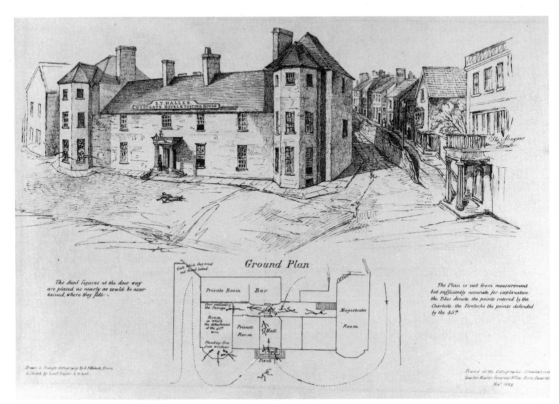

A plan of the Westgate Hotel, dated November 1839; drawn shortly after the rising, it shows where the troops were stationed and where the bodies were found afterwards (Newport Museum and Art Gallery)

Nine men were killed, and when Lieutenant Gray examined the bodies, he found that some of them were equipped with powder and ball cartridges. Pikes and other weapons lay around on the the ground where the insurgents had thrown them as they ran away.

There is some authority for saying that attacking the armed forces of the Crown was, *ipso facto*, levying war against the queen, and there was much dispute as to whether the insurgents knew that the troops were in the room, and whether they actually fired after they realized they were there. It seems clear that they stopped as soon as they saw the soldiers.

This was really the end of the insurrection. Frost ran away and at about 10 o'clock, William Adams, Sir Charles Morgan's park keeper, saw him walking through Tredegar Park, with a handkerchief over his face as if he was crying. He disappeared into a copse, but returned later to Newport.

Later that morning, a warrant for the arrest of Frost and a warrant to search his premises were issued to Thomas Jones Phillips, an attorney and a clerk to the magistrates and another of Prothero's protegés. He went to Frost's home, accompanied by Edward Hopkins, another attorney who was also the Superintendent of Police. Frost was not there, but they searched the house and Mrs Frost gave them every facility to examine her husband's papers.

Phillips also had a warrant against Partridge, a printer who lived nearby, and after leaving Frost's house he went to execute this warrant. He knocked at the door and tried to open it and called 'Partridge!' and Partridge replied that he had gone to bed. Phillips said that he would have to force the door, and did so, and immediately inside

Thomas Phillips, a solicitor who was the Mayor of Newport in 1839. He was wounded in the hip and arm (which was still in a sling when his portrait was painted) and was knighted for his services against the rising (Newport Museum and Art Gallery)

he found Frost, who looked very fatigued. He was taken to the Westgate Inn and searched, and three pistols and a powder-flask and ball were found on him.

In the meantime, at about 6 o'clock on the Sunday evening, Zephaniah Williams had assembled a crowd of men – he told a friend of his, Joseph Stockdale, that he hoped there would be 14,000 there – on the mountain between Ebbw Vale and Nantyglo, and he addressed them as follows: 'My dear chartists, you need not be frightened because we are bound to be at Newport at two o'clock; the soldiers will not touch you.' The men all 'whooped' when he said this, and said they did not care for the soldiers. The reference to 'two o'clock' was the only evidence so support the proposition that the insurgents had intended to attack Newport at that hour.

And so, at about 7.30 p.m., they set off. There may, again, have been 5,000 of them; many were armed with guns and other weapons, and they had been told to bring bread and cheese with them.

Some were dragooned into joining the crowd against their will.

George Lloyd, who lived at Coalbrookvale very close to Williams, was waylaid on his way home and taken along, with a dagger at his chest, and given a mop-stick as a weapon. They broke into houses on the way and dragged the occupants out to join them.

They would have been hard-pressed to reach Risca and their rendezvous with Frost by midnight, even on a fine night. By 11.30 p.m. they had only reached Llanhilleth, about halfway to Risca, where they roused James Samuel, the landlord of the Coach and Horses, and burst into the inn demanding refreshment. Williams himself came in and sat by the fire and drank a pint of beer. The tramway down to Newport ran beside the road, and Williams asked the landlord where he kept his horses, so Mr Samuel sent off his servant, a sixteen-year-old boy, Henry Smith, to fetch a horse and tram, and Williams and several of his men climbed in and set off down the tramway as far as Tyn-y-Cwm.

At Tyn-y-Cwm, at about midnight, they roused Thomas Saunders, a farmer, from his bed. When he got up, he saw a crowd of men, including Williams, carrying lanterns all along the tramway. Many of them went into his barn and stayed to shelter there until 6 or 7 o'clock.

At about 1.30 a.m. the main body reached Abercarn, about halfway between Nantyglo and Newport. There they crowded round the house of James Woolford, a gamekeeper, and threatened to blow his house up if he did not open the door. When he did so, they rushed in and took away three guns. By 6.30 a.m. some of them were at Tydu, about three miles from Newport, where they entered the house of Joseph Anthony and took him off by force.

About a couple of hours later, John Hawkins, a surgeon who practised in Newport, was on the road to Risca to visit a patient when he met a crowd of marching men. He knew Williams personally and told him that there were troops in the town and that he had better go back, but Williams replied: 'Come on, and he would show what the colliers could do in Newport.'

Some of Williams's division may actually have reached Newport at about the time when Frost's men dispersed and fled. Others were still at Tredegar Park when they heard the sound of firing and met their friends in retreat, so they all turned round and went home.

William Jones's division fared no better.

He assembled some of his friends at a racecourse near Pontypool at 2 p.m. on the Sunday and told them to go round the hills and collect the Chartists together, so that by about 10 p.m. a large number of armed men, some 2,000 or 3,000, had gathered at the racecourse. From there they went to the New Inn, about a mile from Pontypool on the Newport road, where William Jones marshalled them – the pikes to go first, then the guns, and the others armed with such weapons as they could get – and directed them to march five abreast to Newport.

As in the case of Williams's division, several men were taken by force and compelled to join the march. About a hundred men, including William Jones himself, invaded the garden of Prothero's house; it is not clear whether they intended to capture Prothero himself, but they certainly seized John Matthews, his gardener, and took him along with them.

It was not until about 10 a.m. on the Monday morning that they reached Malpas Gate on the outskirts of Newport, where they met a man walking in the opposite direction. He told them that he had been at Westgate and what had happened there, so they retreated and dispersed.

It had, in those days, been the usual practice for the preliminary investigation of suspected offences against the State to be carried out by Privy Counsellors, but in this case, the inquiry was conducted by the local magistrates, sitting in the Westgate Hotel. Then, on 19 November, a Special Commission was issued, and Sir Nicholas Tindal (Chief Justice of the Court of Common Pleas), Parke B., Williams J., and Capel Hanbury Leigh (Lord Lieutenant of the County of Monmouth), were appointed commissioners. On 10 December the commission sat and a grand jury was empanelled, and found a true bill for High Treason against John Frost, Zephaniah Williams and William Jones, and nine other men.

The commission then sat as an Assize Court at Monmouth on 31 December. Tindal CJ, Parke B. and Williams J., 'and others Her Majesty's Justices' were on the bench.

The Attorney-General, Sir John Campbell, represented the Crown. He had been called to the Bar while Thomas Erskine was still in practice, and remembered him trying to drill his men in the Inns of Court at the time of the invasion scare of 1805. The other members of the prosecuting team were Sir Thomas Wilde S.-G., Serjeants Ludlow and Talfourd, Mr Wightman and the Hon. J.C. Talbot, instructed by the Treasury Solicitor. Sir Frederick Pollock and Fitzroy Kelly and a Mr Thomas, instructed by William Geach, Frost's stepson, represented the accused.

It is rare for much credit to be given to the attorneys in these cases, but nothing was too much trouble for William Geach. He had himself recently been declared bankrupt (probably as the result of yet another of Prothero's schemes) and had a serious charge of fraud hanging over his head.[3] Yet he found time to visit the Home Secretary in London, on behalf of his stepfather, while the trial was pending. In December, a list of 317 jurors and 236 witnesses was served upon him, and he was confronted by the enormous task of trying to ascertain who they were, and, in the case of the witnesses, what they were likely to say; and of trying to discover witnesses to call on behalf of his client. It was his skill and determination that enabled counsel to cross-examine witnesses so thoroughly; and it has also been said that it was he who drew counsel's attention to the point of law which occupied the court for most of the second day of the trial.

Both Pollock and Kelly were Queen's Counsel.[4] Pollock was standing counsel to the Bank of England and the East India Company, and he had been Attorney-General for a few months in Peel's short-lived Conservative administration in 1834–5. It was ironic that the prosecution was brought by the Law Officers of a reforming government, against reformers who were represented by counsel who were both Tories.

The indictment was an extremely long document, even by the standards of the nineteenth century, occupying no less than ten pages in the report, but it was divided into four counts which in essence alleged:

(i) Levying War in the County of Monmouth contrary to the Act of 1351;
(ii) Levying War in Newport contrary to the Act of 1351;
(iii) Conspiring to depose the Queen, contrary to the Act of 1795;
(iv) Conspiring to levy War to compel the Queen to change her measures and counsels, contrary to the Act of 1795.

All the accused were arraigned and pleaded Not Guilty, and all were removed from the bar except Frost who was to be tried first. Pollock applied to the court that his client, who had recently been unwell, should be allowed the indulgence of a seat, and this was granted.

Steps were then taken to empanel the jury, which gave rise to long arguments on the law. There was a discussion as to whether the jurors should be called in alphabetical order, or whether their names should be placed in a box and drawn out at random. There were further arguments as to the right of the prosecution to challenge jurors. Eventually the following jurors were sworn in:

John Daniel, of Abergavenny, haberdasher
Thomas Davies, of Abergavenny, butcher
Richard Lewis, of Lanvair Discoed, farmer
Edward Brittle, of Mitchell Troy, farmer
James Hollings, of Monmouth, ironmonger
Thomas Jones, of Great House Nash, farmer
Edward Reese, of Lanmartin, miller
Edward Smith, of Chepstow, coachmaker
Christopher John, of Redwick, farmer
William Williams, of Langattock-nigh-Usk, farmer
John Richards, of Chepstow, baker
John Capel Smith, of Chepstow, grocer

No time is mentioned in the report, but it was evidently late now, and Tindal CJ told the Attorney-General that he could hardly be expected to open his case 'at this hour of the evening', with which the Attorney-General concurred. Tindal CJ told the jury that they would have to be kept separate from their families and friends until the trial was over, and arrangements had been made by the sheriff to keep them as comfortable as possible – they were probably accommodated in a local hotel. Then a question arose as to whether Geach should be allowed to see his client before the court sat and after it had risen each day, and it was agreed that he should have access to the prison until 10 o'clock at night and after 7 o'clock in the morning. The court then adjourned until 9 o'clock on the following morning, New Year's Day.

On 1 January the Attorney-General opened the case for the Crown. His speech was not particularly long: he outlined the law in respect of the acts of 1351 and 1795, and set out the facts. Immediately he concluded, Pollock submitted that no list of witnesses had been supplied to his client so as to comply with the Treason Act 1709, under which a person accused of treason was entitled to receive a list of all the witnesses to be called against him, with their professions and places of abode. The requirement appears to be straightforward, but it did in fact give rise to certain

The trial of John Frost at Monmouth. Tindal CJ is presiding, with Parker and Williams JJ; Frost, Jones and Williams are in the dock (Newport Museum and Art Gallery)

problems as to exactly when the list should have been served. Counsel argued this point throughout the entire day. In the evening the court announced that they would reserve the point for the opinion of the judges,[5] and in the meantime the case would proceed. The court then adjourned.

This was not a satisfactory state of affairs, and one would have supposed that the proper course would be to adjourn the case until the judges had expressed their opinion. Pollock raised this issue the following morning, and after some further discussion Tindal CJ intimated that if the judges found in favour of the defendant, he would be pardoned. This, apparently, was the established practice that had existed for centuries, to which Pollock commented: 'Then I can only say that it is high time that that practice was altered by competent authority.' So the case proceeded, and the Crown called its first witness, Samuel Simmons. Once again, Pollock raised an objection, this time on the ground that the witness had not been properly identified. He was said to be resident in the parish of St Woollos in the borough of Newport, but the parish was a very large one and the whole of Newport was in its boundaries. Thomas Prothero was called to explain the situation, and eventually it was ruled that Simmons had been adequately identified. Later in the trial, other witnesses who had not been properly identified were ruled inadmissible.[6]

The case for the Crown lasted for three days until, Saturday 4 January. The crux of the case was that the attack on Newport was the prelude to a general insurrection, and it is necessary to consider carefully the evidence on this issue.

The key witness was James Hodge. The defence objected that his residence had not been adequately identified in the list of witnesses – he had been living at various public houses at the time when the list was served – but the objection was overruled. Hodge gave his evidence to the effect that he had met Frost at Blackwood on the evening of Sunday 3 November, and while he was there a man had said that he had come from Newport, that all the soldiers were Chartists, 'and that they were ready to come up, only for we to go down and fetch them'. It was not clear whether he went voluntarily with Frost's men or not, but somewhere on the outskirts of Newport he said that he had gone to Frost and that the following conversation took place:

> I asked him in the name of God what he was going to do; was he going to attack any place or people. He said he was going to attack Newport, and take it, and blow up or down the bridge, I cannot say which, and stop the Welsh mail from proceeding to Birmingham; that there would be three delegates there to wait for the mail there an hour and a half after time; and if the mail did not arrive, then the attack would commence in Birmingham, and from thence to the North of England and Scotland. . . . I told him he might as well lead us to a slaughter-house to be slaughtered; that he imitated a butcher leading a flock of lambs to a slaughter-house to be slaughtered; and I begged him to desire the men to return to the hills.

Shortly after this, said Hodge, he managed to jump into some brambles and escape.

Matthew Williams was a quarryman from Argoed. In the middle of his examination by Serjeant Ludlow for the Crown, he said, 'Gentlemen, if you please, I would rather speak Welch,' but Ludlow said, 'No, you are doing very well.' Williams went on to say that he had met Frost at a Chartist lodge at Argoed on the Sunday evening, and it was said that there was a plan to go to Newport: 'We were to go there to stop the coaches, and the post and all traffic,' and to guard the town.

John Harford, a collier from Bedwellty, said that some men came to his house at about 6 o'clock on the Sunday evening and told him to come with them and bring a sword. He did so and at about 1 a.m. they reached the Welch Oak, where he heard some of the mob speaking to Frost and asking him if they had not better return. Frost had replied that no they had better not return, and when they asked him what he intended to do, he said, 'First they should go to the new poor-house and take the soldiers and their arms; then he said there was a storehouse where there was plenty of powder; then they would blow up the bridge, that would stop the Welch mail which did run to the north, and then that would be tidings, and they would commence there on Monday night.' Harford managed to escape shortly afterwards, and hid in a cowshed.

This appears to have been the full extent of the evidence called by the Crown to support their proposition that Frost was planning an insurrection, the like of which had not been seen since 1745.

Even if these witnesses could be relied upon (and all of them were severely cross-examined), the whole idea was absurd. There was no direct mail link between Newport and Birmingham. The South Wales mail left Newport in a coach to the ferry across the Bristol Channel, where letters and passengers transferred to a boat. On the other side they were picked up by another coach and taken to Bristol, where the mail was re-sorted for distribution around the country. If the ferry was late, the Birmingham coach would not have waited. The Crown called no evidence as to the times of the postal service – indeed, the Attorney-General seems to have opened the case under the misapprehension that there was a direct service from Newport to Birmingham. And the Crown called no evidence to show that anything untoward had happened that day in Birmingham or anywhere else. If there really was a plan for a general insurrection, it is strange that no knowledge of it had leaked out, but no evidence of such a scheme was ever called.

The case for the Crown was concluded on the Saturday evening, and Sir Frederick Pollock addressed the jury on the Monday. He had, he said, little experience of criminal law:

> Gentlemen . . . to me criminal business is extremely new – a charge of High Treason altogether so. The business of this court, as opposed to that of the other [i.e. civil court], is accompanied by a feeling of interest and anxiety to me so intense, painful and almost overwhelming, that I have on all occasions, where I could with propriety, declined being a party to a criminal prosecution. But on the present occasion I readily say I thought it my duty, when called upon, to undertake this defence. . . . And I am sure that my learned friend will cordially agree with me, that no loyal subject can be better employed than in disproving the existence of Treason, and satisfying you, the gentlemen of the jury, and the public at large, that this is not a case of that complexion, whatever degree of criminality of another sort there may have been.

Pollock spoke, probably, for some six hours. After thanking the judges for the courtesy and patience with which they were conducting the trial, he concentrated on the problem of the Birmingham mail, and outlined the evidence which he was proposing to call for the defence. He concluded:

> Gentlemen, if I have not exhausted the subject, I have nearly exhausted myself, and I have merely to pray that, for the sake of the individual whose counsel I am, for whom, and for those dearer to him than his own life, I implore you to give a calm and a patient consideration to all the circumstances in the case, and to come to a just and, where there is any doubt, to a merciful conclusion.

The principal lines of defence were, firstly, that the object of the attack on the Westgate Inn was to secure the release of prisoners, although it never became clear whether the insurgents knew that there were prisoners in the inn and were trying to rescue them, or whether they were demonstrating in support of Henry Vincent and his fellow prisoners who were in Monmouth gaol. There was evidence that the words spoken to the special constables were not 'Surrender yourselves our prisoners', but 'Surrender your prisoners', or words to that effect. Secondly, it was said that the attack on the soldiers had been an accident. Whether or not the insurgents knew that there were soldiers in the inn, they did not know which room they were in, and they stopped shooting immediately they saw they were there – the mayor and Sergeant Daily being wounded before the insurgents realized what was happening.

Several prosecution witnesses had said that they knew Frost well and had held him in great respect. Other witnesses were called to give evidence as to his good character, including the Rt. Hon. Lord Granville Somerset, one of the Members of Parliament for the County of Monmouth and a political opponent of Frost, who said that, at the time of the Reform Bill agitation in 1831, his brother had been insulted if not assaulted, and that Frost had intervened to prevent violence.

The Revd James Cole, one of the magistrates for the county, produced a letter that Frost had written pleading for an amelioration of the conditions in which Vincent and his fellow-prisoners were being kept. Capel Hanbury Leigh, the Lord Lieutenant of the County, produced a similar letter that Frost had written to him. In this letter, Frost had pointed out that a petition was to be presented to Her Majesty praying for the liberation of these prisoners, and ending: 'I hope, sir, that your influence as lord lieutenant will not be exerted in opposition to the wishes of thousands of the working classes.'

No witnesses were called from the Royal Mail, but Edward Thomas, who was in business as a grocer, tallow-chandler and draper, was familiar with the service, and explained that the mail left Newport at 1 p.m. and was conveyed by ferry across the Bristol Channel, and that the Birmingham coach left Bristol at 4 p.m.

The evidence was concluded sometime on the Monday morning, and Kelly now addressed the jury on behalf of his client. He had practised mostly in mercantile matters and, like his leader, had little experience of the criminal law, but his whole life might have been a preparation for this day. No point was left uncovered. He reviewed the law, both the statutes and the cases. He even achieved a succinct account of the trials of Hardy and Horne Tooke[7] in three sentences:

> The prisoners . . . were charged with a design to subvert the constitution and laws of the country, by setting aside the Parliament and establishing a convention. That was shortly after the French Revolution, when, among the numerous forms of government to which that unfortunate people then resorted, was a Convention of the people; and the prisoners were charged with having, in imitation of their French brethren, designed to overturn the law and government of England, and to establish in its place a Convention similar to that which existed in France.

In that case, and the others to which he referred, the objects attributed to the accused had always been clearly set out by the prosecution so that the defendants knew exactly what charge they had to meet. However, in this case the charges on the indictment were so confusing that it was very difficult to understand what his client was accused of, and there was no evidence whatsoever to suggest that he had been involved in any plan to overturn the constitution. He examined in detail the statements of the witnesses and the story of the Birmingham mail. He pointed out that the Attorney-General, in his opening speech, had alleged that a return of the armed forces which could be mustered was made to the defendants at their meeting on Friday 1 November, but no evidence had been called in support of this allegation. The Attorney-General had alleged that it was the intention of his client to impose 'Charter Law' on the country, but this phrase had never been mentioned by a single witness.[8] The defence had been faced with great difficulties in collecting evidence and witnesses, from the hills, from Bristol, and elsewhere. The Crown had

> boundless resources, they have the purse of the nation; and you and I, and all of us, contribute to the very expenses of this prosecution; they may lay their hands on what public fund they please, they may send at any expense, at any toil and trouble, to all parts of the kingdom as many persons as they think proper, men of talents, means and abilities to procure evidence;

yet they had called no witness at all to prove the timetable of the Birmingham mail, and no witnesses to support their claim that an insurrection was imminent in Birmingham or anywhere else.

At the close of Kelly's speech, Tindal CJ invited Frost to speak on his own behalf, but he replied: 'My lord, I am so well satisfied with what my counsel have said, that I decline saying any thing upon this occasion.'

There followed a short discussion as to whether the court should then adjourn, but Tindal CJ ruled otherwise, and the Solicitor-General replied on behalf of the Crown. After some pleasantries towards Sir Frederick Pollock – they had been at St Paul's School together – he criticised Kelly for some of the remarks that he had made: 'The

Crown had not a tittle of power in this case beyond an ordinary prosecutor,' and even if no one had used the actual phrase 'Charter Law', that was clearly what the defendant had in mind to impose.

He referred to the law in very broad terms: 'What is levying war? The rising of armed men for the purpose of destroying and superseding that state of government which affords protection to the rich and to the poor, which tends to give prosperity to the country, and makes that prosperity conducive to happiness.'

The evidence, he said, indicated a deliberate attempt to take Newport by force, preferably in the middle of the night, and to attack the military. As for the Birmingham mail, he accepted the evidence at face value, and indeed elaborated upon it:

> with previous consultation, with the previous knowledge of an intention that [the letters] should be stopped if possession should be gained of the town, what more certain information could any one of the conspirators at Birmingham want of the success of their enterprise than that the letters from Newport had not arrived?. . . . From Birmingham the like intelligence is communicated to different parts of the kingdom; the consequence of which is, that, like fires bursting out in many places, the means of safety cannot be addressed to each, and thus the common object is promoted.

The Solicitor-General continued his address on the following morning and summarised his case by saying:

> I say that the charge against the prisoner is, that he, believing there was a body of armed men in this country ready to revolt and rebel, raised a large body of armed men, with the intention to take possession of the town of Newport, to supersede the law and the Government, and to give a signal for general insurrection through the kingdom; that the object of that was to overturn the Government. It is immaterial whether he possessed the means; whether his means were adequate to his purpose; whether his purpose was wise or not; whether there was any probability of it being accomplished: for, gentlemen, how much of public distress, how much of murder and ruin, arise from an impotent attempt to affect a revolution!

Tindal CJ now summed up. He commenced by directing the jury to ignore the four separate counts on the indictment, and treat the case as if it was one combined charge of levying war against the queen, which he defined, on the strength of a passage in Foster's *Discourse on Treason*, so as to include all insurrections for redressing national grievances. He proceeded to repeat all the evidence that had been given on both sides. With regard to the evidence of the Birmingham mail, the judge said:

> No doubt whatever can exist, that if it was the immediate intention of the prisoner to take the town, put a stop to all traffic, and prevent communication between Newport and different towns, by a large armed body of men, with the further and ultimate intention of effecting thereby an alteration in the law and government of the country, that such intention, evidenced by the acts referred to, amounts to the offence of High Treason.

With regard to Frost's previous good character, he said:

> The general character of a man will make it often very improbable that he should commit a particular crime. A man which has a general character for honesty is not likely to commit a theft. A man who has a peaceable and well-disposed character, and recommends to others peace, upon occasions of general disturbance, is not likely to be a person who would commit an act of violence by levying war. But it is at best no more than a question of probability, to be put in opposition and weighed against the evidence of the fact.

He again reviewed the evidence relating personally to the defendant, and concluded:

> It lies upon the Crown to prove conclusively against him that the crime of High Treason . . .
> has been made out by the proof brought against him. . . . It is only if the Crown had made it
> out so clearly and conclusively that you cannot entertain a just and reasonable doubt of the
> degree of his guilt that you are to find him Guilty.

To judge by the transcript, the summing-up would appear to have been quite impartial; but everyone present in court seems to have regarded it as virtually a direction to the jury to acquit. At its conclusion, the Attorney-General convened a meeting of prosecuting counsel in his lodgings to decide what course to take on the assumption that Frost would be acquitted, and they were still in conference when a messenger arrived to inform them that a verdict of Guilty had been returned. The jury added: 'My Lords, we wish to recommend the prisoner to the merciful consideration of the court,' and Tindal CJ said that the recommendation would be forwarded to the proper authorities.

The following day Zephaniah Williams was put on trial. He was convicted on 13 January, again with a recommendation to mercy. William Jones was tried on 15 January, found Guilty and recommended to mercy. On 16 January five other men were brought to the bar to withdraw their pleas of Not Guilty and to enter pleas of Guilty, and the Attorney-General stated that he did not propose to proceed against four others, who were formally found Not Guilty.

On the same day, 16 January, Frost, Williams and Jones were brought into court and asked if they had anything to say before judgment was entered. Geach was in court and said that the Attorney-General had assured him that his client would not be brought up for judgment until the point of law, which had been reserved for the judges, had been decided, but Tindal CJ said that the Attorney-General had no authority to give such an assurance.

Geach then raised another point. There had been two jurors on the list, one called John Christopher, and the other Christopher John. It had been the intention of his client to challenge the one who had actually served on the jury, but there had been a misunderstanding as to which was which. The court dismissed this objection and Tindal CJ passed sentence in the usual form on Frost, Williams and Jones. He proceeded to the four who had pleaded Guilty, and intimated that they were likely to be reprieved, but he had to pass sentence in the meantime.

In the following week, the Court of Exchequer Chamber assembled to hear the arguments relating to the list of witnesses. Lord Denman, Chief Justice of the Court of King's Bench, presided, along with Tindal CJ, Lord Abinger CB, and twelve other judges. The case was argued over three days. A majority of the court, nine to six, were of the opinion that the delivery of the list had not been a good delivery in point of law, but a majority of nine to six were of the opinion that the objection had not been taken at the proper time. They were all of the opinion that, if the objection had been taken at the proper time, the only effect would have been the postponement of the trial in order to allow a proper delivery. The result of the determination was, therefore, that the defect was irrelevant and that the conviction was right.

Strong opinions were expressed as to what should be done with the convicts. The aristocracy and the armed forces demanded that they should be executed at once; there were equally strong demands, chiefly from the Chartists, that they should be reprieved. The cabinet discussed their fate on several occasions, and Pollock visited

John Frost in the condemned cell at
Monmouth (Newport Museum and
Art Gallery)

the Home Secretary on no fewer than seven occasions to plead on their behalf. Eventually, Tindal CJ himself intervened, and a decision was reached that they should be reprieved, and transported for life. It was shortly after this, when they were about to depart for Australia, that Geach visited his stepfather at Portsmouth, and found him, apparently a dying man, covered with a tarpaulin on the deck of the ship.

In spite of his ill-health, Frost survived, and he and Williams and Jones all reached Tasmania, where they were, at first, received as honoured guests rather than as convicts; but they soon fell foul of the authorities, and suffered as much as most of the other prisoners in the colony. In 1855 they were all given a conditional pardon, the condition being that they did not return to England. Williams and Jones decided to stay in Tasmania; Jones died in poverty in 1873; Williams, on the other hand, put his knowledge of coal-mining to good use, and made a fortune; he died in 1874.

Frost went to America where he spent a year, but returned to England when the pardon was made unconditional. When he arrived at Newport, the corporation declined to make an official welcome for him, but his friends met him off the Bristol ferry, and paraded him through the town in a coach decked with flowers. Shortly afterwards, he went to London, where he received a tumultuous welcome, and was taken in a procession through the streets.

Frost's wife, Mary, was still alive, although she died shortly afterwards; he and two of his daughters then resided in a cottage in Stapleton, near Bristol. Frost himself wrote a book called *The Horrors of Convict Life* and gave lectures on the same subject. In his ninetieth year he was still planning to write his autobiography, but his health began to decline, and he died, aged 92, in 1877.

John Frost in his old age. He returned to England in 1856 and lived near Bristol, until his death, aged nearly 93, in 1877 (Newport Museum and Art Gallery)

There has been much discussion as to how this uprising came about.

The whole incident seemed so strange that it has been suggested that it was instigated by some *agent provocateur*. Was there some counterpart to George Edwards in the Cato Street conspiracy? If there was, no evidence of such a person came to light during the trial; but subsequently there was a rumour that a spy had infiltrated the movement, and had not only been present at the Westgate Hotel but had fired the first shot; however, it was said that he had then been killed when the troops returned fire.

The ostensible aim of the march on Newport – to release Vincent, Edwards, Dickenson and Townsend from prison – is untenable; they were in Monmouth, not Newport. It is, however, possible that the object was to obtain and imprison hostages to be used as a bargaining counter. In the summer of 1839, Frost had issued a broadsheet in which he recommended that hostages should be taken and kept in a coal-pit – and Thomas Phillips had been singled out by name for this treatment; Frost repeated this idea when he addressed a meeting in Glasgow on 10 June. Prothero would have been another obvious choice and the insurgents did enter his property; Frost may well have surmised that the most likely place to find Phillips would be the Westgate Hotel. Alternatively, Frost may have planned simply to take and hold Newport for a few days, as other Chartists had held Llanidloes during the spring.

But was there evidence to support the assertion of the attorney-general that the rising was planned in conjunction with a mass insurrection in other parts of the country? No such evidence, apart from the matter of the Birmingham mail, emerged at the trial; however, David Williams found a good deal of material – rumours, newspaper reports, memoirs – to suggest that the attorney-general was right.

During the summer, Vincent had told the Convention that the mountains of south Wales could be defended against an army, so was there some strategic plan to create a rising in Wales, to draw troops there from the rest of the country, and enable a general insurrection to take place? There is reason to believe that more was planned in Wales than actually occurred. There was a surgeon in Pontypridd, Dr William Price, who was supposed to have joined the other insurgents with seven cannon – although what he was going to do with them never became clear; but neither he nor his cannon materialized, and he himself thought it wise to leave the country and go to Paris, where he stayed for several months. Then there was a mysterious Pole, Major Beniowski, the delegate for Tower Hamlets at the Convention, who, it was said, was sent to Wales with 138 lb of ball cartridges: it was Beniowski's participation in the affair that gave rise to the rumour that the Russians were behind the rising, in an attempt to overthrow the British government, and that the Russian fleet was in the North Sea to provide support. It also seems certain that the Merthyr Chartists had been expected to join in, although whether they were supposed to take part in the attack on Newport or to make a separate assault on Brecon is uncertain.

Finally there were stories that there was to be a Chartist rising in Lancashire and Yorkshire and elsewhere, timed to take place on 5 November. In particular, an emissary was sent to Feargus O'Connor in Leeds, entreating him to put his words into deeds; and it is said that he promised to do so. In the event, O'Connor decided that it would be prudent to retire to Ireland, sending word to Merthyr that there would be no rising in Yorkshire, and to Yorkshire that there would be no rising in Merthyr.

As for Frost himself, all that he would ever say was that some people had been threatening him and his family: 'Mr Frost, if you will not lead us, neither you nor your family shall live at Newport;' and so he allowed himself to be drawn into the insurrection.

It was not a satisfactory case.

There can be no doubt that Frost and his friends were levying war: they were marching as an army, and were armed with a variety of weapons including firearms. But in order to constitute an offence under the Act of 1351 it had to be shown that they were levying war against the queen. Levying war as part of a general insurrection would have sufficed for this purpose (and also for the purposes of the Act of 1795), but the only evidence of such an insurrection was that of Hodge, with some support from Harford, in relation to the Birmingham mail. It is hard to believe that a jury would have accepted this at face value, but there was, on the other hand, ample evidence of a planned attack upon Newport. Even if the numbers were exaggerated, there can be no doubt that Frost and the other leaders had several hundred, if not several thousand, men under their command – far more than would be required to demonstrate in support of their friends who were in prison. But would an attack upon a town suffice to come within the Act of 1351? There was little authority on this point, and no clear precedent as far as I am aware: it was the sort of issue that should have been raised before the full bench of judges.

Probably the convictions were justified, but it was the last case of its kind. In later years anyone involved in a riotous assembly has been prosecuted for the lesser offence of riot.

CHAPTER TEN

The Trial of Sir Roger Casement (1916)

The trial of Sir Roger Casement took place in the last week of June 1916, his appeal was heard and dismissed three weeks later, and he was executed on 3 August.

Casement was born in Ireland in 1864. He spent many years in government service, for which he was knighted in 1911, and retired from the service in 1913. In the autumn of 1914 he was in Germany, where he was evidently allowed complete freedom of movement, and during the winter he was making speeches to Irish prisoners of war, urging them to join the Irish brigade.

Early in 1916 the Germans were planning to send a shipment of arms to assist the Irish in an uprising, timed to start on 24 April. As part of this scheme Casement and two other men, Robert Monteith and Daniel Bailey, left Germany in a U-boat, U 19, and after a voyage of twelve days they reached the Irish coast near Tralee. They were put in a rowing-boat at about 1 a.m. on 21 April, but the boat overturned and they had to wade ashore. Bailey had to go back two or three times to collect their equipment, some of which they buried nearby. They then walked to an old ruin, known as McKenna's fort, where Casement himself remained, while the other two walked on to Tralee. Casement was arrested soon afterwards with a knapsack in his possession, in which was found a flash-lamp, forty rounds of ammunition and some fragments of a map, and in a coat pocket there was a railway ticket from Berlin to Wilhelmshaven. While the police were escorting Casement from McKenna's fort to Tralee, he tore up some paper and threw it on the ground. On examination this proved to be a code-book containing a straightforward numeric code, e.g. 00611: cease communications with; 00621: await further instructions; etc. Monteith and Bailey were arrested later on the same day. On 23 April Bailey made a long statement to the police in which he gave a detailed description of his journey from Germany and his landing in Ireland.

In the evening of 21 April HMS *Bluebell* intercepted a ship, the *Aud*, flying Norwegian colours, some ninety miles off the south-west coast of Ireland. The *Aud* was instructed to sail to Queenstown, but about three miles from port she ran up the German flag and was scuttled, the crew taking to the boats which then pulled to the *Bluebell*. When the wreck was later examined by a diver, it was found to contain a large number of rifles and ammunition; one rifle was retrieved and identified as a Russian service rifle.

The Law Officers of the Crown decided to prosecute Casement for treason and, following committal proceedings in the middle of May before the Bow Street magistrate, he was tried in the King's Bench Division of the High Court of Justice on 26 June 1916.[1]

The indictment contained one count only, namely of adhering to the enemy contrary to the Treason Act 1351, by aiding and assisting them in Germany between 1 December 1914 and 21 April 1916. Six overt acts were alleged, namely:

(i) On 31 December, 1914, inciting prisoners at Limburg Hahn Camp to forsake their allegiance to the Crown, to join the armed forces of the enemy, and to fight against the Crown;

HIGH COURT OF JUSTICE—K.B. & Chancery Divisions.

Monday, 26th June, 1916

Mr. Justice PETERSON—*continued.*

To follow the L to R Division.

Division IV.—S to Z.—(Master CHANDLER).

With Counsel.

In re Wyles Bros. ld. & Companies Act, 1908
In re Vauxhall Engineering Co. ld. (Selz v. The Company)
In re Thorowgood, dec. (Donne v. Thorowgood)
In re Steer, dec. (Wheeler v. Steer)

To-morrow (Tuesday) the following Business will be taken

Short Causes.

In re The Falmouth Consolidated Mines ld.
Schiff   The Company   fur. con.

Monmouthshire & South Wales Permanent Benefit Building Soc. v. Mansel motion for judgt.

Petitions.

In re George Jennings Peyton & Co. ld. and reduced, In re Cos. (Consolidation) Act, 1908

In re D'Oyly
D'Oyley   Binley

In re The Manbre Saccharine Co. ld. & reduced and In re The Companies (Consolidation) Act, 1908

Adjourned Summonses

13 In re Burr, dec.
Nelson   Burr   adjd. sumns. pt. hd.

15 In re Ellison, dec.
Wethered v. W. Wethered   adjd. sumns.

4 In re Burroughes' Settlement
Burroughes   Fraser   adjd. sumns.

16 In re De Mamin, dec.
Speed   Ingham   adjd. sumns.

17 In re J. R. Roberts, dec.
Williams v. Public Trustee   adjd. sumns.

The next to be heard are :—

18 In re E. F. Smyth, dec.
Edwards   Smyth adjd. sumns. (for Mr. Justice Eve)

20 In re Lord Grimthorpe, dec.
Beckett   Aberdare   adjd. sumns.

21 In re W. Herring, dec.
Herring   Herring   adjd. sumns.

22 In re Jacob Lory, dec.
Hendy   Lory   adjd. sumns.

23 Albert Lee & Co. v. Swinden & Co. ld.
   point of law

24 In re T. J. Gunn, dec.
Harvey   Gunn   adjd. sumns.

25 In re an Application by Williams ld., No. 369,247 & In re the Opposition of Cadbury Bros. ld. & ors. & In re The Trade Marks Act, 1905   motion

LORD CHIEF JUSTICE'S COURT.

Before

The LORD CHIEF JUSTICE OF ENGLAND

Mr. Justice AVORY and

Mr. Justice HORRIDGE.

At 10·15.

The King   Casement
The King   Bailey

NOTICE.

TRINITY SITTINGS, 1916.

King's Bench Divisional Court.

ORDER OF BUSINESS.

For the week ending July 1st.

Tuesday and Friday--Ex parte Motions.

NOTICE.

The Revenue Paper will be taken by Mr. Justice ATKIN on Wednesday, the 12th July next, and following days.

The Cause List for 26 June 1916. Note that the name of Bailey appears immediately after Casement; the Crown originally intended to try the two together, or to try Bailey after Casement. In the end, however, the Crown decided to offer no evidence against Bailey (Library, Royal Courts of Justice)

(ii) and (iii) Similar overt acts on 6 January and 19 February, 1915.

(iv) In January and February 1915, at Limburg Hahn Camp, circulating and distributing and causing to be circulated and distributed among the prisoners of war a leaflet to the same effect;

(v) In December 1914 and January and February 1915, persuading certain prisoners to the same effect;

(vi) On or about 12 April, 1916, setting out from Germany as a member of a warlike and hostile expedition undertaken and equipped by the enemy with a view to landing arms and ammunition on the coast of Ireland for use in the prosecution of the war by the enemy.

The leaflet referred to in overt act (iv) became known as Exhibit 4 during the trial. In view of its importance, it is desirable to set it out in full:

IRISHMEN!

Here is a chance for you to fight for Ireland!

You have fought for England, your country's hereditary enemy.

You have fought for Belgium, in England's interest, though it was no more to you than the Fiji Islands!

Are you willing to fight for your own country?

With a view to securing the National Freedom of Ireland, with the moral and material assistance of the German Government, an Irish Brigade is being formed.

The object of the Irish Brigade shall be to fight solely for the cause of Ireland, and under no circumstances shall it be directed to any German end.

The Irish Brigade shall be formed and shall fight under the Irish flag alone; the men shall wear a special, distinctively Irish uniform and have Irish officers.

The Irish Brigade shall be clothed, fed, and efficiently equipped with arms and ammunition by the German Government. It will be stationed near Berlin, and be treated as guests of the German Government.

At the end of the war the German Government undertakes to send each member of the Brigade, who may so desire it, to the United States of America, with necessary means to land. The Irishmen in America are collecting money for the Brigade. Those men who do not join the Irish Brigade will be removed from Limburg and distributed among other camps.

If interested, see your company commanders

Join the Irish Brigade and win Ireland's independence!

Remember Bachelor's Walk![2]
God save Ireland!

A remarkable feature of the case is the Crown's failure to plead Casement's landing in Ireland as an overt act. In *R. v. Preston* (1691) a similar point had arisen in reference to the venue of a trial in Middlesex: Preston was accused of adhering to the enemy in various parts of the country, but the only overt act alleged in Middlesex was that he had embarked on a boat from the Surrey steps on the north bank of the Thames on his way to join the enemy. Lord Holt CJ had ruled that this was a valid overt act. On this basis Casement's disembarkation from a boat on the Irish coast, equipped with material supplied by the enemy, was manifestly an overt act, and, assuming that Ireland was part of the realm,[3] it would have been an overt act in the realm. In that event the principal line of defence adopted by Casement's advisers, namely that the overt acts alleged had been committed out of the realm and were therefore outside the scope of the Act of 1351, would have disappeared, and they would have been forced back on the argument that his activities did not constitute adhering to the enemy.

Casement's conduct, in the middle of the First World War, could hardly have been expected to evoke sympathy in England, but this does not excuse the attitude adopted by members of the English legal profession. An Irish solicitor in practice in London, Mr Gavan Duffy, a family friend of the Casements, undertook the defence, but his partners insisted on dissolving the partnership in consequence. In spite of the urgency of the matter, eight days elapsed before he was allowed to see his client, who was held in the strictest custody in the Tower. In a hurry he then briefed two Welshmen, Mr Artemus Jones and Prof. J.H. Morgan (Professor of Constitutional Law in London University and Reader in the same subject to the Inns of Court, and also a personal friend of Casement), to represent the defence at Bow Street. It is said that Sir John Simon KC and Mr Gordon Hewart KC were both offered the brief for the defence at the trial and both refused it, whereupon Mr Duffy approached his brother-in-law, Serjeant Sullivan KC.[4]

Serjeant Sullivan was also reluctant to act, and in his case there were certain technical difficulties. As a Serjeant of the Irish Bar,[5] he was not allowed to act against the Crown in Ireland. It was uncertain if this rule applied in England, but if it did, it was waived. Furthermore, although a KC in Ireland, he was a junior member of the English Bar with no practical experience in this country, and he had a busy practice in his home country, which was on the verge of insurrection. Superimposed on the professional and political difficulties were those of a personal nature: when the two men met each other for the first time in Brixton Prison (to which Casement had now been transferred) they seem to have taken a dislike to each other at first sight. Casement disagreed with his counsel's views as to the correct method of conducting the case, while Serjeant Sullivan seems to have regarded his client as a megalomaniac.

The case commenced on 26 June 1916 in the Royal Courts of Justice before Viscount Reading CJ, and Avory and Horridge JJ. The Crown was represented by Sir Frederick Smith A.-G., Sir George Cave S.-G., and Messrs A.H. Bodkin, Travers Humphreys and G.A.H. Branson, instructed by the Director of Public Proscections. Casement was represented by Serjeant Sullivan, Mr Artemus Jones and Professor Morgan, instructed by Mr Duffy assisted by Mr Michael Doyle of the American Bar.

Before the commencement of the trial, Serjeant Sullivan applied to have the indictment quashed on the ground that it disclosed no offence in law, but the court ruled that such an application was to be postponed until the close of the case for the Crown. The jurors were then called, and Serjeant Sullivan exercised his right to challenge no less than thirty-seven – probably an error of judgment on his part, for his object appears to have been to select the roughest-looking members of the panel, whereas a proper defence would have been more likely to succeed before a more educated jury. It was nearly midday before the following jury was finally sworn in:

Frederick Wheeler, Willesden, shipping clerk
Ernest West, Willesden, schoolmaster
John Watts, Willesden, warehouseman
Albert Abbott, Palmers Green, clerk
Herbert Scoble, Hackney, clerk
Richard Scantlebury, Hackney, agent
Albert Scopes, Hackney, leather merchant
John Burdon, Wandsworth, mechanical engineer
William Card, Ealing, baker
William Cole, Chelsea, coachman
Hyman Saunders, Hackney, tailor
Albert Ansley, Palmers Green, bank clerk

After the Attorney-General had opened the case for the Crown, he called two witnesses on formal matters, followed by five Irishmen who had all been captured by the enemy in the early days of the war, and were later repatriated under an exchange scheme. These were John Cronin of the Royal Munster Fusiliers, Daniel O'Brien of the 19th Hussars, John Robinson of the Royal Army Medical Corps, William Egan of the Royal Irish Rifles, Michael O'Connor of the Royal Irish Regiment, Michael Moore of the Royal Army Medical Corps, and John Neill of the 18th Royal Irish. They had for a time been held in separate camps, but were later congregated at Limburg Hahn with about 2,500 other Irish prisoners.

They gave evidence that Casement had addressed them on various occasions and had tried to persuade them to join an Irish Brigade to fight for Ireland. There was some disagreement as to when they would go to Ireland – O'Brien and Neill thought that it would not be until after the end of the war, whereas Cronin, Robinson and Moore thought that it would be as soon as the Germans had won a naval victory. There was no suggestion that they should fight for Germany (although Neill said that they would be sent to join the Turks against Russia; this suggestion was not, however, pursued by the Crown). The witnesses agreed that if they joined the Irish Brigade they would be the guests of the German government until they went to Ireland. They were also told that if they stayed in Germany until the end of the war, they would be given £10 or £20 and sent to America.

All these witnesses were shown Exhibit 4 and agreed that they had seen copies in the camp. It is significant that none of the witnesses said that it was connected with the defendant. No evidence was given at any time that Casement had written it, or was responsible for distributing it, or had any knowledge of it. Nor indeed, was it ever formally produced, and no explanation was given as to how it came into the hands of the prosecution.

About fifty men joined the Irish Brigade, and there was some suggestion that those who refused had their rations reduced or were sent to a punishment camp.

These witnesses concluded their evidence at the end of the first day of the trial. On the following day various witnesses described what had happened on 20 and 21 April 1916 near Curraghane on the Irish coast. Michael Hussey had seen a light out at sea, John M'Carthy found a boat that had come ashore in the middle of the night, Mary Gorman saw three men walking past her home at 4.30 a.m. and she recognized one of them as the defendant, while Sgt. Hearn of the Royal Irish Constabulary examined the boat and a knapsack found nearby, which contained a map and some ammunition, and other items, and he and Constable Riley went to McKenna's fort, where they found Casement. This evidence, and the evidence of the code and the railway ticket, appears to have been placed before the court under overt act (vi), namely that Casement had set out from Germany with the object of landing arms and ammunition in Ireland for the prosecution of the war against England. After that, two other police officers described how Casement was brought from Ireland to London.

Witnesses were also called relating to the *Aud*, but there was no evidence to show that Casement was in any way connected with this incident.[6]

The Crown then called Lieutenant-Colonel Gordon, of the Directorate of Military Intelligence at the War Office, who was questioned about the map fragments which had been found in Casement's possession, and he expressed the opinion that they provided sufficient material to construct a map of Ireland.[7]

Finally, they called evidence relating to the arrest of Bailey. The prosecution had planned to charge Casement and Bailey together on a conspiracy charge, but had changed their minds when Bailey agreed to give evidence for the Crown. However, he was in fact never called as a witness.

One might have supposed that at some stage of the proceedings, the defence would have submitted that Exhibit 4 was inadmissible. No such submission was made, and so, at the very end of the case for the Crown, the Solicitor-General now submitted that it was admissible. A short argument ensued, but the court ruled that, although there was no evidence to connect the document with the defendant, it was nevertheless admissible and it was read to the jury.

After the close of the case for the Crown, Serjeant Sullivan moved to quash the indictment on the ground that a person could not be guilty of adhering to the enemy 'out of the realm'. This was the principal issue that was argued at the trial, and subsequently before the Court of Criminal Appeal. The salient features of this argument are as follows:

Firstly, the wording of the Act, according to the Crown, meant 'If a man be adherent to the King's enemies in his realm (giving to them aid and comfort in the realm) or elsewhere.' That is to say that the words in brackets become a gloss to the term 'adherent', and the treason of being adherent to the king's enemies could therefore be committed either in the realm or elsewhere. In any event treason by adhering to the enemy was more likely to be committed abroad than at home – it would be inconceivable that parliament should provide immunity for a person committing treason in the very situation in which he was most likely to commit it.

In answer to this, the defence argued that the only possible meaning of the Act was 'If a man be adherent to the King's enemies in his realm (giving them aid and comfort in the realm or elsewhere).' When the Act was passed the Crown had subjects, particularly in France, who were outside the realm, and who might be called upon to fight for their feudal superiors against the Crown – far from being absurd, the Act was framed so as to protect such persons from a charge of treason unless they actually came within the realm.

Secondly, there was a long line of cases in which persons had committed treason abroad and had been tried and convicted in England, from *de Weston* and *de Gomenys* in 1377 to *Lynch* in 1903. But the defence argued that most of these cases were, for one reason or another, irrelevant or unreliable or had been wrongly decided.[8]

Thirdly, there was a line of statutes in which parliament had expressly made offences treasonable if committed within the realm or without. This would have been superfluous if the Act of 1351 meant what the Crown said it meant. The clear inference to be drawn from this line of legislation was that when parliament intended to make it treasonable to assist the enemy out of the realm, it said so in express terms. All these Acts had expired or had been repealed, some as recently as 1863. If parliament had wished to renew these provisions in 1914, it could have done so. In fact this was not done.[9]

The arguments lasted for much of the second and third days of the trial. The court then delivered judgment. Lord Reading CJ and Avory and Horridge JJ all gave assenting judgments; they accepted the arguments of the Crown and rejected the submission.

As parliament had passed the Criminal Evidence Act of 1898, it would have been open to Casement, had he so wished, to give evidence on oath which would have been subject to cross-examination. Instead, he chose to make an unsworn statement from the dock. He said emphatically that he had never asked any Irishman to fight for Germany, he rejected the insinuations that he had had the rations of Irish prisoners reduced or had had Irishmen sent to punishment camps for refusing to join the Irish Brigade, and he rejected the suggestions that he had ever asked for or received a penny from the German government. He also criticized the Attorney-General for having referred, in his opening speech, to the rising in Ireland although no evidence had been called on that issue: 'Since the rising has been mentioned, however, I must state categorically that the rebellion was not made in Germany, and that not one penny of German gold went to finance it.'

Towards the end of the day Serjeant Sullivan addressed the jury, doing so on the basis that his client had been recruiting for Ireland and only in the interests of Ireland, and he analysed the evidence with that object in view. Before he concluded his speech, however, he was taken ill, and the court was adjourned.

On the following morning Mr Jones informed the court that his leader was unable to appear, so he now, with the permission of the court, continued to address the jury and he embarked on a new line of argument, namely that Casement's conduct did not constitute 'aid and comfort':[10]

> Gentlemen, you are dealing with the language of a statute passed almost six hundred years ago, and the meaning of these words 'aid and comfort' at that time, I suggest to you, was something rather different from the words 'aid and comfort' as they are used today. Aiding and comforting the enemy means supplying them with information or with forces or with material for the purpose of levying war against the King, and you have to be satisfied in your own mind that Sir Roger Casement's intention when he was in Germany was to use the Irish brigade for the purpose of fighting Germany's battles against England.

At this point Lord Reading CJ interrupted him, and said that it was his intention to direct the jury in the following terms:

> I shall tell the jury that 'giving aid and comfort to the King's enemies' means assisting the King's enemies in the war with this country, and that any act which strengthens or tends to strengthen the enemy in the conduct of the war against us would be giving aid and comfort to the King's enemies, and that any act which weakens or tends to weaken the power of this country to resist or to attack the enemy equally is giving aid and comfort to the King's enemies.

In earlier treason cases counsel had addressed the jury, often at very great length, on matters of law without interruption from the bench, but Mr Jones did not pursue this matter any further. Instead he turned his attention to the state of affairs in Ireland, and suggested that his client might have been properly prosecuted, under the Defence of the Realm Act, for importing arms into that country, but not for treason.

The Attorney-General now replied on behalf of the Crown. Among other matters, he asked what motive the defendant could have had for going to Germany in the first place – no explanation had ever been given. He stressed the evidence that the Irish Brigade was to go to Ireland after Germany had won a battle at sea, and the finding of the code where the defendant had dropped it after his arrest.

Lord Reading CJ now summed up. He opened his address with a remarkable passage:

> You have had the advantage . . . of hearing the defence in this case conducted by Mr Sullivan until this morning, with the assistance of his juniors. There are some persons who . . . are inclined to rebel against the notion that a member of the English bar, or members of it, should be found to defend a prisoner on a charge of treason against the British State. I need not tell you, I am sure, gentlemen, that if anyone has those thoughts in his mind he has but a poor conception of the high obligation and responsibility of the bar of England. It is

the proud privilege of the bar of England that it is ready to come into court and to defend a person accused, however grave the charge may be. . . . It is a great benefit in the trial of a case, more particularly of this importance, that you should feel as we feel, that everything possible that could be urged on behalf of the defence has been said in this case after much thought, much study, much deliberation, and particularly by one who has conducted the defence in accordance with the highest traditions of the English bar.

It is difficult to believe that it had escaped the attention of the Lord Chief Justice that leading members of the English bar had refused to come into court to defend Casement, and that his defence had been conducted entirely by members of the Irish and Welsh bar. Whether counsel had said everything that could be said is another matter, and is certainly open to question.

He then reviewed the law and the evidence. With regard to Exhibit 4, he conceded that there was no evidence to connect it with the defendant, but said that the jury could consider it if they wished to do so, and he said much the same about the *Aud*. As far as the code was concerned, it was, he said, obvious that Casement must have had this in his possession in concert with Germany.

The jury retired at 2.53 p.m. and returned at 3.48 p.m. with a verdict of Guilty. When Casement was asked if he had anything to say why the court should not pass sentence and judgment upon him to die, he took the opportunity to make a long speech on behalf of his country, and of the current situation in Ireland. Lord Reading CJ then sentenced him to death.

It may be that Casement could have applied for a stay of execution, followed by an appeal to parliament, under s. 2 of the Treason Act; however that may be, he did in

Sir Roger Casement leaving the Royal Courts
of Justice, 1916 (Press Association)

fact appeal to the Court of Criminal Appeal. Two grounds of appeal were set out: (i) that the offence of adhering to the enemy could not be committed abroad, and (ii) that Lord Reading CJ's definition of adhering to the enemy was wrong and that the jury had thereby been misdirected.

At the hearing of the appeal, Serjeant Sullivan abandoned the latter ground, apparently without his client's consent, so this issue was left without any further consideration. No authorities were ever cited in support of Artemus Jones's definition of 'giving aid and comfort to the enemy', but it may be said with some confidence that there had not been a single case in England, at any rate since the revolution of 1688, in which anyone had been convicted of, or even prosecuted for, adhering to the enemy, except for conduct which fell squarely within his definition – cases of espionage such as *R. v. de la Motte*, or of serving in the armed forces of the enemy. In all these cases the nature of the offence was self-evident and the judges rarely troubled to define it. There were, however, some Irish authorities in support of the definition put forward by Lord Reading CJ, to the effect that adherence to the enemy was constituted by any act to promote their interests.

The appeal therefore proceeded on the issue which Lord Reading CJ had postponed – the motion to quash the indictment. Serjeant Sullivan argued the case before Darling, Bray, Lawrence, Scrutton and Atkin JJ on 17 and 18 July 1916. The court did not call upon the Attorney-General in reply, and the appeal was dismissed. Darling J. delivered the judgment of the court in terms similar to those employed by Lord Reading CJ.

At common law there was a procedure whereby a person convicted of a criminal offence might appeal to the House of Lords, but subject to the surprising requirement

An artist's impression of the Court of Criminal Appeal hearing the appeal of Sir Roger Casement. Mr Justice Darling is presiding; Serjeant Sullivan is addressing the Court (Government Art Collection)

that he could only do so with the consent of the Attorney-General, the senior prosecuting officer of the Crown. Even more surprisingly, parliament retained this rule in the Criminal Appeal Act 1907 (which had established the Court of Criminal Appeal), by laying down that a defendant might appeal from the Court of Criminal Appeal to the House of Lords only if he obtained the certificate of the Attorney-General that the decision of the Court of Criminal Appeal involved a point of law of exceptional importance, and that it was desirable in the public interest that a further appeal should be brought.

Accordingly, Serjeant Sullivan, Mr Jones and Mr Duffy all wrote letters to the Attorney-General requesting him to grant the certificate, but he refused to do so. At the end of July Mr Jones and Professor Morgan went to see the Attorney-General and urged upon him the importance of the matter, but he maintained his attitude, and indeed is said to have told them that the matter was 'trivial'. They also complained that the Government was making use of Casement's diaries to prejudice the press and the public against him. Professor Morgan consulted Professor Holdsworth, and wrote a final letter to the Attorney-General, to which no reply was received.

Casement was executed in Pentonville Prison at 9 a.m. on 3 August 1916.

It has been alleged that, two years later, Professor Morgan met the Attorney-General who conceded that the point was an important one, but said that if he had given his certificate and the conviction had been quashed on a technicality, feeling against Casement had been so strong that the government might have been brought down. It might be said, therefore, that the refusal of the certificate was justifiable as not being 'in the public interest'.

CHAPTER ELEVEN

The Trial of William Joyce (1945)

Two or three weeks after the beginning of the Second World War in 1939 Albert Hunt, a Detective Inspector of the Special Branch at New Scotland Yard, was twiddling the knob of his radio and heard a voice saying that Folkestone and Dover had been destroyed. As he was stationed at Folkestone, and knew that there had been no enemy activity either there or at Dover, he was somewhat surprised. He recognized the voice as that of William Joyce, to whose speeches he had listened on several occasions in the five years prior to the war.

William Joyce was born in New York on 24 April 1906, the son of an Irishman who had been in America for twelve years and had become a naturalized US citizen; William himself was therefore a US citizen. In about 1909 the family returned to Ireland, and William went to school at the College of St Ignatius Loyola in Galway. There he was involved in a fist-fight with another boy (he was an excellent boxer) and suffered a broken nose; as this was never properly set, the injury left him with a nasal drawl which was later to become familiar on the radio. He took some part in the turbulent Irish troubles, but his family moved to England in 1921 and settled in Dulwich.

In London, Joyce enrolled as a part-time student at Birkbeck College in the University of London, and also in the OTC – on occasions he attended tutorials in uniform and with his rifle. He also joined an early version of the Fascists – British Fascisti Ltd. When he was attending an election meeting in Lambeth in October 1924 he was assaulted – by 'Jewish Communists', he always alleged – and his face was slashed with a razor from mouth to ear; a terrible scar remained for the rest of his life. Nevertheless, he continued with his studies and in 1927 obtained a first class degree in English Literature; he married his first wife at about the same time.

During the 1930s Joyce joined Sir Oswald Mosley's British Union of Fascists, and for a time was his deputy leader. He was, in his way, a brilliant orator, a master of the English language and a master of invective and insults. In 1933 he was involved in a riot at Worthing, for which he was prosecuted at Lewes Assizes; but he briefed Sir Patrick Hastings who persuaded the judge that there was no case to go to the jury.

Joyce now became dissatisfied with Mosley, and formed his own, and more extreme, party, the British National Socialist League, whose policy seemed difficult to distinguish from Hitler's; and while his followers dwindled in number, his tone became more shrill, especially against Communists and Jews; on two occasions he was prosecuted for minor assaults, but was acquitted. At this time he left his wife, and in 1937 married Margaret White, a fellow party-activist.

On 4 July 1933 Joyce applied for a British passport, stating that he was a British subject: whether he knew that he was, by birth, a US citizen or whether he genuinely believed that he was British has never been ascertained. His decision to leave England for Germany just before the outbreak of war does not seem to have been premeditated. His passport expired in 1938 and he renewed it for one year; it expired again in the following summer, and on 24 August 1939 he renewed it again; it expired again on 1 July 1940. On 26 August, he and Margaret left England, and arrived in

Berlin on the following day; but, so far from being welcomed with open arms as they had hoped, they were warned that they would at once be interned as enemy aliens if war broke out. They decided, therefore, to return to England, but found that they had insufficient funds for the railway fare.

However, Joyce happened to have one or two contacts in Berlin, and on 18 September he entered into a contract with the Reichfundfunk, the German broadcasting service; within a week or two he was broadcasting to England. At first, he was probably acting on the instructions of his employers (which may explain why the announcement heard by Inspector Hunt was such nonsense, compared with the much more sophisticated, and much more sinister, broadcasts later in the war); and it was at this time that he acquired the nickname by which he is usually remembered – Lord Haw Haw.

During the winter of 1939/40, Joyce wrote a book called *Twilight Over England*; in the Preface he described himself 'as a daily perpetrator of High Treason'; the book was published in the following September, with a print-run of 100,000 copies, most of which were circulated among British prisoners of war. By 1945 the British authorities were presumably aware of this book, but it was never mentioned at the trial; it may be that, in the absence of an admission from Joyce, there would have been insuperable difficulties in proving that Joyce had actually written the words which appeared in the printed text.

In the autumn of 1939, Anna Volkov, a virulent anti-Semite of Russian origin living in London, was working in conjunction with a clerk in the US Embassy in London; he intercepted messages between Churchill and Roosevelt, and she forwarded them to Berlin through friendly embassies. On 10 April 1940 she handed a letter, addressed to 'Herr W.B. Joyce, Rundfundhaus, Berlin', containing some significant material relating to affairs in England, and a code-word to acknowledge its receipt, to the Romanian embassy. However, it was intercepted and copied before being forwarded to Germany; a few days later Joyce acknowledged its receipt in one of his regular broadcasts. Anna Volkov was arrested and tried for espionage, and was sentenced by Tucker J. to ten years imprisonment; in the course of the trial, Tucker J. expressly referred to Joyce as a traitor. No mention was made of the correspondence between Anna Volkov and Joyce at the latter's trial, although this was *prima facie* an overt act of adhering to the enemy and one which, one would have thought, could have been proved without undue difficulty.

In September 1940 Joyce was granted German nationality, and four years later he received the 'War Service Cross' from Hitler; later in the same year he received a German passport and a certificate that he was a member of the Volkssturm. He broadcast regularly until 30 April 1945.

As the war drew to a close, Joyce's employers provided him and his wife with a passport in the name of Wilhelm Hansen and sent him to Hamburg, and from thence to Flensburg near the Danish frontier; for a few days this was the capital of the Third Reich. Towards the end of May, the town was occupied by British troops, and on 28 May when Joyce was out for a walk he saw two British officers, Captain Lickorish and Lieutenant Perry (the latter was a Jew) looking for firewood; he pointed out to them that there were 'a few more pieces over there', and Lieutenant Perry asked him: 'You wouldn't happen to be William Joyce, would you?' Instead of replying, Joyce put his hand into his pocket to take out his new passport, but Lieutenant Perry thought he was reaching for a weapon, so he shot him, causing flesh wounds in both of his thighs. He was then taken to Luneberg Hospital where, two days later, he was interviewed by

IM NAMEN
DES DEUTSCHEN VOLKES
VERLEIHE ICH

dem Hauptkommentator
William Joyce
in Berlin-Charlottenburg

DAS
KRIEGSVERDIENSTKREUZ
1. KLASSE

Führerhauptquartier, den 1. September 1944.

DER FÜHRER

The decoration awarded by Adolf Hitler to William Joyce, and presented to him by a senior member of the staff of the Rundfunkhaus. The first signature is that of Hitler (From the DPP file relating to the trial of Joyce, reproduced by permission of the Controller of Her Majesty's Stationery Office)

Captain Scarden of the Intelligence Corps. Captain Scarden cautioned him, and Joyce made a lengthy statement in which he set out his family history, and explained why he had joined the German broadcasting service. The gist of what he said was that he had always admired what Hitler had done, and that he was doing his best to bring about a reconciliation between Germany and England.

While Joyce was recovering in hospital in France, parliament passed the Treason Act 1945, specifically, so it has been said, to facilitate his trial. The new Act was principally procedural, but abolished various safeguards which had traditionally been regarded as desirable to protect defendants in cases of treason, and in particular the requirement under the Treason Act 1695 for calling at least two witnesses to one, or one witness each to two overt acts. In the event Detective Inspector Hunt was the only witness called to identify Joyce's voice in any broadcast covered by count 3, which was the vital count in the indictment.[1]

On 28 June Joyce appeared before the Bow Street magistrate and was committed for trial in July. However, the case was postponed until September to enable the defence to obtain evidence that Joyce was a United States citizen. The indictment contained three counts; as the Treason Act 1945 laid down that the procedure in treason trials was to be assimilated to that in cases of murder, the indictment was drafted according to modern practice, each count commencing with a Statement of Offence, and a description of the overt acts being replaced by Particulars of Offence. In each case the Statement of Offence simply alleged adhering to the enemy contrary to the Act of 1351, and the particulars alleged may be summarized as follows:

Joyce was wounded at the time of his arrest, and was taken to the Luneberg Hospital. He is shown here in the grounds of the hospital (Times Newspapers Ltd)

(i) broadcasting propaganda on behalf of the enemy between 18 September 1939 and 29 May 1945;
(ii) purporting to become naturalized as a subject of Germany;
(iii) broadcasting propaganda on behalf of the enemy between 18 September 1939 and 2 July 1940.

The first two counts depended upon the assumption that Joyce was a British subject (and there was some evidence that he was). The significance of the third count was that it covered the period while Joyce's British passport was still in force, and the Crown based its case against him primarily on the ground that, even if he was an alien, he still owed allegiance to the Crown as long as he held the passport.

The trial commenced on 17 September 1945 at the Old Bailey before Tucker J. Sir Hartley Shawcross A.-G. appeared for the Crown with Mr A.L. Byrne and Mr Gerald Howard, instructed by the Director of Public Prosecutions. Joyce was represented by Mr G.O. Slade KC, Mr Derek Curtis-Bennett KC and Mr James Burge, instucted by Messrs Ludlow & Co. Joyce pleaded Not Guilty, and a jury (whose names are not recorded) was sworn in.[2]

The Attorney-General opened the case for the Crown by reciting Joyce's history before and during the war, and reading the statement which he had made soon after his arrest. He explained the legal situation and the difference between counts 1 and 2 and count 3 – a distinction which, Slade KC said later that afternoon, he had not understood until then.[3] The Crown called a witness from the records office of the

University of London OTC, who produced documents relating to Joyce's application and enrolment in the corps, and an officer from the passport office who produced his applications for a passport and its renewal.

The Crown then called Albert Hunt, who recounted what he had heard in the autumn of 1939. He added that he had heard the same voice on various later occasions until 1944, and had taken a note of what was said. In cross-examination he was asked whether he could have been mistaken in recognizing the defendant's voice, but he asserted that he was not mistaken.[4]

Finally the prosecution called Captains Lickorish and Scarden, Samuel Salzedo, who translated the documents that had been produced (most of which related to events which had occurred after 2 July 1940, and were therefore only relevant to counts 1 and 2), and Chief Inspector Bridges of New Scotland Yard, who had interviewed Joyce on his return from France.

Slade KC now submitted that Joyce was a United States citizen, but, although some evidence to that effect had been produced, Tucker J. ruled that, at that stage, the case should proceed on the basis that he was a British subject. Slade KC then addressed the jury, solely on the issue of nationality, and called a series of witnesses who established beyond all question that Joyce was a United States citizen. At the close of the case for the defence, the Attorney-General stated that he no longer wished to press the case on counts 1 and 2.

One would have supposed that the defence would have now applied for the jury to be discharged, so that the trial could be recommenced before a new jury on count 3 alone, but no such application was made and the case proceeded.[5]

It was now well into the second day of the trial and the rest of the day was spent in arguments on the law, the Attorney-General submitting that Joyce owed allegiance to the Crown on the ground that he was the holder of a British passport and Slade KC arguing in reply. The latter was still addressing the court when it adjourned.

Slade KC resumed his address on the following morning, but he now raised a new point which, it would appear, Mr Burge had discovered overnight – namely that as Joyce was an alien, the court had no jurisdiction to hear the case at all.

The failure of the defence to raise this issue at an earlier stage is indeed remarkable. The English courts have jurisdiction to try any offence committed by anyone in England; on rare occasions parliament has conferred jurisdiction upon them to try offences committed by British subjects abroad, but it is almost unknown for parliament to confer jurisdiction to try offences committed by aliens abroad – cases of piracy being about the only exception to the general rule.[6] Furthermore, there is a well-known procedure for raising the issue, namely by entering a plea to the jurisdiction before the commencement of the trial.

The Attorney-General replied, and Tucker J. ruled, without giving any reasons, that 'I shall direct the jury on count 3 that on 24 August, 1939, when the passport was applied for the prisoner, beyond a shadow of doubt, owed allegiance to this country, and that . . . nothing happened at the material time to put an end to the allegiance that he then owed.'

Slade KC then addressed the jury, primarily on the basis that Inspector Hunt's evidence could not be relied upon, the Attorney-General replied, and Tucker J. summed-up. Most of the summing-up was on the issue of allegiance and the passport, and the judge dealt only briefly with the other aspect of the law, namely the meaning of the terms 'adhering to the enemy' and 'giving aid and comfort to the enemy'. On this topic he said simply that 'adhering to the King's enemies and aiding and comforting them means nothing more than actively throwing in your lot with the enemy', or actively assisting the enemy. Then he quoted a passage from *R. v. Casement*, although he referred to it as a 'famous case *after* the last war'.[7]

The jury retired at 3.37 p.m. and returned at 4 o'clock with a verdict of Guilty.

Following his conviction Joyce appealed to the Court of Criminal Appeal (Viscount Caldecote CJ, and Humphreys and Lynskey JJ). The appeal was heard from 30 to 31 October, and dismissed on 1 November 1945. The Attorney-General then issued his certificate for a further appeal to the House of Lords (Viscount Jowitt LC, and Lords Macmillan, Wright, Porter and Simmonds). The appeal was heard from 10 to 13 December 1945 and dismissed on 18 December, and Joyce was hanged on 3 January 1946. It was not until 1 February 1946 that their Lordships gave their reasons for dismissing the appeal. The Opinion of the House was delivered by the Lord Chancellor, with Lords Macmillan, Wright and Simmonds concurring. Lord Porter, dissenting, would have allowed the appeal.[8]

There were various issues of law which were, or could have been, raised.

(1) Adhering to the enemy out of the realm. J.W. Hall, in his book on the trial, written for the *Notable British Trials* series, stated that the decision in Casement's case 'definitely settled the law on this point and it was no longer open to Joyce's counsel'. But, even if the Court of Criminal Appeal regarded itself as being bound by its previous decision, the matter could certainly have been reopened in the House of Lords. However, this issue was never raised.

(2) Giving aid and comfort to the enemy. Apart from Tucker J.'s direction on this issue, this question was never mentioned.

(3) Jurisdiction. This issue was argued at the trial, and again before the Court of Criminal Appeal, and appears to be unanswerable. However, Viscount Caldecote CJ said that he and his colleagues had experienced 'some difficulty in understanding precisely the grounds upon which the submission was made', and referred to the Treason Act of 1543 (which conferred power on the courts to try treason committed abroad, but without reference to aliens) and by referring to *R. v. Casement* as authority for the proposition that the court did have jurisdiction to try aliens for offences committed abroad – although, of course, the point had never been considered in that case. In the House of Lords the Lord Chancellor disposed of the matter summarily.

(4) Allegiance. The Crown based its case against Joyce on the ground that, although an alien, his possession of a British passport meant that he still owed allegiance to the Crown even when he was in Germany. This argument was founded on a resolution of the judges in 1707, 'assembled at the Queen's command', and reported in Foster's *Crown Cases*. The passage reads:

> And if such alien, seeking the protection of the crown and having a family and effects here should during a war with his native country go thither and there adhere to the King's enemies for purposes of hostility, he might be dealt with as a traitor. For he came and settled here under the protection of the Crown: and though his person was removed for a time, his effects and family continued still under the same protection.

The prosecution's contention was that this principle extended to the holder of a passport on the ground that the Crown was under a duty to protect the holder of a passport who was, therefore, under a corresponding duty of allegiance to the Crown.

In answer to this, Slade KC argued that the resolution of the judges was an extrajudicial statement of no legal effect, that there was no reason to believe that its text was correctly stated, that it could not in any event be extended to the possession of a passport, that a passport was merely a means of identification, and that the passport issued to Joyce was a nullity since the Crown had no power to issue a passport to an alien.

In spite of these arguments, the House of Lords upheld the decison of Tucker J. and the Court of Criminal Appeal.

J.W. Hall, writing only a few months after Joyce's trial and execution, commented that he had found, along with a universal reprobation of Joyce's conduct, 'an almost equally universal feeling, shared by lawyers and laymen, servicemen and civilians, that . . . the decision was wrong, and that an unmeritorious case made bad law'. There was a strong and widespread feeling, he added, not that Joyce should have been reprieved, but that he should not have been convicted.

Many traitors have remained faithful to their principles to the bitter end. On 18 August 1746 Lord Balmerino, on the scaffold on Tower Hill, while about to kneel before the block, declared: 'O Lord! reward my friends, forgive my foes, bless King James, and receive my soul.' Three centuries later, on 3 January 1946, in the condemned cell at Brixton while he was waiting for the hangman, Joyce wrote his last letter to his wife: 'I salute you, Freja, as your lover for ever; Sieg Heil! Sieg Heil! Sieg Heil!'

Adhering to the Enemy 'Out of the Realm'

The cases[1] cited by the Crown in *R. v. Casement* in support of their submission that the offence of adhering to the enemy could be committed abroad were: *de Weston* and *de Gomenys* (1377) for surrendering the castles of Outrewyk and Ardes in Flanders, *Lord Wentworth and others* (1588) for conspiring to surrender Calais, *O'Rurke and Perrot* (1591–2) for adhering to the enemy in Ireland, *Lord Middleton and others* (1695) for assisting the enemy in France, *the Duke of Wharton* (1729) for conspiring with the Spaniards to attack Gibraltar, *Platt* (1777) (an application for habeas corpus to release a prisoner detained in England for an alleged treason in Georgia), *Cundell* (1808) for assisting the French in Mauritius, dicta in *R. v. Mulcahy* (1868), and *Lynch* (1903). In the last case the defendant had been accused of adhering to the enemy in the South African Republic during the Boer War. It had been argued on his behalf by Avory KC (who, as Mr Justice Avory, was a member of the court which tried Casement) that this treason could not be committed abroad, but the court, relying on *R. v. Vaughan* (1696), ruled that it could and Lynch was convicted and sentenced to death.

The arguments of the defence in respect of these cases were as follows. De Weston and de Gomenys were convicted on impeachment or attainted by parliament. The case of Lord Wentworth could not be relied upon, as Calais was still arguably part of the realm in 1588. Likewise, in respect of O'Rurke and Perrot, Ireland was part of the realm in the sixteenth century. Lord Middleton and others never appeared before a court and were simply outlawed without trial, so the case was of no weight, and the same applied to the Duke of Wharton. Remarks in *R. v. Platt* and *R. v. Mulcahy* were clearly obiter. Lynch had been wrongly convicted, as the case proceeded on the strength of *R. v. Vaughan* although the facts showed that Vaughan had been on the narrow seas, and therefore within the realm at the material time, so the case had been misunderstood. In the last resort, the only two cases in which anyone had been unequivocally convicted in judicial proceedings of adhering to the enemy out of the realm were *R. v. Cundell* and *R. v. Lynch*.

The line of statutes under which certain forms of conduct were expressly made treasonable even if committed abroad is:

The Treason Act 1534, having made it treasonable to assist the king's enemies in certain specified ways within the realm, went on to make the same offences treasonable if committed out of the realm. The Treason Act 1552 contained terms almost identical with those of the Act of 1534.

The Mutiny Act 1703, after reciting that there was no effective way of governing HM's forces out of the realm, declared that if any officer or soldier held any correspondence with the enemy, or gave them advice or intelligence, or treated with them, or entered into any conditions with them, he should be guilty of treason (an entirely superfluous piece of legislation, it would seem, if the Act of 1351 meant what Lord Reading CJ said it did).

The Treason Act 1795 also made certain acts treasonable if committed 'within the realm or without'.

'Aid and Comfort'

English cases of giving 'aid and comfort' to the enemy since 1688: *R.* v. *Preston* (1691) and *R.* v. *Crosby* (1695) were two cases of supplying information to the French with a view to making war on England and deposing William III. *R.* v. *Charnock*, *R.* v. *Freind* and *R.* v. *Cook* (1696) all arose out of a plot to assassinate the king and overthrow the regime. *R.* v. *Gregg* (1708), *R.* v. *Hensey* (1758) and *R.* v. *Tyrie* (1782) were all cases, like *R.* v. *de la Motte*, of sending military intelligence to the enemy, and so were *R.* v. *Stone* (1796) and *R.* v. *O'Coigley* (1798). Cundell (1808) joined the French in Mauritius and acted as a sentry over his fellow prisoners of war, Lynch (1903) and de Jager (1907) joined the armed forces of the Boers, and Ahlers (1914) was instrumental in assisting the return of German nationals of military age to Germany after the outbreak of war.

In Ireland, in *R.* v. *Finney* (1797) there was positive evidence of a plot to assist the French, and Chamberlain J. said that adherence to the enemy consisted in doing any act to promote their interests. In *R.* v. *Sheares* (1798) the defendants were prosecuted for compassing the death of the king and adhering to the enemy, although the evidence of assistance to the French was very slender. In that case Mr Curran, counsel for the defence, made a submission very similar to that of Artemus Jones, but in his summing-up Carleton CJ said:

> Aid or comfort afforded to the King's enemies in the realm or elsewhere, whereby they may be strengthened, or better enabled to carry on war, armaments or enterprise against us, or to defend themselves, or whereby the King's hands might be weakened, are acts of adherence to his enemies; any act whereby the relative power of the enemy might be promoted if done with that intent is a treasonable adherence . . .

But later on he qualified this by adding:

> It is of the essence of that charge that the act done must be with the imputed intent of aiding the King's foreign enemies. The evidence is a conspiracy to raise war, and open rebellion, to take the camp, City of Dublin, the Castle, the lord lieutenant and privy council . . . you are therefore to consider whether you can infer that this rising was acted upon with a view to aid the French. That intent is absolutely necessary. It is a matter of notoriety that the French have been upon the coast the winter before last, and might possibly be expected again.

Finally, in *R.* v. *Bond*, also in 1798, Chamberlain J. said that adherence to the enemy is:

> An offence which consists of any act, conspiracy or attempt, directly or indirectly, to assist any power at war with the King, and for the public safety it has always been held that this offence is complete, although such conspiracy or attempt shall not have been attended with success: and I cannot give a stronger instance of this species of treason than entering into a conspiracy (in time of war) to raise an armed force of the King's subjects to act against his authority, and with an intent to call for the assistance of the enemy should they invade the kingdom.

The Farnley Wood Conspiracy[1]

The Restoration of Charles II was generally accepted by the nation at large – but not, apparently, in the West Riding of Yorkshire where a conspiracy was hatched to restore the Republic.

The leader of this conspiracy was Captain Thomas Oates, of Morley, who had been an officer in the Parliamentary army. Other members were his son Ralph; Joshua Cardmaker, Luke Lund, John Ellis, William Westerman and John Fossard – all of Morley; John Nettleton of Dunningley; Timothy Crowther and Robert Oldred of Dewsbury; Richard Oldred – known as the Devil of Dewsbury; Israel Rhodes of Woodkirk; John Locock of Bradford; William Dickenson, Thomas Westerman and Edward Webster – all of Gildersome; Robert Scott of Alverthorpe; and John Holdsworth of Churlwell. It appears that they assembled, along with many other men (the numbers said to have met varies between 50 and 300), on 12 October 1663 in Farnley Wood, about three miles to the south-east of the centre of Leeds. There they dug a trench (or made use of a trench which already existed), and declared for a 'christian magistracy' and a 'gospel ministry'.

There is some suggestion that they were in correspondence with John Lambert, the Parliamentary general, who was now in exile in Guernsey, but it is unlikely that he would have risked his life by supporting such an undertaking.

How far the conspiracy proceeded is not clear. According to one account, they planned to attack York, but were surrounded by troops and were captured in the wood. It seems clear that Ralph Oates was captured, and he disclosed the names of many of the other conspirators. According to another account, they learnt that troops had been despatched to disperse them, so they withdrew and returned to their own homes where they were arrested. It is said that all the prisons in the north were full.

On learning of this conspiracy, the king appointed a Special Commission of four or five judges, and many of the conspirators appeared before them and were convicted and sentenced to death.

Another man who appeared before the same commission was Peter Mason, a joiner from Holbeck, 'an excellent workman but a very wicked drunken and bad man, a great Theife who the Assizes before these 21 men were tryed and executed was comitted to Yorke Castle for stealing a white horse from Mr Thomas Fenton of Hunslett and endeavoured to chainge his Cullour by dying him blue'. However, he was spared, on condition that he 'should be the Topman to hang those persons that were condemned with him'. This he agreed to do and evidently did so with great relish, 'holding his bloody knife in his mouth when he had been quartering the bodyes of men without any concern'. Afterwards he boasted of his achievements and was so hated that he fled to Ireland, and 'maid his exit upon a pare of Gallowes for some heinous fact by him there committed'.

Three of those sentenced were Robert Atkins, a salter and oil-drawer who had been in business at Timble Bridge, Henry Watson a clothier from Leeds Ridge, and John Errington a clothdresser from Leeds Kirkgate. The execution was fixed for Tuesday 19 January 1664, which was the Leeds market-day, 'soe persons might be present and see the tragicall end of those three persons'. They were brought on horseback to the great ash tree in Chapel Allerton, from where they were drawn on a sledge to the place of execution on Chapel Allerton Moor. Atkins's body was buried in his own garden near the old Church of Leeds, the others near the gallows on the moor. Their heads were set on iron spikes upon the Moothall End, and there they remained until 3 April 1677, when 'being a very windy day towards night were all blowne down, severall persons very narrowly escaping with their Lives & were in great dainger to be slaine, but thro' the providence of god not one was hurt'.

Several others were executed, presumably at the usual place of execution at York (near the Knavesmire Racecourse); others were reprieved or detained in prison until the next assize.

Notes

Introduction
1. The declaration alleged, *inter alia*, that the Crown had refused to assent to laws and had forbidden governors to pass urgent legislation, had maintained standing armies without the consent of the local legislatures, declared the colonists out of protection and waged war against them, plundered their coasts and towns, transported foreign mercenaries to suppress them, cut off their trade, and imposed taxes without their consent. (It may be noted in passing that the imposition of taxes without consent, traditionally regarded as the vital issue, came very low on the list of complaints.)
2. The original was in French.
3. Subsections (v) and (vi) were repealed in the nineteenth century, section 2 in 1948.
4. See Wharam, *The Treason Trials, 1794.*

Chapter 1: The Essex Rebellion (1601)
1. The Earl of Essex was living in a house that had previously belonged to the Earl of Leicester, and is marked 'Leycester House' on Norden's map of London.
2. i.e., imprison them.
3. The dots after 'Poly' are in the original, as if the scribe had failed to catch the words.

Chapter 2: The Trial of Sir Walter Raleigh (1603)
1. The editor of the *State Trials* at vol. 2, 46, quotes a passage from Bishop Kennett's edition of Wilson's *Life of James I*; I have been unable to trace any further details of this work.
2. Arabella was the grand-daughter of Margaret, the sister of Henry VIII, and therefore had some claim to the throne.
3. According to the *Shorter Oxford Dictionary*, the term 'bye' in this context is simply the name of a plot against James I, as distinguished from the 'main plot'.
4. An accomplice or person who acts as a decoy.
5. *Judges* 15.
6. Campion, a Jesuit, had been convicted and executed in 1580.
7. Queen Elizabeth died on 24 March 1603.
8. A round board, traditionally believed to have been the Round Table of King Arthur, hung then and still hangs in the Hall of Winchester Castle. I have been unable to discover why this case was tried at Winchester, but as there is a reference to the plague, the courts may have been evacuated.

Chapter 3: The Gunpowder Plot Trial (1606)
1. The King's Book is reprinted in the *State Trials*, vol. 2, 195–202; no information is given as to the origin of the report of the trials themselves. A full bibliography of matters relating to the Gunpowder Plot is to be found in Nicholls, *Investigating the Gunpowder Plot.*
2. No evidence emerged at the trial as to where the gunpowder came from. In strict law, the Crown had a monopoly of the manufacture of gunpowder, but according to Glenys Crocker, *The Gunpowder Industry* (Shire Publications Ltd, 1986), gunpowder was being made illegally in various parts of the country, in particular in Southwark and Lambeth.
3. I am indebted to Mrs Patricia Godfrey, the Local Studies Librarian of the Dover Library, for informing me that William Brook, Lord Cobham, was the Lord Warden of the Cinque Ports from 1558 to 1597, when he was succeeded by his son Henry Brook, Lord Cobham, who was dismissed following his conviction – see chapter 2 above.
4. According to Peter Fleming, *Invasion, 1940* (Hart-Davis, 1957), pp. 249–50, the Germans were planning to bring about 12,000 horses across the Channel, but never mastered the problem of disembarking them on a hostile shore.

Chapter 4: The Trial of Alice Lisle (1685)
1. 'Judge Jeffreys' spelt his name in various ways; in the law reports he is usually spelt 'Jefferies'. The joint appointment has been questioned – see Montgomery Hyde, *Judge Jeffreys*, p. 210 n. 3.
2. *Notes and Queries* 155 (1928), 149.

Chapter 5: The Gordon Riots: the trial of Lord George Gordon (1781)

1. The use of the word 'Scotch' is now regarded as incorrect, but was in regular use in the 18th century.
2. See p. 92 below; there were rumours at the time that the county associations were preparing to use armed force against the government.
3. For accounts of the riots, see Bibliography.
4. Now Kenwood.
5. For an account of Erskine's early life, see Wharam, *The Treason Trials, 1794*, pp. 108–12 and 114–16.
6. 'Lord' was a courtesy title that Lord George Gordon held as the son of a peer; he himself was not a peer and therefore not entitled to trial in the House of Lords.
7. James Wallace did not receive the knighthood, usually bestowed on attorneys-general. The solicitor-general was the son of John Manfield – he inserted the 's' later; he was no relation of the chief justice.
8. *Edinburgh Review* 16 (1810), 102.
9. Boswell's *Life*, 6 April 1781. Charles Dickens, on the other hand, understood the real reason why Lord George had been acquitted; see *Barnaby Rudge*, 'Chapter the Last'.
10. It is thought that about twenty men were summarily executed by the military (in addition to those killed during the course of the riots); about a hundred were subsequently put on trial for offences connected with the riots, and many, including James Jackson, were convicted and executed.

Chapter 6: The Trial of Francis Henry de la Motte (1781)

1. The author of the letter was de la Motte. Although he was a Frenchman and was writing to his fellow-Frenchman, he often referred to the English as 'we'.
2. But according to N.A.M. Rodger in his life of Lord Sandwich, *The Insatiable Earl* (Harper Collins, 1993), p. 211, the government had been aware of the French spy ring for some time.
3. The text in the *State Trials* is based on the transcript of Joseph Gurney's shorthand note.
4. John Heath, esq.; Mr Heath is believed to have been the only judge of the old Superior Courts or of the modern High Court of Justice who has refused to accept the knighthood traditionally bestowed on HM Judges.
5. At a time when most wars were directed against the monarch personally, it became the custom to include a count of Compassing the king's death in cases based on adherence to the enemy, and this practice continued, as a formality, until the end of the eighteenth century.
6. According to George Croly, *Life of George IV* (1830), p. 38, a naval clerk called Ryder had been put into an office at Plymouth where he communicated the Admiralty signals to the enemy.

Chapter 7: The Pop Gun Conspiracy: the Trial of Robert Thomas Crossfield (1796)

1. See Wharam, *The Treason Trials, 1794*.
2. The text in the *State Trials* is based on the transcript of Joseph Gurney's shorthand note.
3. A cartel was a written agreement for the exchange of prisoners, and a cartel-ship was a ship employed for this purpose.
4. Blackstone's *Commentaries*, vol. 4, 357.
5. During the years after the Revolution, there was a fashion in France for planting symbolic Trees of Liberty – some 60,000 are said to have been planted between 1789 and 1793. The tree almost invariably selected for the purpose was the Lombardy Poplar, because of its association with the word for 'people'– *peuple/peuplier* in French, *populus/populus* in Latin – and it became a regular feature of the broadsheets of the period. The fashion was revived in 1848, and again in 1889, and two years later Monet painted his series of Poplars on the Epte, see Prof. Paul Tucker, *Monet in the '90s* (Yale, 1989). In England any sort of tree, or even a pole, seems to have sufficed. The trees were sometimes decorated with symbols of liberty, rather like a Christmas tree.
6. Abraham Newland was the chief cashier of the Bank of England, whose signature appeared on bank notes; contemporary notes were referred to as 'Abraham Newlands'.

Chapter 8: The Cato Street Conspiracy: the Trial of Arthur Thistlewood (1820)

1. It was assumed, at least in the early stages of the trial, that a dinner party had been arranged; it may well be, however, that no dinner had been planned, and that the announcement in the press was designed to trap the conspirators.
2. The Manchester Massacre, or the Battle of Peterloo, occurred on 16 August 1819. It is probable that about a dozen people were killed and many more injured when the Manchester Yeomany attacked the gathering. Lurid and exaggerated reports of the event circulated rapidly.
3. Wax-end is the thread coated with cobblers' wax used by shoemakers.

4. Fitzclarence was the illegitimate son of the Duke of Clarence, later King William IV.
5. It appears that a conductor was a rank, probably equivalent to a corporal.
6. Contrary to his usual practice, the editor of the *State Trials* gives no provenance for this report, but it is presumably the transcript of the official shorthand note. See further, Stanhope, *The Cato Street Conspiracy.*
7. The times of the speeches are not given, but can be calculated roughly from the length in the report.
8. See Henderson, *Recollections of John Adolphus.*
9. Adolphus did not name the Act, but legislation was being passed at this period to diminish the risk of fires in built-up areas.

Chapter 9: The Chartist Rebellion: the Trial of John Frost (1839–40)
1. A transcript of Joseph and Thomas Gurney's shorthand note of this trial was published by Saunders & Benning (successors to J. Butterworth & Son), 43 Fleet Street, in 1840. The case is also reported in IV St. Tr. (N.S.) 85 and, briefly, in 9 Car. & P. 129 (*English Reports*, vol. 173, 771). See also Williams, *John Frost.*
2. Usually described by the witnesses as a 'bow' window, but clearly a bay with three straight sides.
3. He was prosecuted and convicted shortly afterwards on a serious fraud charge, and sentenced to transportation.
4. It was not the practice in those days to add the letters QC (or KC) after the name of leading counsel.
5. There was no criminal appeal court in those days, but points of law which arose in criminal trials could be referred to the whole bench of judges, sitting in the Court of Exchequer Chamber.
6. This seems at first sight to be a highly technical point. However, the purpose of serving a list of witnesses upon the accused was to enable him to find and interview the witnesses, and this could not be achieved unless they were adequately identified.
7. See Wharam, *The Treason Trials, 1794.*
8. In fairness to Campbell A.-G. it must be pointed out that some of the witnesses whom he intended to call were held to be inadmissible (see note 6, above). It may be that they would have given the evidence in question.

Chapter 10: The Trial of Sir Roger Casement (1916)
1. This case is reported in full in Hyde, *The Trial of Sir Roger Casement.*
2. On 26 July 1914, a cargo of arms and ammunition from Hamburg was unloaded on the Irish coast near Dublin; a party of Volunteers met the ship and escorted the cargo towards Dublin; most of them dispersed on the way, but a few were still walking together when they reached Bachelor's Walk; some troops of the Scottish Borderers then fired upon them, killing three and injuring about thirty (see Sir James O'Connor, *History of Ireland* (Edward Arnold, 1926), vol. 2, pp. 202–3.
3. It may have been open to argument, but Ireland was probably, in law, part of the realm as long as it remained part of the United Kingdom. According to Serjeant Sullivan in his autobiography, *The Last Serjeant* (Macdonald, 1952), p. 270, 'If Casement had been charged with his Irish venture, he would have had to be tried in Ireland.' No authority was cited in support of this proposition, and I know of none.
4. There was also the problem of negotiating fees. The Bar appears to have forgotten that it was contrary to professional etiquette to accept any fee for defending a person charged with treason. See Lord Campbell, *Life of Lord Erskine*, in his *Lives of the Chancellors*, p. 678n. Serjeant Sullivan and Mr Artemus Jones charged £530 and £325 respectively for their appearance at the trial, although Prof. Morgan declined to accept any fee.
5. Although the rank of Serjeant has never been expressly abolished, no serjeant at the English Bar has been appointed since 1875. Appointments continued for some time in Ireland, and Serjeant Sullivan was the last to hold the title.
6. According to Hyde, *The Trial of Sir Roger Casement*, Casement discussed the *Aud* at an interrogation at Scotland Yard, and admitted that he had full knowledge of the ship's cargo and intentions, but no evidence of this discussion was presented at the trial.
7. It would appear that the map had originally been complete, and had been torn up – possibly in the hope that it would not be recognized.
8. See Appendix 1.
9. See Appendix 1.
10. See Appendix 2.

Chapter 11: The Trial of William Joyce (1945)

1. If Sir Walter Raleigh was correct in saying that two witnesses were required at common law, then it would be arguable that the repeal of the Act of 1695 had simply resurrected the common law rule.
2. The case is reported in full in Hall, *The Trial of William Joyce*; it is reported in the Law Reports at [1946] AC 347; for further material on the case, see Bibliography. Solicitor and counsel were assigned and paid under the Poor Prisoners' Defence Act 1930, the forerunner of the Legal Aid scheme.
3. At NBT 83: 'Until I heard my friend the Attorney-General open the case on the third count I had not appreciated there was any distinction between it and counts 1 and 2.' This is an astonishing statement. It is incredible that none of Joyce's lawyers addressed their minds to this count, asking themselves or their client what significance was to be attached to the date 2 July 1940, and therefore realizing that this was related to the expiry of the passport.
4. There were widespread reports that Lord Haw Haw was announcing the destruction of towns which were known not to have been attacked, and the sinking of ships, usually HMS *Ark Royal*, which were known not to have been sunk. It may well be, however, that these broadcasts were made by someone else. Later broadcasts definitely made by Joyce (the transcripts of which are included in Hall, *The Trial of William Joyce*, Appendix 7) were well researched and carefully worded. The possibility that Inspector Hunt wrongly attributed this early broadcast to Joyce cannot be excluded.
5. In his summing-up Tucker J. told the jury to bring in verdicts of Not Guilty on counts 1 and 2, but never, as far as I can see, warned them to disregard the evidence given under those two counts.
6. More recently parliament has conferred power on English and Scottish courts to try offences committed on drilling rigs in international waters.
7. My italics.
8. In the opinion of Lord Porter, the trial judge had misdirected the jury on a relatively minor matter, which did not affect the general principle.

Appendix 1

1. Full references may be found in Wharam, 'Casement and Joyce', *Modern Law Review* (1978), 681.

Appendix 3

1. This account of the Farnley Wood Conspiracy is based on Allen, *New and Complete History of the County of York*. I am indebted to Geoffrey Forster, the librarian of the Leeds Private Library, for drawing my attention to this work. It would be interesting to know how many other similar occurrences are hidden away in local records.

Bibliography

GENERAL

Blackstone's *Commentaries on the Laws of England*, 4 vols, 1765–9
Campbell, Lord John. *Lives of the Chancellors*, 1845–8
——. *Lives of the Chief Justices*, 1847–9
Coke, Sir Edward. *Institutes*, 4 vols, 1628–44
Frost, Sir Michael. *Discourse on Treason: Crown Cases*, 1762
Howell's *State Trials*, 33 vols, 1816–26
Wharam, Alan. *The Treason Trials, 1794*, Leicester University Press, 1992

CHAPTER 1: THE ESSEX REBELLION (1601)

Howell's *State Trials*, vol. 1, cols 1333–1452

CHAPTER 2: THE TRIAL OF SIR WALTER RALEIGH (1603)

Howell's *State Trials*, vol. 2, cols 1–60
Irwin, Margaret. *That Great Lucifer*, Chatto & Windus, 1960

CHAPTER 3: THE GUNPOWDER PLOT TRIAL (1606)

Howell's *State Trials*, vol. 2, cols 159–358
Nicholls, Mark. *Investigating the Gunpowder Plot*, Manchester University Press, 1991
  [includes a comprehensive bibliography]

CHAPTER 4: THE TRIAL OF ALICE LISLE (1685)

Howell's *State Trials*, vol. 11, cols 297–382
Helm, P.J. *Jeffreys*, Robert Hale, 1966
Montgomery Hyde, H. *Judge Jeffreys*, Harrap, 1940
Muddiman, J.G. (ed.) *The Bloody Assizes*, Notable British Trials, Wm Hodge & Co.,
  1929

CHAPTER 5: THE GORDON RIOTS: THE TRIAL OF LORD GEORGE GORDON (1781)

Howell's *State Trials*, vol. 21, cols 485–652
de Castro, J. Paul. *The Gordon Riots*, Oxford University Press, 1926 [includes extracts
  from eye-witness accounts]
Hibbert, Christopher. *King Mob*, Longmans Green & Co., 1959
Nicholson, John. *The Great Liberty Riot of 1780*, BM BOZO, 1985 [an unorthodox
  view of the riots]

CHAPTER 6: THE TRIAL OF FRANCIS HENRY DE LA MOTTE (1781)

Howell's *State Trials*, vol. 21, cols 564–816

CHAPTER 7: THE POP GUN CONSPIRACY: THE TRIAL OF ROBERT THOMAS CROSSFIELD (1796)

Howell's *State Trials*, vol. 26, cols 1–222

CHAPTER 8: THE CATO STREET CONSPIRACY: THE TRIAL OF ARTHUR THISTLEWOOD (1820)

Howell's *State Trials*, vol. 33, cols 682–956
Henderson, Emily. *Recollections of the Public Career and Private Life of John Adolphus, the Eminent Barrister and Historian*, Cautley Newby, 1871
Stanhope, John. *The Cato Street Conspiracy*, Jonathan Cape, 1962

CHAPTER 9: THE CHARTIST REBELLION: THE TRIAL OF JOHN FROST (1839–40)

Williams, David. *John Frost: A Study in Chartism*, University of Wales Press, 1939, repr. Evelyn, Adams & Mackay, 1969 [includes much contemporary material]

CHAPTER 10: THE TRIAL OF SIR ROGER CASEMENT (1916)

Montgomery Hyde, H. *The Trial of Sir Roger Casement*, Notable British Trials, Wm Hodge & Co., 2nd (revised) edn, 1960 [includes the transcript of the evidence at the trial]

CHAPTER 11: THE TRIAL OF WILLIAM JOYCE (1945)

Hall, J.W. (ed.) *The Trial of William Joyce*, Notable British Trials, Wm Hodge & Co., 1946 [includes the transcript of the evidence at the trial]
Selwyn, Francis. *Hitler's Englishman*, Routledge & Kegan Paul, 1987
West, Rebecca. *The Meaning of Treason*, Macmillan, 1949, repr. Penguin Books, 1965

APPENDIX 3

Allen, Thomas. *New and Complete History of the County of York*, Hinton, 1828

Index

Page numbers in italics denote illustrations.